EVERYDAY HANDBOOKS

GRAMMAR, RHETORIC AND COMPOSITION

FOR HOME STUDY

Richard D. Mallery

ASSOCIATE PROFESSOR OF ENGLISH

NEW YORK UNIVERSITY

BARNES & NOBLE, INC.

• PUBLISHERS
• BOOKSELLERS
• FOUNDED 1873

Printed in the United States of America

PREFACE

WHETHER OR NOT you write and speak easily on some or many topics, there are undoubtedly times when you feel the need of turning to a book in which you can check some point about which you are in doubt. *Grammar, Rhetoric, and Composition for Home Study* should be helpful to you on such occasions; but it does more than provide information about specific details of English usage. We have brought together here in systematic form all the essential rules of good usage in English.

In studying this book you will find that the basic problem of all writing is simple and at the same time difficult, namely, the construction of a sentence. Your task also includes the arranging of single sentences into paragraphs. After very complete sections on the sentence and paragraph, with many examples and exercises for home study, the book then deals with the arrangement of written material in larger units such as articles, essays, and stories.

The Index will make it possible for you to find information about specific points or rules by immediate reference to the appropriate page. However, it is our hope that you will want to use this book to review the whole subject of good English. We therefore urge you to begin with Chapter I and to take up the topics in order.

Chapter I introduces you to the basic requirements of good writing, provides you with preliminary definitions, and then gives suggestions for finding a subject about which to write.

Chapter II deals with the eight parts of speech which are the basis of English grammar. Chapter III is devoted to syntax, or the question of sentence structure. Mastery of the principles dealt with in these two chapters will enable you to arrange words effectively in sentence form. In Chapter IV certain common errors in sentence structure are discussed. The grouping of sentences in paragraphs is treated in Chapter V. And Chapter VI deals with larger forms of composition.

Chapters VII and VIII are devoted to mechanical matters, including punctuation, capitalization, abbreviation, contraction, hyphenation, numerals, italics, and manuscript form.

Chapter IX deals with diction, or the choice of words. It focuses your attention on a very vital question: Are the words in your sentences the best words to convey your meaning to someone else? Too often a writer fails to make himself understood because he forgets that what is clear to him may not be clear to the reader. This chapter helps you to find the right word and the right phrase.

Chapter X, on style, indicates what it is that gives character and individuality to writing.

The Appendix shows how card catalogues in public libraries can be used most effectively in locating desired books, and outlines standard methods for preparing papers requiring library research. At the end of the book you will find the Answers to the exercises.

For permission to reprint copyrighted passages, our thanks are due to publishers, authors, or authorized representatives, as follows: Doubleday, Doran and Company, Inc., for a passage from "Literary Taste: How to Form It", by Arnold Bennett, copyright, 1927. Farrar & Rinehart, Inc., New York, and Faber & Faber, Ltd., London, for a passage from *Chaucer,* by G. K. Chesterton. Ginn and Company for two passages from *Ancient Times,* by J. H. Breasted. Harcourt, Brace and Company, Inc., for "Holding A Baby", by Heywood Broun. Harper & Brothers for passages from Mark Twain's *Autobiography* and from *The Mind in the Making,* by James Harvey Robinson. Harper & Brothers and Chatto & Windus for passages from *Point Counter Point,* by Aldous Huxley. Houghton Mifflin Company, as authorized publishers of the Works of Bret Harte, for "The Outcasts of Poker Flat". J. B. Lippincott Company and the author, for the essay "Style" from *Streamlines,* by Christopher Morley. Miss Amy Loveman, of *The Saturday Review of Literature,* for permission to quote the article "New Dimensions in Information", by Miss Loveman. The Macmillan Company, and Macmillan & Co., Ltd., for brief passages from *The Golden Bough,* by J. G. Frazer, and *Words and Their Ways,* by Greenough & Kittredge. G. & C. Merriam Company for permission to reproduce a page from *Webster's Collegiate Dictionary,* Fifth Edition. The Modern Library, Inc., for a passage from Ludwig Lewisohn's essay "Literature and Life", originally published in *A Modern Book of Criticism,* edited by Mr. Lewisohn. The New York *Times* for a passage from "Topics of the Times" of May 23, 1943. The *New Yorker* for a passage from an article called "Opportunity". Charles Scribner's Sons for a passage from *The Inn of Tranquillity,* by John Galsworthy. The Viking Press, Inc., for a passage from *While Rome Burns* (copyright, 1934), by Alexander Woollcott.

R. D. M.

GRAMMAR, RHETORIC, AND COMPOSITION
FOR HOME STUDY

CONTENTS

CHAPTER I

THE WRITING PROCESS

ALL OF US have to do a good deal of writing and we naturally want to express ourselves as well as possible. We want to be able to communicate our thoughts to others by speaking or writing accurately, convincingly, and gracefully.

Thinking, speaking, and writing are closely related to each other. If you think clearly and are familiar with the essential rules of good English, you will speak and write with the confidence that comes from complete awareness of the problem which you are tackling and from a sense of having had the necessary training.

Whether your writing consists chiefly of personal correspondence or business reports or articles or stories, you will want to be grounded in the fundamentals of grammar and rhetoric. You must know these fundamentals so well that they seem as natural to you as the spelling of your own name. Remember that the rules of grammar, rhetoric, and composition apply to both writing and speaking. In the course of studying the principles of good writing and putting them into practice, you will find that you are attaining greater ease and correctness in speaking as well as advancing steadily toward mastery of the writing process.

RULES AND STANDARDS OF GOOD WRITING

A good sentence does not write itself. Good essays do not just "happen." The man or woman whose letters or articles or stories you admire has mastered the rules and conventions which must be followed in all acceptable writing. You as a person interested in writing will also have to master these rules and conventions if you are to communicate your thoughts successfully. These rules and standards are important. Until you have mastered them, you will be handicapped, for you will lack the *tools* of the writing craft.

I

THE MEANING OF GRAMMAR, RHETORIC, AND COMPOSITION

Consider, first of all, the implications of the words which make up our title: *grammar, rhetoric,* and *composition:*

Grammar deals with the parts of speech, with the variations in the form of words when used in different constructions, and with the relationship between different words within the sentence. You will discover that the rules of grammar are quite definite and that it is possible to say that, under certain circumstances, one form of a word is correct and other forms are incorrect.

Rhetoric deals with the choice of words (diction) and with the effective arrangement of words (style). Rhetoric, in short, is the art of writing well in prose.

Composition is concerned with the "putting together" of parts to form a whole: words into sentences, sentences into paragraphs, and paragraphs into longer units such as essays and narratives. This arrangement is essential to all artistic production—and especially to writing.

Although less rigid than the rules of grammar, the rules of rhetoric, and composition nevertheless do provide us with standards of good diction and good style. These "rules of good English" are the outgrowth of generations of experiments in the art of using words for communication.

SOME USEFUL DEFINITIONS

At this point it will be helpful to state briefly what we mean by certain terms which we shall use in our discussion of written English. For convenience of reference we shall group these definitions and explanations of terms under four headings: The Parts of Speech, Other Grammatical Terms, Punctuation Marks, and Capital Letters. It should be borne in mind that most of these short definitions will be expanded and discussed in later chapters.

THE PARTS OF SPEECH

First, let us examine the traditional **eight parts of speech:**

1. **Noun**	Word used as the name of a person, place, thing, condition, or quality.
2. **Pronoun**	Word used in place of a noun.
3. **Verb**	Word which states or asserts something about a person, place, or thing.

2

4. **Adjective**	Word which modifies the meaning of a noun or pronoun.
5. **Adverb**	Word which modifies the meaning of a verb, adjective, or another adverb.
6. **Preposition**	Word which connects a noun or pronoun (with or without modifiers) with the main body of the sentence.
7. **Conjunction**	Word which joins two or more words, phrases, or clauses.
8. **Interjection**	Word used as an exclamation to express sudden emotion.

OTHER GRAMMATICAL TERMS

In discussing the relationships of the various parts of a sentence to each other, it is convenient to use the following terms:

1. **Subject**	The word or words naming the person or thing about which something is asserted.
2. **Predicate**	The word or words which assert something about the subject.
3. **Object**	The word naming the person or thing directly or indirectly affected by the action of the verb.
4. **Predicate Nominative**	The word or words used after a linking verb to complete the meaning of the verb and to identify or describe the subject.
5. **Phrase**	A group of words forming a unit but not containing a predicate.
6. **Clause**	A group of words containing both a subject and a predicate, but constituting less than a complete sentence.
7. **Substantive**	A noun or pronoun.
8. **Antecedent**	The substantive to which a pronoun refers.
9. **Appositive**	A word or group of words used to explain another word or group of words. The explaining word or group is said to be "in apposition" to the word or group which it explains. Usually the appositive follows directly after the word or words to which it is in apposition.

3

10. **Singular**	The form of a word which refers to *one* person, thing, or instance.
11. **Plural**	The form of a word which refers to *more than one* person, thing, or instance.
12. **Inflection**	Changes in the *form* of a word corresponding to certain changes in the way in which the word is used.
13. **Conjugation**	Systematic arrangement of the various changes in the *forms* of a verb.
14. **Infinitive**	The first principal part of a verb; it is usually preceded by *to*, as in *to write*, and it is used as a noun.
15. **Participle**	An adjective derived from a verb.
16. **Gerund**	A noun derived from a verb.
17. **Syntax**	That part of grammar which deals with sentence structure.

Punctuation Marks

Punctuation marks help make clear the structure of a composition by dividing it into sentences and paragraphs and by dividing the sentence into its several parts. Generally speaking, we may say that punctuation marks are intended to indicate significant pauses. These may be comparatively long pauses between independent thoughts, or short pauses after phrases or clauses to aid the reader in grasping them as units, or very brief pauses to separate individual words from one another. The marks of punctuation (all of which are discussed fully in Chapter VII) are as follows:

,	**Comma**	Mark indicating a very short pause.
.	**Period**	Mark indicating a full stop. (Also used after abbreviations.)
;	**Semicolon**	Mark indicating a longer pause than does the comma.
:	**Colon**	Mark indicating that something, usually a list, is to follow.
—	**Dash**	Mark indicating an abrupt pause.
?	**Question Mark**	Mark placed at the end of a complete question.

4

!	Exclamation Point	Mark placed at the close of an expression of sudden emotion.
'	Apostrophe	Mark indicating the omission of letters in a word.
-	Hyphen	Mark which connects two parts of a word.
" "	Quotation Marks	Marks indicating the beginning and end of a passage given exactly as used by someone else.
' '	Single Quotation Marks	Marks used for a quotation within a quotation.
( )	Parentheses	Marks indicating the beginning and end of a passage only loosely connected with a sentence or paragraph. (A "parenthesis" is a pair of these marks.)
[ ]	Brackets	Marks used in the same way parentheses are used, but setting apart the enclosed material even more than parentheses do.

CAPITAL LETTERS

There are two principal uses of capital letters: (1) to show the beginning of a new thought unit, and (2) to show that a word is a proper noun or a proper adjective. Always capitalize the first word of a sentence. Always capitalize honorary titles when they precede a proper name. In titles of books and in other headings, all important words are ordinarily capitalized. For a fuller discussion of Capitalization, see Chapter VIII.

DICTION

The rules of diction, as has been mentioned, are much less rigid than are the rules of grammar. The problems of diction are problems of usage, and usage varies widely. Consequently, you will want to examine your own word habits carefully. Are you sure that you understand the words you use? Are they the best words with which to convey your meaning? How often do you consult the dictionary? Are you making an effort to enlarge and improve your vocabulary?

Remember that good English conforms to certain traditional

standards. Use words that can be readily understood today. Use words that will be intelligible in all parts of the country. Use words and expressions that are in good repute. Use words that are exact. Chapter IX is devoted to these standards of diction.

BASIC REQUIREMENTS OF GOOD WRITING

There is a great deal more to the writing process, however, than merely learning rules and applying them. You must have *a subject worth writing about* and some *clear thoughts on the subject,* as well as an ability to compose *effective sentences* which conform to *standards of accuracy.* This book aims to aid you in selecting subjects, in organizing your thoughts clearly, and in expressing yourself easily and correctly.

Confident writing is the best writing, and confidence in writing comes from the ability to write good sentences that are the result of clear thinking and are presented in acceptable form. You may be inclined to feel that subject matter is more important than mechanical form. It is undoubtedly true that having something to say is more important than is meticulous punctuation. But the good sentence is the clear sentence—the sentence which reveals its meaning immediately. Whenever the reader's attention is distracted even for a moment away from the thought embodied in the sentence to the unusual structure of the sentence, to the vagaries of punctuation, or to the unorthodox spelling of the words, the author of the sentence has failed. The purpose of writing is, as we have pointed out, to communicate thought. A sloppy manuscript is usually evidence of sloppy thinking. Careless handwriting, misspelled words, lack of essential marks of punctuation—these interpose a barrier between author and reader. Careful attention to the mechanical form of your paper will help you to develop good habits of writing and thinking.

BASIC STEPS IN THE WRITING PROCESS

Let us turn now to the fundamentals of composition. Four problems must be settled before you can commence any writing. They are, briefly stated, these:

> Finding a Subject
> Limiting the Subject
> Evaluating the Material
> Planning the Paper

Once you have begun your composition you will pass through these three stages:

> Writing the First Draft
> Revising the First Draft
> Making the Final Copy

We shall now take up in turn all of these basic steps in the writing process.

Finding a Subject

There are a number of good methods to follow in looking for a subject. Here are some suggestions:

Perhaps you keep a diary. Develop it; you will find that it contains many topics which are good subjects for essays.

Perhaps you have been neglecting to answer letters from your friends. Answer them; letter writing is excellent practice in composition.

Whenever you can, choose subjects that interest you. The things you like to talk about are usually excellent subjects for your papers.

Get yourself a notebook and begin at once noting down possible topics for compositions. Many professional writers have notebooks in which they jot down suggestions and hints for future essays or stories, interesting words, curious phrases, and scraps of overheard conversation.

Here are more specific points, to help you get started:

(1) Write down everything that has happened during the last day or two in diary form. Then search through what you have written for theme topics of various kinds.

(2) Hunt through a newspaper for topics. Find at least ten on the first page.

(3) What makes your family different from others?

(4) What was the most frightening experience you ever had? the most amusing? the most humiliating?

(5) What tools have you used? What machines can you operate? List them.

(6) What items in the newspaper do you regularly skip over? Why? Read one or two and list the reasons why they do not interest you.

7

(7) Draw up a list of unusual persons known to you. Indicate in a word or two why you consider them unusual.

(8) Attempt a definition of the word *hobby*. What are your hobbies? What other unusual ones have you heard of?

(9) Make a list of buildings to describe.

(10) Make a list of twenty episodes in your own life history for later autobiographical treatment. Do not hesitate to include items that seem unimportant now. Try, of course, to select significant ones.

Begin at once to organize and classify your experience. For example, here are some *general headings:*

(1)	Jobs	(11)	Hobbies
(2)	Sports	(12)	Pets
(3)	Food	(13)	Aversions
(4)	Amusements	(14)	Relatives
(5)	Friends	(15)	Travel
(6)	Vacations	(16)	Customs
(7)	Clubs	(17)	Sleep
(8)	Education	(18)	War
(9)	Etiquette	(19)	Science
(10)	Morals	(20)	Religion

Other headings will occur to you.

LIMITING THE SUBJECT

Do not try to handle too broad a topic. Focus your attention on a small subdivision or phase of a general subject. "Human Progress," for example, is clearly not a good title for an essay of five hundred or even five thousand words. But "My Best Summer Vacation" can be treated vividly in a short paper. Vague generalizations about "Human Progress through the Ages" will seem like a vast subject to your reader; but the topic "The Outstanding Event of the Past Month" will keep you within bounds and consequently will enable you to develop your points fully and concretely.

Examine the list of general headings given above and any others that you may have noted down in your notebook. Since it is obvious that you can say something about some phase of every one of these subjects, begin at once to focus your attention upon these limited and more useful phases of these subjects. Follow some such procedure as this in your notebook:

GENERAL SUBJECT	PHASE OF THE SUBJECT
1. Clubs.	(1) When I Was Treasurer
	(2) Seconding the Motion
	(3) Joiners
	(4) My Father Is a Joiner
	(5) How I Learned to Cooperate
	(6) Our Athletic Club
	(7) The Club and the Union
	(8) Why George Always Wants to Be President
	(9) Reading the Minutes
	(10) Robert's Rules of Order
2. Food	(1) Dinner at Home
	(2) Dinner with Relatives
	(3) Dinner on a Jet
	(4) How to Bake a Cake
	(5) How to Plan a Balanced Diet
	(6) A Meal I'll Never Forget
	(7) The Stove of the Future
	(8) Our Camp Cook
	(9) A Picnic Experience
	(10) The Bride's First Meal

Evaluating the Material

It should be abundantly clear by this time that you have plenty of material. Your next problem is to decide what to use and what to discard. If your subject is personal you will have no trouble deciding upon the accuracy of your information. If, however, your subject is not based upon personal experience—if it is derived, that is, from books and other secondary authorities—you will want to convince yourself that you have investigated the field with some thoroughness, that the material you have assembled is trustworthy and accurate, that you have consulted the best authorities. You will want, also, to differentiate between facts and opinions of major importance and those that are of lesser importance.

The best plan is to compose a *one-sentence statement* of your purpose. Until you have such a statement, you cannot evaluate your material efficiently. Therefore, make a habit of writing in your notebook one-sentence statements for your limited subjects. Such a sentence will help you achieve unity not only by setting limits to your paper but also by reminding you of your point of view.

It is helpful to write with a specific reader in mind. Always try to visualize your reader. Invent one if necessary. What impression do you want to make on him? How much does he already know about the subject? Is it your purpose to entertain and possibly amuse him, or to give him information, or to convince him of the need for doing something? Adopt some such scheme of entries as this:

(1) *Subject:* Organizations
(2) *Limited Subject:* Seconding the Motion
(3) *Purpose:* I wish to describe Mr. Granby, the club member who seldom speaks except to second the motion.

(1) *Subject:* Organizations
(2) *Limited Subject:* What we learned by forming a club.
(3) *Purpose:* I wish to convince my reader that a local athletic club for city boys will produce two important results.

PLANNING THE PAPER

Having established and stated your purpose, you must next draw up a tentative plan for your paper. Often your sentence statement will suggest how to arrange your material. Are you going to explain how to change a tire? Trace the several steps in normal order. Is your purpose to give three reasons for studying French? Begin with the one upon which there is sure to be agreement and lead up by way of the second to the third and most important of all. The plan of your paper will depend upon your material and above all upon your purpose and point of view. Are you going to tell a story? Begin with something happening, indicate briefly what has happened before to produce this situation, work through a series of crises to one major crisis, and conclude. The same material may lend itself to expository treatment or to pure description. In each instance the plan will be different, but no matter what sort of writing you have in mind, one thing you must do: make a plan before you start. (Each of the types of composition—narration, description, exposition—will be fully discussed in Chapter VI.)

A pleasant way to learn about structure is to try to uncover the framework of some essay or story written by a practising author. In your notebook, make an outline—not too long—of a magazine article you have enjoyed reading. Consider the problem of the beginning and the end. Copy some examples of good opening paragraphs and state briefly why you consider them good. Do the same for concluding paragraphs. Ask yourself what the author has accomplished in each paragraph. Does he stop abruptly? Does he summarize what has gone before? Make a note of your opinions.

From your list of possible topics, select one and write it down. Then draw up a list of eight or ten questions that might be asked about it by someone who has heard that you have written on this topic. It is often helpful to be able to anticipate such questions. Moreover, answering them supplies you with something definite to say. Here is a sample:

Topic: Binding Books at Home
Questions:
    (1) How expensive is it?
    (2) How much equipment is necessary?
    (3) Are there several kinds of bindings?
    (4) How satisfactory is the "cloth" cover?
    (5) Can glue be made at home?
    (6) Which leathers are most satisfactory?
    (7) What do you mean by "end-papers"?
    (8) How long does it take to bind a book?
    (9) Should I plan to do several at once?
    (10) How do I begin?
    (11) Can I bind magazines and pamphlets?

Perhaps you will not find it expedient to answer all of these questions in one paper. You may want merely to write informally about the pleasures of book-binding as a hobby. You may want to narrate your first (and, it may be, disastrous) attempt to rebind a worn and battered book. Or again, you may want to give simple instructions for home binding. Whatever your purpose, you must make a plan, so that you will know what to include and, more important perhaps, what to omit.

For a short personal essay no formal outline will be necessary. If, however, you are going to write a long, factual and perhaps argumentative article, you will be well advised to write down a list of the several points you wish to make, in the order in which you wish to treat them. Remember that an outline is merely a tool. Do not hesitate to change it whenever in the progress of your writing you feel that a change will make for greater clarity or emphasis. Sample outlines for your guidance will be found on pages 310–312.

WRITING AND REVISING THE FIRST DRAFT AND MAKING THE FINAL COPY

Write your first draft in pencil as rapidly as you can. Do not pause for detailed changes; do not fret about neatness. Put your manuscript aside for a time before you begin revising it. Then go to work systematically and doggedly, examining each sentence and each paragraph as objectively as you can. If you stumble over a word or a phrase, the chances are your reader will also stumble. Read the offending passage aloud. Try various ways of phrasing the idea involved. Be on the alert constantly for violations of unity. Remind yourself that every word in a short article must bear upon the topic. Do not wander into side paths, however delightful they may seem. If you do compose a phrase which you like but which is not needed in your short article, save it for some other time. When you have eliminated all extraneous matter and have applied strict tests of correctness and effectiveness to the material which you intend to use, you will have completed the revision of your first draft.

You will then be ready to make the final copy of your manuscript. This will consist not only in copying the material as it stands in your revised draft, but in bearing in mind the rules of good appearance which are often spoken of as "manuscript form." The standards of manuscript form are discussed at the end of Chapter VIII.

EASE IN WRITING

Most of us recognize good English when we *read* it or *hear* it, even if we have no idea how the writer has obtained his effects. However, those of us who have tried at one time or another to communicate our thoughts in *writing* have soon come to recognize that, as Alexander Pope expressed it, "true ease in writing comes from art, not chance." The chapters which follow are intended to help you attain this "true ease" by supplying you with the tools of the writing process.

CHAPTER II

GRAMMAR: THE PARTS OF SPEECH

ENGLISH WORDS are classified in various ways to show how they are used in sentences. In studying Grammar we are concerned with words which serve the same purpose, and with the relationship between words in sentences. In this chapter we shall discuss the eight classifications of words according to purpose, which are known as the **eight parts of speech**; in Chapter III we shall turn to **syntax** and consider how words are related to each other in sentences. The eight parts of speech are: **nouns, pronouns, verbs, adjectives, adverbs, prepositions, conjunctions,** and **interjections.**

THE NOUN

Nouns are words used to indicate names of persons, places, or things. If we add that nouns also indicate qualities, ideas, and activities, we have a rough but convenient statement of what the word **noun** means. The following words are nouns: *man, city, blanket, friendliness, democracy, manufacture.*

CLASSES OF NOUNS

All nouns may be divided into two groups: common nouns and proper nouns. A **common noun** is the name of a kind or class of person, place, or thing: *traveller, town, brush.* A **proper noun** is the name of a particular person or place: *William Shakespeare, United States.* It should be noted that proper nouns are always capitalized.

Common nouns may be divided into three groups. For example, some grammarians classify them as **abstract, concrete,** and **collective.** Names of qualities, actions, and ideas we call **abstract** nouns; and names of particular objects we call **concrete** nouns. Thus, *neatness* and *fear* are abstract; *knife* and *boy* are concrete.

Jury, herd, audience, team, group, and similar words are called **collective** nouns, for each indicates by means of its singular form a group of persons or objects. Whenever we are thinking of the group as a whole we use a singular verb, as, for example, in the sentence:

The jury *is* composed entirely of men.

When we are thinking primarily of the individual members of the group, we use a plural verb, as in this sentence:

The jury *were taken* to the courthouse in three automobiles.

Be careful not to treat the same collective noun first as singular and then as plural in the same sentence:

I think the committee *is* going to have *its* (not *their*) hands full today.

(See also Agreement of Subject and Verb on page 62.)

PROPERTIES OF NOUNS

English nouns have four characteristics, usually called **properties:** gender, person, number, and case.

GENDER

The **gender** of nouns is determined by sex, and we speak of nouns denoting the male sex as of MASCULINE GENDER, those denoting the female sex as of FEMININE GENDER, and those denoting things of no sex as of NEUTER GENDER. Thus *man, father, husband, brother, son, king, prince, hero* are masculine; and *woman, mother, wife, sister, daughter, queen, princess, heroine* are feminine. Examples of neuter nouns are *house, door, window, street, water, sky, tree, life, hope, happiness.*

As will be noted by comparing the examples of masculine and feminine nouns given above, the two words are sometimes closely related in form, as in *prince* and *princess,* and in *hero* and *heroine.* Sometimes the corresponding words have entirely different forms as in *husband* and *wife,* and in *son* and *daughter.* In learning pairs of corresponding masculine and feminine words, it is necessary to note the exact ending of the feminine form where the two words are related; thus we have:

MASCULINE	FEMININE
baron	baroness
hero	heroine
executor	executrix

14

And where the forms are different, both members of the pair must be noted:

bachelor	spinster
nephew	niece
gander	goose

Such nouns as *child, cousin, neighbor, teacher, visitor* may refer either to masculine or feminine, and are therefore classified as of COMMON GENDER.

PERSON

Person (a property of nouns, pronouns, and verbs) shows whether the noun represents the speaker (FIRST PERSON), the one spoken to (SECOND PERSON), or the one spoken of (THIRD PERSON). The noun itself does not change in form; it is known to be in the first, second, or third person because of the relation it bears to other words in the sentence. A noun is said to be in the FIRST PERSON SINGULAR if it is in apposition with the pronoun *I:*

I, *Andrew,* take thee, Elizabeth, to be my wedded wife.

In the following sentences we have nouns in the second and third persons, indicating the person spoken to and the person spoken of:

Andrew, be there on time.
Andrew is never late.

NUMBER

A noun in English is either singular or plural in **number:** SINGULAR, if it denotes one person or thing; PLURAL, if it denotes more than one.

A noun which is "regular" forms its plural by the addition of *s* to the singular form:

SINGULAR	PLURAL
girl	girls
picture	pictures
lamb	lambs

Certain nouns add *es* to the singular:

(1) Nouns ending in *ch, s, sh, x,* or *z* add *es:*

fox	foxes
patch	patches

15

(2) A number of nouns ending in *o* add *es:*

volcano	volcanoes
Negro	Negroes
hero	heroes

but there are exceptions:

studio	studios
piano	pianos

(3) Nouns ending in *f* or *fe* change *f* to *v* and add *es:*

life	lives
calf	calves
elf	elves

(4) Nouns ending in *y* preceded by a consonant or *qu* change *y* to *i* and add *es:*

baby	babies
lily	lilies
soliloquy	soliloquies

But nouns ending in *y* preceded by a vowel merely add *s* to the singular form:

valley	valleys
chimney	chimneys

A noun which is "irregular" forms its plural by retaining the older plural form of *en* or *ren:*

child	children
ox	oxen

or by a vowel change:

man	men
foot	feet
tooth	teeth

A few nouns are unchanged in the plural:

sheep
swine
trout
deer

16

Some nouns have two plural forms, one regular and the other irregular. The regular plural of *brother* is *brothers*; *brethren* means "member of the same group." *Fishes* is the regular plural of *fish* and suggests a certain number counted individually; *fish* as a plural suggests quantity or species.

Some nouns are plural in form and singular in meaning:

> mathematics
> politics
> news

And a noun plural in form may, if used collectively, be treated as singular:

> Ten years is a long time.

Most compound nouns form the plural by adding *s* to the end of the last word: SINGULAR—*high school;* PLURAL—*high schools.* When the first member is more important, as in *father-in-law,* add *s* to this member: *fathers-in-law.*

CASE

A noun is said to be in the NOMINATIVE CASE (the subject of a sentence) if it denotes the person or thing acting, in the POSSESSIVE CASE if it denotes the person or thing possessing, and in the OBJECTIVE CASE (the object of a verb or preposition) if it denotes the person or thing acted upon.

Nominative and objective cases involve no change in the form of the noun and can usually be determined only by the word order of the sentence. Note the following sentence:

> The *father* punished the *child* for *disobedience.*

Here *father* is in the nominative case since it is the subject, *child* is in the objective case since it is the direct object of the verb *punished,* and *disobedience* is in the objective case since it is the object of the preposition *for.*

In the sentence which follows we have examples of various types of Nominatives:

> The *meeting* having ended, Arthur Johnson, our *president,* said: *"George,* you are the best *secretary* we have ever had."

Here *meeting* has no direct connection with a verb and is called the Nominative Absolute; *president* is in the nominative case, since it is in apposition with the subject, *Arthur Johnson; George* is the Nominative of Direct Address; and *secretary* is the Predicate Nominative, since it is a noun in the predicate referring to the subject, *you*.

The POSSESSIVE CASE does involve a change in the form of the noun. If the noun is singular, possession is shown by adding the apostrophe (') and *s;* if the noun is plural, by an apostrophe after the *s:*

> the girl's name
> the girls' names

The following special usages may be noted:

(1) Plural nouns not ending in *s* form the possessive by adding *'s:*

> the men's interests
> the children's games

(2) Compound words, names of firms, and the like add *'s* at the end:

> his sister-in-law's question

(3) If the singular ends in *s* and the word is short, *'s* is added to form the possessive:

> Keats's poems
> Jefferson Davis's term of office

(4) If the singular ends in an *s*-sound and the following word begins with an *s*-sound, the apostrophe only is added:

> Louis' sister
> for goodness' sake

(5) English idiom sometimes requires a double possessive:

> that book of George's

THE PRONOUN

A **pronoun** is a word used in place of a noun, to avoid repetition of the noun to which it refers. The word *he,* for example, has no meaning unless it can be referred to a previous noun (which is known as the "antecedent" of the pronoun). Naturally, the connection between pronoun and antecedent must be immediately and unmistakably clear.

> Ernest always keeps his dictionary close at hand, for he regards it as an indispensable aid to writing.

In this sentence *Ernest* is the antecedent of *his* and *he*; *dictionary* is the antecedent of *it*.

CLASSES OF PRONOUNS

In English we speak of five kinds of pronouns: personal, relative, interrogative, demonstrative (or definite), and indefinite.

PERSONAL PRONOUNS

Pronouns which stand directly for names of persons, places, or things are called **personal** pronouns: *I, you, he, she, it, we,* and *they.*

> *You* drive for the first hour; then *I* will take over.
> *It* is an interesting story.
> *We* ought to reach Pittsburgh by four o'clock.
> *They* will be waiting impatiently.

Compound forms of certain personal pronouns are made by the addition of *self* or *selves*. These compound forms are called "reflexive" if they are in the predicate of a sentence and refer back to the subject. They are called "intensive" if they reinforce or give emphasis to another word in the same part of the sentence.

> He injured *himself* last week. (reflexive)
> I insist upon seeing them *myself*. (reflexive)
> You *yourself* must be very happy about it. (intensive)
> The governor *himself* will be at the meeting. (intensive)

CAUTION: Do not use the compound form as the subject of the sentence.

> James and *I* often go hunting.
> (NOT: James and myself often go hunting.)

RELATIVE PRONOUNS

The **relative** pronouns—*who, what, that* and *which*—refer to antecedents and, at the same time, introduce dependent clauses. *Who* applies to persons; *what* applies to things; *that* can refer to either persons, animals, or inanimate objects; *which* is not applied to persons, but does refer to animals or inanimate objects:

> He is a man *who* is bound to succeed.
> He asked me to give you *what* you wanted.
> This is the house *that* Jack built.
> Here is the spot of *which* I was telling you.

There is another distinction, however, based on whether the reference is general or specific. *That* is usually more general, and *which* more specific:

> There are a great many houses *that* I like.
> This is the house *which* I like best.

Compound forms of the relative pronouns are formed by adding *ever* or *soever:*

> *Whoever* comes first will have the best seat.
> *Whatever* he wants, give it to him.
> Do it *whichever* way you prefer.

INTERROGATIVE PRONOUNS

The **interrogative** pronouns—*who, which,* and *what*—are used in asking "direct" questions:

> Just *what* do you mean by that?
> *Who* came to the door when you knocked?
> *Which* will you have?

Interrogative pronouns are also used in indirect questions (that is, questions which are only a part of the thought of the sentence, and consequently are not followed by a question mark):

> I want to know *what* you mean by that.

DEMONSTRATIVE PRONOUNS

The **demonstrative** pronouns—*this, that, these,* and *those*—point definitely to persons or things to which they refer:

> *This* is my plan.
> *These* are my plans.
> *That* is the house I mentioned..
> *Those* are the boys he told us about.

INDEFINITE PRONOUNS

Indefinite pronouns point out persons and things but do so less definitely than do the demonstratives:

> *Some* stayed away from the meeting.
> *Several* were kept home because of illness.
> *Few* stayed away of their own accord.

The principal words functioning as indefinite pronouns are:

all	everything
any	few
anybody	neither
anyone	nobody
anything	none
each	one
either	several
everybody	some

PROPERTIES OF PRONOUNS

PERSON AND GENDER

The personal pronouns vary in form to show a change in **person;** other pronouns do not. *I* and *we* are in the first person, representing the speaker; *you* is in the second person, representing the one spoken to; and *he, she, it,* and *they* are in the third person, representing the one spoken of.

Personal pronouns in the third person singular vary in form to show a change in **gender.** *He* is masculine, *she* is feminine, and *it* is neuter.

NUMBER

A pronoun is either singular or plural in **number** depending upon the number of the antecedent. Change of number in personal pronouns is shown by change of form, except that the pronoun for the second person is the same for singular and plural:

SINGULAR	PLURAL
I will work now.	*We* will work now.
You will work now.	*You* will work now.
He will work now.	*They* will work now.
She will work now.	*They* will work now.
It will work now.	*They* will work now.

21

The demonstrative pronouns *this* and *that* are singular and *these* and *those* are plural. Indefinite pronouns are either singular (*one, someone, each*) or plural (*few, all, many*). Interrogative and relative pronouns do not change in form to indicate change in number:

> *This* is the short-story *which* I enjoyed.
> *These* are the short-stories *which* I enjoyed.

CASE

Personal pronouns and a few relative pronouns show change in case by a change in form:

NOMINATIVE CASE

	SINGULAR	PLURAL
FIRST PERSON	I	we
SECOND	you	you
THIRD	he, she, it	they

POSSESSIVE CASE

FIRST	my (mine)	our (ours)
SECOND	your (yours)	your (yours)
THIRD	his, her (hers), its	their (theirs)

OBJECTIVE CASE

FIRST	me	us
SECOND	you	you
THIRD	him, her, it	them

Relative pronouns show the following variations:

> NOMINATIVE CASE: who, that, which
> POSSESSIVE CASE: whose
> OBJECTIVE CASE: whom, that, which

AGREEMENT OF PRONOUN AND ANTECEDENT

A pronoun refers to a previous substantive (noun or pronoun) and must agree with this "antecedent" in person, number, and gender.

> Janet always likes to have people think of *her* as a very busy person.

In this sentence the pronoun *her* is third person, singular number, and feminine gender to agree with the antecedent noun *Janet* which is also third person, singular number, and feminine gender. Notice that the pronoun need not be in the same case as the antecedent. *Janet* is nominative; *her* is objective.

Observe that the following words are singular and that when one of them is used as an antecedent it requires a singular pronoun:

another	every	nobody
any	everybody	no one
anybody	everyone	one
anyone	kind	person
anything	man	somebody
each	many a one	someone
either	neither	sort

(The pronoun *none* may be treated either as singular or as plural.)

The following sentences are designed to illustrate the agreement of pronoun and antecedent:

Everybody says *he* will do *his* best to follow the printed instructions.

One reads *his* list carefully; another merely glances rapidly through *his*.

Each is aware of how important the warnings are to *him*.

Neither of the two can be expected to do more than *his* share.

This sort of emergency always has *its* exciting moments.

Somebody, of course, is bound to forget what *he* should do.

Unless special emphasis is required, use the masculine pronoun to refer to two antecedents of different gender:

Every man and woman is expected to do *his* duty.

Every man and woman is expected to carry out *his* or *her* duties promptly.

A collective noun as antecedent requires a singular or plural pronoun depending upon the sentence:

The boat-crew yesterday won *its* fifth straight race.

The boat-crew pulled on *their* sweaters.

In the first of these sentences the boat-crew is thought of as a unit; in the second sentence the members are thought of as individuals.

If a single pronoun refers to two antecedents, it should agree with the nearer antecedent:

> I am sure that either Sam or his two friends will lose *their* way on this trip.
>
> They spent the afternoon talking about the college courses and the professors *whom* they particularly did not approve of.

THE VERB

Verbs are words which say or assert something about a person, place, or thing. A verb may make a statement, ask a question, or give a command. A verb may express action, occurrence, or mode of being. The italicized words in these sentences are verbs:

> The young student *became* interested.
> *Will* you *do* something for me?
> Harry *is reading* a new novel.

KINDS OF VERBS

Verbs are either "transitive" or "intransitive." **Transitive** verbs require an object; **intransitive** verbs do not:

> Mrs. Jones *bakes* wonderful pies. (transitive)
> She *walks* rather rapidly. (intransitive)

Some verbs are listed in the dictionary as both transitive and intransitive. The verb *ran* has one meaning in the sentence

> The horse *ran* away. (intransitive)

and a different meaning in

> The women *ran* a bazaar at the fair. (transitive)

Verbs are either "principal" verbs or "auxiliary" verbs. **Principal** verbs are verbs complete in themselves; **auxiliary** verbs are verbs joined to the principal verb in order that the idea of the verb may be expressed more fully:

> She *speaks*. (principal verb)
> She *will* speak. (auxiliary verb)

Auxiliary verbs most often met with are:

be	may	should
can	must	shall
do	ought	will
have		would

Verbs are either "regular" or "irregular." If a verb forms its past tense and past participle by adding *d* or *ed* to the present tense (or simple form of the verb) we speak of it as a **regular** verb. Most verbs in English are conjugated regularly. An **irregular** verb forms its past tense and past participle by some internal change in the word. It should be noted that all auxiliary verbs are irregular.

	PRESENT	PAST	PAST PARTICIPLE
REGULAR	permit	permitted	permitted
IRREGULAR	am	was	been
IRREGULAR	do	did	done

PROPERTIES OF VERBS

A number of technical terms are used to describe the various **properties** of a verb: **voice, mood, tense, person,** and **number.**

VOICE

Verbs are active or passive in **voice.** If the subject of a verb is represented as performing the action, we speak of the verb as being in the ACTIVE voice:

> He *gave* me the money.

If the subject is acted upon, we speak of the verb as being in the PASSIVE voice:

> The money *was given* to me.

MOOD

Verbs are said to be in one of three **moods:** INDICATIVE, SUBJUNCTIVE, or IMPERATIVE. Mood shows the manner in which the state of being or action of the verb is to be regarded.

(1) The INDICATIVE mood is the mood which states a fact or asks a question:

> We *are* uneasy about it.
> *Are* we uneasy about it?
> They *say* that we *are* uneasy about it.
> We *are* not uneasy about it.

(2) The SUBJUNCTIVE mood suggests that something is uncertain, imagined, desirable or undesirable, or contrary to fact. As a general rule, the subjunctive is found in a dependent clause, introduced by a conjunction such as *if, though, lest, that, till,* or *unless:*

> If I *were* you, I should not worry.
>
> Suppose the worst *should happen*. You have taken every precaution.
>
> It is essential that you *be* on the alert.

(3) The IMPERATIVE mood expresses a request or a command. The subject is usually omitted:

> *Introduce* me to your friend.
>
> *Do* not *slam* the door.

TENSE

Tense means the time of the action indicated—present, past, future. Action in the present requires the PRESENT TENSE:

> She *is* at home.

Action in the past requires the PAST TENSE:

> She *was* at home yesterday.

And action expected to take place in the future requires the FUTURE TENSE:

> She *will be* at home all next week.

Present, past, and future tenses deal with actions as taking place at the time indicated. If the action is thought of as completed (or "perfected"), we say that the verb is in the PRESENT PERFECT (or PERFECT), PAST PERFECT, or FUTURE PERFECT tense:

> She *has been* on her vacation. (perfect)
>
> She *had been* on her vacation when I saw her last week. (past perfect)
>
> She *will have been* on her vacation by the time I see her next. (future perfect)

PERSON AND NUMBER

A verb must agree with its subject in person and number.

The verb is said to be in the FIRST, SECOND, or THIRD **person** depending upon whether it shows that the action is that of the speaker, the person spoken to, or the person spoken of.

The verb is said to be either SINGULAR or PLURAL in number SINGULAR if the action or state expressed is that of one person or thing; PLURAL if it is that of more than one:

	SINGULAR	PLURAL
FIRST PERSON	I buy	we buy
SECOND PERSON	you buy	you buy
THIRD PERSON	he buys	they buy

The conjugation tables will show that most English verbs have the same form for all persons, with the exception of the third person singular. The older form for the second person singular and plural (*thou art, thou buyest, ye buy,* and the like) is now seldom used except in poetry. Current English requires *you* in both singular and plural. The irregular verb *be* presents such conjugated forms as:

I am
you are
he is

all of which must be memorized. The full conjugation is given on pages 32 and 33.

The number of a verb agrees with the number of the noun or pronoun which is the verb's subject. Collective nouns and nouns which indicate amounts and measurements are sometimes troublesome. Note that a plural verb is required in the sentence

Two cups of sugar *are* then added.

because the verb agrees with the plural noun "cups." However, a singular verb is required in the sentence

Ten years *is* a long time.

because the expression "Ten years" is used in a collective sense meaning a "period of ten years."

FINITE AND INFINITE VERBS

Finite verbs possess the properties of voice, mood, tense, person, and number. They must be distinguished sharply from the so-called **infinite** verb-forms—infinitive, participle, and gerund—which are not limited as to number, person, and mood.

THE INFINITIVE

The **infinitive** is a verbal noun because it has the properties of both a noun and a verb. The sentence

> *To see* her is *to love* her.

contains two infinitives: *to see* and *to love*. The word *to,* originally a preposition, is now regarded as part of the infinitive and is called the "sign" of the infinitive. Sometimes it is omitted as in

> Make him *stop*.

It is usually omitted when an auxiliary verb is used. The uses of the infinitive include the following:

> as subject: *To win* is his main desire.
> as object: They wanted to *linger*.
> as adjective: This is a point *to be noted*.
> as adverb: We went yesterday *to see him*.

THE PARTICIPLE

The **participle** is a "verbal adjective." The present participle of regular verbs is formed by adding *-ing* to the "stem" or "root-form" of the verb. The past participle of regular verbs has the same form as the past indicative. The past perfect participle consists of the past participle preceded by the word *having*.

STEM	PRESENT PARTICIPLE	PAST PARTICIPLE	PAST PERFECT PARTICIPLE
look	looking	looked	having looked
measure	measuring	measured	having measured

The participle may be used:

as an adjective to modify a noun:

> *Barking* dogs seldom bite.
> The *threatening* letter alarmed him.

as a verb-form taking an object:

> *Giving* him the message, I left at once.

as a verb-form modified by an adverb:

> *Muttering* incoherently, the old man walked away.

The **gerund** is a "verbal noun." The present tense of the gerund is formed by adding *-ing* to the stem and is thus identical in spelling with the present participle. It differs, however, in use. The gerund may be used in the several ways a noun is used:

as subject of a verb:

> *Walking* is good exercise.

as object of a verb:

> He taught *swimming*.

as predicate noun:

> Seeing is *believing*.

as a verb-form taking an object:

> *Answering* questions was her job.

The gerund often has a subject, either in the possessive or objective case:

> *Alfred's coming* to town was unexpected.
> Can you picture *him winning* first prize?

The gerund is often used in a phrase:

> *After studying* for six hours, he gave up.

CONJUGATION

To **conjugate** a verb is to arrange its inflectional forms according to a standardized plan. Such an arrangement is an expansion of three forms of the verb, called the **principal parts of the verb:** the INFINITIVE, the PAST TENSE FORM, and the PAST PARTICIPLE.

	INFINITIVE	PAST TENSE	PAST PARTICIPLE
REGULAR	call	called	called
IRREGULAR	speak	spoke	spoken

Observe that the second principal part is always used alone to indicate simple past action or state:

> He *called* on the mayor yesterday.
> They *spoke* at length.

But the third principal part is always used in a verb-phrase, never alone:

> When he *had called* out the ten names, he left the stage.
> We *have spoken* of her frequently.

The full conjugation of a verb makes use of the following scheme for all tenses and moods in both active and passive voice:

INDICATIVE MOOD

PRESENT TENSE

ACTIVE VOICE

	Singular	*Plural*
FIRST PERSON	I call	we call
SECOND PERSON	you call	you call
THIRD PERSON	he calls	they call

A condensed conjugation uses only the third person, singular number of the verb, as in the following "synopsis" of the regular verb *to call:*

PRINCIPAL PARTS: **call, called, called**

INDICATIVE MOOD

	Active	*Passive*
PRESENT	he calls	is called
PAST	he called	was called
FUTURE	he will call	will be called
PERFECT	he has called	has been called
PAST PERFECT	he had called	had been called
FUTURE PERFECT	he will have called	will have been called

SUBJUNCTIVE MOOD

		Active	*Passive*
PRESENT	(if) he call	be called
PAST	(if) he called	were called
PERFECT	(if) he have called	have been called
PAST PERFECT	(if) he had called	had been called

IMPERATIVE MOOD

PRESENT	call	be called

PRESENT	(to) call	be called
PERFECT	(to) have called	have been called

GERUND

PRESENT	calling	being called
PERFECT	having called	having been called

PARTICIPLE

PRESENT	calling	being called
PAST		called
PERFECT	having called	having been called

The **progressive form** of the verb, which shows action going on at the time referred to, consists of the appropriate form of the verb *to be* plus the present participle. The **emphatic form** makes use of the appropriate form of the verb *to do* plus the stem.

	SIMPLE FORM	PROGRESSIVE FORM	EMPHATIC FORM
PRESENT	he calls	he is calling	he does call
PAST	he called	he was calling	he did call

Synopsis of the irregular verb **to drive**
PRINCIPAL PARTS: **drive, drove, driven**

INDICATIVE MOOD

	Active	*Passive*
PRESENT	he drives	is driven
PAST	he drove	was driven
FUTURE	he will drive	will be driven
PERFECT	he has driven	has been driven
PAST PERFECT	he had driven	had been driven
FUTURE PERFECT	he will have driven	will have been driven

SUBJUNCTIVE MOOD

PRESENT	(if) he drive	be driven
PAST	(if) he drove	were driven
PERFECT	(if) he have driven	have been driven
PAST PERFECT	(if) he had driven	had been driven

31

PRESENT   drive   be driven

INFINITIVE

PRESENT	(to) drive	be driven
PERFECT	(to) have driven	have been driven

GERUND

PRESENT	driving	being driven
PERFECT	having driven	having been driven

PARTICIPLE

PRESENT	driving	being driven
PAST		driven
PERFECT	having driven	having been driven

The verb **to be**

PRINCIPAL PARTS: **be, was, been**

INDICATIVE MOOD

Active

PRESENT	I am; he is; we, you, they are
PAST	I, he was; we, you, they were
FUTURE	I, we shall be; he, you, they will be
PERFECT	I have been; he has been; we, you, they have been
PAST PERFECT	I, he, we, you, they had been
FUTURE PERFECT	I, we shall have been; he, you, they will have been

SUBJUNCTIVE MOOD

Active

PRESENT	(if) I, he, we, you, they be
PAST	(if) I, he, we, you, they were
PERFECT	(if) I, he, we, you, they have been
PAST PERFECT	(if) I, he, we, you, they had been

IMPERATIVE MOOD

PRESENT   be

	INFINITIVE
PRESENT	(to) be
PERFECT	(to) have been

	GERUND
PRESENT	being
PERFECT	having been

	PARTICIPLE
PRESENT	being
PAST	been
PERFECT	having been

LIST OF IRREGULAR VERBS

The following list includes most of the so-called irregular verbs: those that form the past tense and the past participle otherwise than by adding -ed. The principal parts of these verbs must be memorized.

PRESENT	PAST	PAST PARTICIPLE
abide	abode	abode
arise	arose	arisen
be	was	been
bear	bore	borne
bear	bore	born
beat	beat	beaten
become	became	become
beget	begot	begotten
begin	began	begun
behold	beheld	beheld
bend	bent	bent
beseech	besought	besought
bet	bet	bet
bid	bid (bade)	bid (bidden)
bind	bound	bound
bite	bit	bitten
bleed	bled	bled
blow	blew	blown
break	broke	broken
breed	bred	bred
bring	brought	brought

33

PRESENT	PAST	PAST PARTICIPLE
build	built	built
burst	burst	burst
buy	bought	bought
cast	cast	cast
catch	caught	caught
choose	chose	chosen
cleave	clove (cleaved, cleft)	cloven (cleaved, cleft)
cling	clung	clung
come	came	come
cost	cost	cost
creep	crept	crept
crow	crew (crowed)	crowed
cut	cut	cut
deal	dealt	dealt
dig	dug	dug
do	did	done
draw	drew	drawn
drink	drank	drunk
drive	drove	driven
eat	ate	eaten
fall	fell	fallen
feed	fed	fed
feel	felt	felt
fight	fought	fought
find	found	found
flee	fled	fled
fling	flung	flung
fly	flew	flown
forget	forgot	forgotten
forsake	forsook	forsaken
freeze	froze	frozen
get	got	got
give	gave	given
go	went	gone
grind	ground	ground
grow	grew	grown
hang	hung	hung
hang	hanged	hanged
have	had	had
hear	heard	heard
hide	hid	hidden
hit	hit	hit
hold	held	held
hurt	hurt	hurt

PRESENT	PAST	PAST PARTICIPLE
keep	kept	kept
know	knew	known
lay	laid	laid
lead	led	led
leave	left	left
lend	lent	lent
let	let	let
lie	lay	lain
lose	lost	lost
make	made	made
mean	meant	meant
meet	met	met
pay	paid	paid
read (*pron.* "reed")	read (*pron.* "red")	read (*pron.* "red")
rid	rid	rid
ride	rode	ridden
ring	rang	rung
rise	rose	risen
run	ran	run
say	said	said
see	saw	seen
seek	sought	sought
sell	sold	sold
send	sent	sent
set	set	set
shake	shook	shaken
shine	shone	shone
shoe	shod	shod
shoot	shot	shot
show	showed	showed (shown)
shut	shut	shut
sing	sang	sung
sink	sank	sunk
sit	sat	sat
slay	slew	slain
slide	slid	slid
sling	slung	slung
slink	slunk	slunk
smite	smote	smitten
sow	sowed	sowed (sown)
speak	spoke	spoken
speed	sped	sped
spend	spent	spent
spin	spun	spun

PRESENT	PAST	PAST PARTICIPLE
split	split	split
spread	spread	spread
spring	sprang	sprung
stand	stood	stood
steal	stole	stolen
stick	stuck	stuck
sting	stung	stung
stink	stank (stunk)	stunk
stride	strode	stridden
strike	struck	struck (stricken)
string	strung	strung
strive	strove	striven (strived)
swear	swore	sworn
sweep	swept	swept
swim	swam	swum
swing	swung	swung
take	took	taken
teach	taught	taught
tear	tore	torn
tell	told	told
think	thought	thought
thrive	throve (thrived)	thrived (thriven)
throw	threw	thrown
thrust	thrust	thrust
tread	trod	trodden
wake	woke (waked)	woke (waked)
wear	wore	worn
weave	wove	woven
weep	wept	wept
win	won	won
wind	wound	wound
wring	wrung	wrung
write	wrote	written

AUXILIARY VERBS

There are eight *auxiliary* verbs, or verbs which combine with other verbs and modify the meaning of the verb with which they combine. These auxiliary verbs are: **be, can, do, have, may, must, shall,** and **will.** Some of these have full conjugations of their own. All of them may be used to form what are known as verb-phrases; for example: I **will** *go;* It **might** *have been done;* They **must** *agree.*

Forms of the verb **may**

PRESENT   I, he, we, you, they **may**
PAST   I, he, we, you, they **might**

Forms of the verb **can**

PRESENT   I, he, we, you, they **can**
PAST   I, he, we, you, they **could**

Potential Mood of Various Auxiliary Verbs

PRESENT TENSE

I
he
we   **may, can,** or **must** *work, eat, agree*
you
they

PRESENT PERFECT TENSE

I
he
we   **may, can,** or **must** *have worked,* etc.
you
they

PAST TENSE

I
he
we   **might, could, would,** or **should** *work,* etc.
you
they

PAST PERFECT TENSE

I
he
we   **might, could, would,** or **should** *have worked,* etc.
you
they

37

Forms of the verb do

Do is used as an auxiliary for emphasis, interrogation, or negation. It is used only in the present and past tenses of the indicative and subjunctive moods, and in the imperative.

PRESENT INDICATIVE   I **do,** he **does,** we, you, they **do** *work*
PAST INDICATIVE   I **did,** he **did,** we, you, they **did** *work*
PRESENT AND PAST
  SUBJUNCTIVE   (If) I, he, we, you, they **do** *work*
IMPERATIVE   **Do** *work*

Forms of the verb have
(As an auxiliary to form Perfect Tenses)

PRESENT PERFECT   **I have** *worked,* he **has** *worked;* we, you, they **have** *worked*

PAST PERFECT   I, he, we, you, they **had** *worked*

SEMI-AUXILIARIES

Ought and **let** are called semi-auxiliaries. **Ought** is used only in the present indicative and is followed by the infinitive form of the verb with which it is combined, as in I **ought** *to work.* **Let** is most often used with the infinitive (without *to*) and the objective case of the pronoun, as in **Let** *him work.*

USE OF **Shall** AND **Will**

A. Use the form given below to express SIMPLE FUTURITY or EXPECTATION on the part of the person speaking:

I shall do it   We shall do it
You will do it   You will do it
He will do it   They will do it

B. Use the form given below to express DETERMINATION, DESIRE, COMMAND, THREAT, PROMISE, WILLINGNESS, and INTENTION on the part of the person speaking:

I will do it   We will do it
You shall do it   You shall do it
He shall do it   They shall do it

SPECIAL USAGES:

    (1) In courteous commands, use the form "you will":

        You will submit your report by Monday.

    (2) Conventional formulas often require "will":

        Sergeant, you will lead your men to the barracks.
        The meeting will come to order.

    (3) When an adjective conveys the idea of willingness, use *shall* in the first person; but, with an adverb use *will:*

        I shall be most happy to do it for you.
        We shall be glad to do it.
        We will gladly do it. (adverb)

C. In questions, use whatever form is expected in the answer. This means that in questions *shall* must be used for the first person:

        Shall I write to him?
        Shall we be on time?

Either *shall* or *will* is used in the second and third persons depending upon the answer expected:

Shall you leave early? ANSWER: I shall. (pure future)
Will you do it no matter what happens? ANSWER: I will. (determination)
Will they see it? ANSWER: They will. (pure future)
Shall he be told? ANSWER: He shall. (necessity)

USE OF **Should** AND **Would**

A. The rules for the use of *should* and *would* are in general the same as those for *shall* and *will:*

    I should like to do it. (simple futurity)
    I would do it if I dared. (determination)
    We should very much enjoy doing it. (simple futurity)
    Should you buy it if it is offered for sale? EXPECTED ANSWER: I should. (simple futurity)
    Would you buy it if you could? EXPECTED ANSWER: I would. (determination)

B. Use *should* in first, second, and third persons to express general obligation, expectation, or condition:

> We should have questioned him more closely.
>
> If he should happen to be there tomorrow, we must speak to him.
>
> He really should be there at least by five o'clock.

C. Use *would* in first, second, and third persons to express an habitual or customary action or to express a wish:

> > Once a week Herbert would go to the library.
> >
> > Lose weight? Would that I could!

Indirect Discourse

After verbs of SAYING, TELLING, THINKING, and the like, use the past tense and the past perfect tense for the present and past respectively of direct discourse:

Direct	Indirect
They said: "We are unwilling to go to the meeting."	They said they were unwilling to go to the meeting.
They said: "Williams told us it was not an important one."	They said that Williams had told them it was not an important one.

But observe that universal or permanent truths are expressed by the present tense:

The teacher said: "A straight line is the shortest distance between two points."	The teacher said that a straight line is the shortest distance between two points.

In writing indirect discourse, use *shall, will, should,* or *would* as required in direct discourse:

Direct	Indirect
Will you be at home?	They asked him whether he would be at home or not.
As far as I know, I shall be at home all evening.	He told them that as far as he knew he should be at home all evening.
We shall call on him.	We think that we shall call on him.
I shall not be going out. (simple futurity)	You say that you shall not be going out.
I will wait until you come. (determination)	You tell us that you will wait until we come.

THE ADJECTIVE

Adjectives are words which indicate a quality or condition. "An *old* man," "the *late* mayor," "a *lonely* farm" are expressions in which the noun is modified in a certain way and in which the meaning is rendered more exact. "I am *weary*" and "She seems *pleased*" show that adjectives may modify pronouns as well.

Classes of Adjectives

Adjectives may be classified as Descriptive, Limiting, and Proper Adjectives.

DESCRIPTIVE ADJECTIVES

Descriptive adjectives indicate a quality or a condition:

> her *blue* dress
> *bright* colors
> the *redecorated* apartment
> his *smiling* answer

LIMITING ADJECTIVES

Limiting adjectives indicate number or quantity, or point out limits. The *articles* "the" and "a" and "an" are limiting adjectives (see pp. 44–45).

> my *only* ambition
> the *ninth* inning
> *ten* cents

PROPER ADJECTIVES

Proper adjectives, as the name suggests, come from proper nouns:

> *American* soldiers
> *Bolivian* tin

Proper adjectives often become in effect simple descriptive adjectives and lose their capital letters except at the beginning of a sentence:

> *melba* toast
> *pasteurized* milk

Position of Adjectives

Usually in English sentences, the adjective precedes the noun it modifies, as in all the examples given thus far. If an adjective follows its noun, we may be sure that the writer avoids the usual pattern for some good reason. In some contexts, it is more emphatic to say *joy unspeakable* than *unspeakable joy*. The nouns *anything, everything, nothing,* and *something* are regularly followed, not preceded, by an adjective, as in these expressions:

> everything *imaginable*
> nothing *unpleasant*
> something *interesting*

English idiom sometimes requires that the adjective follow the noun. Notice that the second of the two following sentences is correct:

> She was an *eager* girl to study.
> She was a girl *eager* to study.

Certain fixed forms, such as court *martial* (rather than *martial* court) and William the *Conqueror,* must be learned by observing the usage of the best writers. Notice that the name George V is read as "George *the* Fifth," the adjective being itself modified by the article *the.* The problem of the predicate adjective will be dealt with in the chapter on Syntax.

Comparison of Adjectives

We may express a greater or less degree of a quality by the device of **comparison,** and adjectives may be said to be POSITIVE, COMPARATIVE, or SUPERLATIVE in "degree." For example, the expressions:

the *old* house	the *simple* plan
the *older* house	the *simpler* plan
the *oldest* house	the *simplest* plan

show the "regular" forms of comparison, that is, by adding -*er* and -*est* for the comparative and superlative degrees. Usually there is no real problem of spelling involved. Note however that the mute *e* in *simple* is dropped when -*er* or -*est* is added, and *y* changes to *i* in *pretty, prettier, prettiest.*

Examples: *young, younger, youngest; late, later, latest; lazy, lazier, laziest.*

A second method of comparison is to place the word "more" before the positive form of the adjective to form the comparative; and the word "most" to form the superlative:

> It is *likely*.
> It is *more likely*.
> It is *most likely*.

Words of several syllables and also participles are almost always compared by using "more" and "most" rather than by adding "er" and "est":

POSITIVE	COMPARATIVE	SUPERLATIVE
unusual	more unusual	most unusual
learned	more learned	most learned
willing	more willing	most willing

Both of the methods described show comparison in ascending or increasing series. However, the words *less* and *least* may be prefixed to show comparison in a descending or decreasing series:

> It is *likely*.
> It is *less likely*.
> It is *least likely*.

Certain English adjectives have a fixed form in comparative and superlative which must be learned. The following list contains the majority of such "irregular" adjectives:

POSITIVE	COMPARATIVE	SUPERLATIVE
bad	worse	worst
far	farther (further)	farthest (furthest)
good (well)	better	best
little	less	least
many (much)	more	most

Adjectives Which Cannot Be Compared

Some adjectives cannot be compared. Examples are (1) adjectives like *unique* ("the one of its kind"), *perfect,* and *circular;* and (2) the numerals and articles: *ten* dollars; *the* book.

A thing cannot be *more* or *less* unique, *more* or *less* everlasting, or *more* or *less* untouchable. There can be, logically, no degrees of "uniqueness." We may, of course, speak of something as being *not quite* or *almost* unique or *not quite* or *almost* perfect, but we should avoid such expressions as *more empty* and *most unendurable*. The following list contains examples of adjectives which, strictly speaking, do not admit of comparison:

absolute	ideal
basic	meaningless
chief	mortal
comparative	obvious
complete	omnipotent
contemporary	perfect
devoid	possible
empty	primary
entire	replete
essential	simultaneous
eternal	ultimate
everlasting	unanimous
fatal	unendurable
final	unique
full	universal
fundamental	whole
harmless	worthless

Several adjectives beginning *in-* belong in this group; for example, *inadmissible, inevitable, indestructible,* and *incessant*.

NUMERALS

Numbering adjectives, or "numerals," are either **cardinals** or **ordinals,** the first group indicating number absolutely and the second indicating a certain relative position in a series. *One, two, three, four, twenty,* and the like are cardinals, whereas *first, second, third, fourth, twentieth,* and the like are ordinals.

ARTICLES

There are two **articles:** the words *a* (or *an*) called the **indefinite** article and the word *the* called the **definite** article. The article is really a limiting adjective and is used, either alone or with other adjectives, to modify a noun. The indefinite article *a* is used before words beginning with a consonant sound, as in:

a year

a man

a unit

44

An is used before words beginning with a vowel sound, as in:

> *an* umbrella
> *an* hour
> *an* unusual day

Notice that **sound,** not spelling, determines the use of *a* or *an,* and that our choice depends upon the word immediately following the article:

> *an* uncle
> *a* rich uncle

The definite article *the* is separated from the noun by the modifying adjective or adjectives if there àre any:

> *the* sky
> *the* beautiful sky
> *the* beautiful blue sky

THE ADVERB

Adverbs may modify verbs, as in these sentences:

> She smiled *contentedly.*
> The news travelled *fast.*

Adverbs may modify adjectives:

> The applicant was *under* twenty-one.

Adverbs may modify other adverbs:

> I know that all *too* well.

Adverbs that modify a whole clause or sentence are called **sentence adverbs:**

> *Unfortunately,* no one saw him do it.

We can often identify adverbs by asking if the words in question tell WHERE, HOW, WHEN, or TO WHAT EXTENT something is done. *Today, simply, here, now,* and *more* are examples.

In the following table, **certain familiar adverbs are** grouped according to meaning:

> TIME: *now, when, then, finally, never, lately*
> PLACE: *where, there, here, below, far, downstairs*
> MANNER: *well, ill, how, otherwise*
> DEGREE: *more, less, too, completely, much, equally*
> CAUSE OR PURPOSE: *why, therefore, wherefore, consequently*
> NUMBER: *first, secondly, thirdly*

Yes is called an **affirmative** adverb, and *no* and *not* are called **negative** adverbs. When an adverb is used in asking a question, either direct or indirect, it is called an **interrogative** adverb:

> *How* are you feeling?
> They cannot tell *why* he did it.

In the last sentence, *why* is not merely an interrogative adverb; it is also a **relative** or **conjunctive** adverb because, in addition to modifying the verb *did, why* relates the dependent clause *why he did it* to the independent clause *They cannot tell.* The following sentence makes use of an adverb, *before,* with the force of a conjunction:

> I want to see him *before* the play begins.

COMPARISON

Adverbs, like adjectives, are compared in two ways. Commonly, they make use of *more* and *most* or *less* and *least,* as in these expressions:

slowly	more slowly	most slowly
often	less often	least often
eagerly	more eagerly	most eagerly

Some adverbs which are identical in spelling with adjectives add *-er* or *-est* to the positive form:

tight	tighter	tightest
hard	harder	hardest
early	earlier	earliest
close	closer	closest

A few adverbs are compared irregularly. The following list shows the chief variations from the usual pattern:

POSITIVE	COMPARATIVE	SUPERLATIVE
badly	worse	worst
far	farther (further)	farthest (furthest)
late	later	latest (last)
little	less	least
much	more	most
near	nearer	nearest (next)
well	better	best

PLACING OF ADVERBS

Adverbs, as we have seen, may modify verbs, adjectives, other adverbs, or whole clauses or sentences. In general, the adverbs must be so placed in the sentence that the reader will have no hesitation in deciding which word the adverb modifies. Hence, the adverb should be placed as near as possible to that word. *Almost, even, ever, just,* and *only* sometimes cause trouble.

Because the adverb is misplaced, the following sentences are ambiguous:

> The teacher *only* pointed out one mistake.
> The boy polished the car *almost* until it shone.
> We *just* asked for a few minutes of his time.

By placing the adverb close to the word it modifies, we make the sentences immediately clear:

> The teacher pointed out *only* one mistake.
> The boy polished the car until it *almost* shone.
> We asked for *just* a few minutes of his time.

THE PREPOSITION

An important connective is the **preposition,** which combines with a noun or pronoun to form a prepositional phrase. The noun or pronoun is called the "object" of the preposition. The preposition shows the relation between this object and other words in the sentence.

> The children scampered *down* the street, but they were stopped *at* the corner *by* their father, who was returning *from* his office.

Down, at, by, and *from* are prepositions. Each is used to introduce a prepositional phrase and to show how the object of the preposition is related to certain other words. In the phrase *at the corner,* for instance, *at* shows "where" they were stopped. The phrase is thus equivalent to an adverb.

The following list contains the principal prepositions used in English:

aboard	concerning	regarding
about	considering	respecting
above	down	round
across	during	since
after	for	through
against	from	throughout
along	in	till
amid	inside	to
among	into	toward (s)
around	like	under
at	near	underneath
before	of	until
behind	off	unto
below	on	up
beneath	onto	upon
beside (s)	outside	via
between	over	with
beyond	past	within
by	per	without

Note that a number of the words in this list are participles. Words like *concerning, considering,* and *regarding* are often used with prepositional force as in these sentences:

> *Considering* his extreme youth, he has done well indeed.
> I spoke to him *regarding* his future plans.

Sometimes a phrase has the force of a preposition:

according to	due to
ahead of	in place of
apart from	in spite of
as far as	in view of
back of	on account of
because of	owing to
contrary to	

Sometimes prepositions are used as adverbs, as in these sentences:

> She was careful not to fall *down*.
> They came to the meeting simply to look *on*.
> Please stand *by* for a moment.

When a preposition, as often happens, becomes closely associated with a certain verb, we have what amounts to a compound verb. The following sentences show that certain prepositions are inseparable from their verbs even in the passive:

> The relatives *smiled at* the baby.
> The baby was *smiled at* by the relatives.

Idiomatic English requires that we distinguish *attend* from *attend to* and *look in* from *look into, look over, look up,* and *look upon.* We may *laugh with* a person; it is something else again to *laugh at* him. (See also Glossary of Faulty Expressions in Chapter IX, pp. 253–275.)

THE CONJUNCTION

A **conjunction** is a word used either to connect words, phrases, clauses, or sentences or to show how one sentence is related to another. We may arrange conjunctions, for convenience, in three principal groups: **coordinating, subordinating,** and **correlative** conjunctions.

COORDINATING CONJUNCTIONS

In the following sentences the conjunction *and* is used: first, to connect two nouns; secondly, to connect two prepositional phrases; and thirdly, to connect two independent clauses in a compound sentence.

> They had bacon *and* eggs for breakfast.
> The ball sailed over the wall *and* into the field.
> Our players were ready *and* the game began.

In the next example, *and* is used to show the relationship between two sentences.

> When I went to Esther's wedding, I naturally expected to see the Andersons. *And,* sure enough, there they were.

A coordinating conjunction serves to join two elements of equal grammatical value. Some grammarians distinguish several subdivisions of the coordinating conjunction, such as "disjunctive," "adversative," and "copulative," but for our purposes it will be sufficient to list the important members of the coordinating group. They are:

> and
> but
> or
> nor
> for (when it is used to mean "the reason is that")
> yet

For and *yet,* as coordinating conjunctions, are usually found in formal, rather than in colloquial, usage.

> I am convinced that the two young men will succeed in their new business, *for* I have observed their work over a period of years.

Yet is properly an adverb, but in this sentence it is a coordinating conjunction, roughly equivalent to *but:*

> Her new hat was an astonishing mass of velvet and feathers, *yet* oddly enough it was attractive.

Careless writers sometimes use *while,* properly a subordinating conjunction, as a coordinating conjunction having the force of *and.* Since *while* suggests simultaneous action, the following sentence is absurd:

> The first course consisted of soup *while* the second was filet of sole.

SUBORDINATING CONJUNCTIONS

Subordinating conjunctions, as the name suggests, are words used to indicate that one element is subordinate to another in a sentence.

> *After* the door closed, Ruth heaved a sigh of relief.

> *If* I reach Forty-second Street before one o'clock, I shall be glad to get it for you.

> Albert wants to get his application in *before* it is too late.

In these sentences, we observe that the words *after, if,* and *before* indicate that the clauses which they introduce are related to and dependent upon the main clause of the sentence. We shall have further examples of the choice of subordinating connectives when we come to discuss the complex sentence. But at this point we shall list the principal subordinating conjunctions, arranged, for convenience of reference, alphabetically. These conjunctions may be used to denote such relations as REASON, TIME, PURPOSE, CONDITION, RESULT, PLACE, and COMPARISON.

after	so that
although	so . . . as (that)
as	such . . . as (that)
as if	than
as long as	that
as often as	though
as soon as	till
as though	unless
because	until
before	what
but that	whatever
even if	when
for the purpose of	whence
how	whenever
if	where
in case	wherever
inasmuch as	which
in order that	whichever
in spite of	while
in that	whither
lest	who
notwithstanding	whoever
now that	why
provided that	with a view to
since	

CORRELATIVE CONJUNCTIONS

Correlative conjunctions are those used in pairs or in a series.

They replied that they felt *neither* unusual cold *nor* unusual warmth.

Either we must make up our minds at once *or* we must resign ourselves to doing without it.

Both Frederick *and* his cousin became ill during the Christmas vacation.

Correlatives are used to connect parallel sentence elements. The careful writer will make sure that the correlatives in his sentence join elements of equal grammatical value. The following sentence illustrates the danger of misplacing a correlative:

> We could tell that a storm was brewing by both the rising wind and by the angry looking clouds.

A slight change gives us a better sentence:

> We could tell that a storm was brewing *both* by the rising wind *and* by the angry looking clouds.

Neither requires *nor,* as in:

> He had *neither* eaten *nor* slept in two days.

Not may take either *or* or *nor* depending on the emphasis desired:

> He would *not* sleep *or* eat.
> He would *not* sleep, *nor* would he eat.

The following list contains the correlatives most often met with:

> not only . . . but also
> though . . . yet
> whether . . . or
> either . . . or
> neither . . . nor
> both . . . and
> so . . . as
> if . . . then
> as . . . as

Pronouns and Adverbs as Conjunctions

It is clear from the preceding lists that relative pronouns, such as *who, which,* and *what,* are often used to show the relation of one clause to another. So with relative adverbs. *Where, when, whence, since, how, why, before, after,* and other adverbs often serve as subordinating conjunctions.

> No doubt I shall see you *before* I leave.
> He is the man *who* lent the money to me.
> *When* she will get a raise, she doesn't know.
> We could not be sure *what* he meant.

52

Relative pronouns afford no especial problem. It is important, however, to distinguish coordinating conjunctions from what are called **conjunctive adverbs**. The following list contains the chief conjunctive adverbs of this special group:

accordingly	nevertheless
also	notwithstanding
besides	otherwise
consequently	so
furthermore	still
hence	then
however	therefore
likewise	thus
moreover	

These words should be regarded as adverbs, except when they are used to connect two independent clauses. Notice that in this sentence the word *otherwise* serves to connect two independent clauses:

> We must leave promptly at eight-thirty; *otherwise* we shall miss the first part of the ceremony.

The full form of the sentence, however, requires the regular coordinating conjunction in addition to the conjunctive adverb.

> We must leave promptly at eight-thirty, *for* otherwise we shall miss the first part of the ceremony.

In the first sentence, the semicolon is used to show that the coordinating conjunction has been omitted. The second sentence requires the comma before the conjunction *for*.

Use of As, As If, and Like

The preposition *like* should not be used as a conjunction in place of *as* or *as if*. *Like* requires a noun or pronoun without a verb. *As* and *as if* require a clause.

> She acted *as if* (not *like*) she had never been in a theater before.
> The student pronounced the French words just *as* (not *like*) the teacher told him he should.
> *Like* most beginners, he worried about details.
> He plays the piano *like* (not *as*) an expert.

53

THE INTERJECTION

An **interjection** is a word or a group of words used to voice an exclamation. It is usually independent of the rest of the sentence; often it serves as an introduction:

> *Oh!* He's going to fall!
> *Pshaw!* I knew I couldn't do it.
> *What!* Is it possible?

Some words are pure interjections. Note, however, that most parts of speech can be used as interjections:

> *Ridiculous!* I don't believe it!
> *My!* What a hot day it is!
> *Helen!* This can't be Helen!

EXERCISES

A. Give a common noun that corresponds to each of the following proper nouns:

Example: *Proper noun,* Yankee Doodle; *common noun,* song.

(1) Denver	(6) France
(2) New Jersey	(7) Paris
(3) Bosphorus	(8) Apennines
(4) Sicily	(9) Rhone
(5) Caspian	(10) Peru

B. Give the plural form of each of these nouns:

(1) turkey	(6) ox
(2) cargo	(7) man
(3) knife	(8) echo
(4) swine	(9) phenomenon
(5) son-in-law	(10) index

C. Study the following sentences from *The Return of the Native* by Thomas Hardy, and follow the instructions given below:

(1) Along the road walked an old man. (2) He was whiteheaded as a mountain, bowed in the shoulders, and faded in general aspect. (3) He wore a glazed hat, an ancient boat-cloak, and shoes; his brass buttons bearing an anchor upon their face. (4) In his hand

was a silver-headed walking-stick, which he used as a veritable third leg, perseveringly dotting the ground with its point at every few inches' interval. (5) One would have said that he had been, in his day, a naval officer of some sort or other.

(6) Before him stretched the long, laborious road, dry, empty, and white. (7) It was quite open to the heath on each side, and bisected that vast dark surface like the parting-line on a head of black hair, diminishing and bending away on the furthest horizon.

(8) The old man frequently stretched his eyes ahead to gaze over the tract that he had yet to traverse. (9) At length he discerned, a long distance in front of him, a moving spot, which appeared to be a vehicle, and it proved to be going the same way as that in which he himself was journeying. (10) It was the single atom of life that the scene contained, and it only served to render the general loneliness more evident. (11) Its rate of advance was slow, and the old man gained upon it sensibly.

(12) When he drew nearer he perceived it to be a spring van, ordinary in shape, but singular in colour, this being a lurid red. (13) The driver walked beside it; and, like his van, he was completely red. (14) One dye of that tincture covered his clothes, the cap upon his head, his boots, his face, and his hands. (15) He was not temporarily overlaid with the colour: it permeated him.

(16) The old man knew the meaning of this. (17) The traveller with the cart was a reddleman—a person whose vocation it was to supply farmers with redding for their sheep. (18) He was one of a class rapidly becoming extinct in Wessex, filling at present in the rural world the place which, during the last century, the dodo occupied in the world of animals. (19) He is a curious, interesting, and nearly perished link between obsolete forms of life and those which generally prevail.

INSTRUCTIONS

C-1. List all the singular nouns.

C-2. List all the plural nouns.

C-3. List all the adjectives in sentences (6) and (7).

C-4. List all the adverbs in sentences (16), (17), (18), and (19).

C-5. The word *stretched* in sentences (6) and (8) is a verb. Is it transitive or intransitive?

55

C-6. Point out the antecedent of each of these pronouns:

    a. *it* in sentence (9)

    b. *he* in sentence (12)

    c. *it* in sentence (13)

    d. *he* in sentence (13)

    e. *it* in sentence (15)

C-7. List the present participles in sentences (16), (17), (18), and (19).

C-8. List the infinitives in sentences (8), (9), (10), and (11).

D. The following sentences contain examples of regular and irregular verbs. Find all the finite verbs and label regular verbs R and irregular verbs IR:

    (1) The decayed officer, by degrees, came up alongside his fellow wayfarer, and wished him good evening. (2) The reddleman turned his head, and replied in sad and occupied tones. (3) He was young, and his face, if not exactly handsome, approached so near to handsome that nobody would have contradicted an assertion that it really was so in its natural colour. (4) His eye, which glared so strangely through his stain, was in itself attractive—keen as that of a bird of prey, and blue as autumn mist. (5) He had neither whisker nor moustache, which allowed the soft curves of the lower part of his face to be apparent.

E. These sentences are ambiguous. Re-write them, changing the position of the adverbs whenever necessary to avoid ambiguity:

    (1) I only went as far as the corner.

    (2) Almost I had given up hope.

    (3) I do not ever expect to have to do this again.

    (4) Philip merely said to the policeman that he was waiting for a friend.

    (5) She knows a girl who almost had the same kind of operation on her throat as she had.

    (6) She nearly had to stay in the hospital for six weeks.

    (7) She only could see her relatives.

F. Re-write, using whichever italicized word is correct for the sentence:

    (1) Pedro seemed (*happy, happily*) when I last saw him.

    (2) He is (*a, an*) Ecuadorian citizen.

(3) He had never before been in (*a, an*) American home.

(4) His brother and (*I, myself*) were in school together.

(5) Everybody who sees them (*is, are*) impressed by their manner.

(6) One of the two boys (*is, are*) tall; the other (*is, are*) fairly short.

(7) Pedro has invited my wife and (*I, me*) to visit him next summer.

(8) I don't know of anyone (*who, whom*) I would rather spend a few weeks with.

(9) Pedro is a young man (*who, whom*), we are sure, will entertain us royally.

(10) He belongs to a tennis club that holds (*their, its*) tournaments during August.

(11) Pedro says that he looks forward to (*us, our*) coming.

(12) He says he can just picture (*us, our*) getting our first glimpse of Ecuador.

(13) Three weeks, we are afraid, (*is, are*) going to seem all too short a time.

(14) He said that he (*will, would*) let us know later about transportation.

(15) Neither my sister (*nor, or*) her husband (*has, have*) ever been out of the country before.

G. Re-write, using whichever italicized word is correct for the sentence:

(1) We found that the storm had (*shook, shaken*) the flagpole severely.

(2) The workmen (*did, done*) what they could to repair the damage.

(3) We expected to find that it had (*blown, blew*) away.

(4) When the sun had (*rose, risen*) next morning, we could see that two trees had (*fell, fallen*) and that several branches had been (*tore, torn*) from a third.

(5) Several window panes were (*broke, broken*), and the house had (*become, became*) quite dilapidated in general appearance.

H. Find the finite verbs, and find the verbals (gerunds, participles, and infinitives) in these sentences:

(1) She decided that walking was good exercise.

(2) The scowling man strode along, looking straight ahead and muttering to himself.

(3) May I borrow your pencil for a moment?

(4) Several glowing embers were thrown violently from the fireplace.

(5) George is my brother-in-law's cousin, not mine.

(6) I tried to learn backgammon last summer.

(7) During the long winter evenings, Stedman pored over his account books.

(8) Leonard was forced to admit that Hazel had been right about not going.

(9) How shall we estimate the effect upon the professional class?

(10) I believe it, although he denies it.

CHAPTER III

GRAMMAR: SYNTAX

Syntax is that part of grammar which deals with the structure of the sentence.

PHRASE, CLAUSE, AND SENTENCE

Because we shall speak not only of **sentences** but of **phrases** and **clauses,** let us begin by defining these terms.

A **phrase** is a group of related words, without subject or predicate, used as a single part of speech. The following expressions are phrases:

> *for Christmas*
> *to the river*
> *opening his eyes*
> *to give full details*

A **clause** is a group of related words containing a subject and a predicate. A clause may be classified as independent or dependent; it may be restrictive or non-restrictive; it may be used as an adjective, as an adverb, or as a noun. The following expressions are clauses:

> *where he went*
> *that the snow was falling*
> *which melted at once*
> *if we are not careful*
> *we went out early*
> *I am positive*

Later in the chapter we shall have more to say about the various kinds of phrases and clauses. For the moment it will be enough to remember that a clause is distinguished from a phrase by having a subject and a predicate. (See also pp. 190–191.)

A **sentence** is a group of related words, or sometimes a single word, which MAKES A STATEMENT, ASKS A QUESTION, EXPRESSES A WISH OR COMMAND, or VOICES AN EXCLAMATION OR INTERJECTION.

SENTENCE ELEMENTS

Every sentence may be divided into two parts: the **subject** and the **predicate;** many sentences contain a **complement** and **modifiers** as well. Disregarding for the moment such "sentence words" as *Yes* and *No,* and such single-word sentences as *Stop,* we may proceed to a consideration of the four **sentence elements:** subject, predicate, complement, and modifiers.

THE SUBJECT

As the first step in analysis, we separate the sentence into **subject** and **predicate.** Note the sentence:

> Sparks fly upward.

Here the words *fly upward* tell something about the *sparks.* If, then, we call *sparks* the subject and *fly upward* the predicate, we have a general rule as follows:

> The **subject** consists of the word or words about which something is said by the word or words making up the **predicate.**

In the following examples, the subject is in italic type:

> *Christmas* comes but once a year.
> *The troops* attacked at dawn.
> *Rumors* travel fast.
> For longer than he cared to admit, *he* had been a student.

Subjects are called **simple subjects** if they consist of a noun or a noun-equivalent:

> *Dogs* bark.
> *He* arrived early.
> *I* expect to work late tonight.

A sentence may have a **compound subject:**

> *Golf and tennis* are good exercise.
> *Books, papers, and pencils* were scattered on the desk.

The **complete subject** consists of the simple subject plus all its modifiers:

> *Noisy and excited groups of girls* were collecting in the hallways.

THE PREDICATE

The **predicate** is the word or words which express what is said about the subject, and consists of the verb, together with such words as may be needed to complete its meaning. The predicates in the next sentences are in italic type:

> The sun *rises.*
> The time *has come.*
> We *must be on our way.*

The predicate may consist of the verb and all its modifiers, and we speak of the **complete predicate** by analogy with the **complete subject.** Four kinds of complete predicates follow:

(1) A verb plus a predicate adjective, predicate noun, or predicate pronoun:

> She *is wealthy.*
> Roosevelt *became president.*
> It *is I.*

(2) A verb plus an object:

> Dogs *chase squirrels.*
> Everyone *wishes to know.*
> The boy *dropped the parcels.*

(3) A verb plus a direct object and an indirect object:

> They *gave him ten dollars.*
> He *showed me the new novel.*

(4) A verb plus an object and a predicate noun or predicate adjective:

> We *called our old car "Peter."*
> Such talk *will drive me mad.*

The verb, or simple predicate, must agree with the subject in person and number. If the subject is singular, as in

> The doctor was praised for his work,

the verb is singular (*was praised*); if plural, as in

> The doctors were praised for their work,

the verb is plural (*were praised*). Compound subjects are plural unless they are considered as a unit:

> Doctors and nurses *were* in attendance.
>
> Friends, neighbors, and acquaintances *were waiting* outside.

But subjects of this type require the singular:

> Two and two *is* four.
>
> A mile and a quarter *separates* us from our goal.

Observe especially that the expressions *along with, with,* and *together with* do not make the subject plural:

> The doctor, together with the nurse, *is working* feverishly.

Observe that the verb agrees with the subject and not with the predicate noun:

> The part of the vacation that he enjoys *is* the motor-boat trips.
>
> Motor-boat trips *are* the part of the vacation he enjoys.

In the first sentence, the subject is singular (*part*) and requires a singular verb (*is*). In the second sentence, the subject is plural (*trips*), and the author has correctly used a plural verb (*are*). In sentences involving correlatives, the verb agrees in person and number with the subject that is nearer to the verb:

> Either he or you *are* to go.

In this sentence, the nearer subject (*you*) is second person, singular number. In the next sentence,

> Neither the soloist nor the members of the chorus *like* this auditorium,

the nearer subject (*members*) is third person, plural number. It is frequently advisable to re-cast sentences of this sort, especially in informal writing.

An **expletive** is a word that fills in, usually being added for emphasis or smoothness. When a sentence contains the expletive *there* or *it*, the real subject occupies the position of the predicate noun and the verb agrees with the real subject:

> There *are* thirty days in September.
> It *is* she.

The Complement

The **complement** is a word that completes the meaning of the verb:

> My brother is learning French.

Here the word *French* completes the meaning of the verb *is learning* by answering the question: "What?" Complements may be divided into two classes as follows:

(1) **direct object:**

> Snow covered the *ground*.
> Bring the *shovels* over here.
> We shall need *them*.

In these sentences, the words *ground, shovels,* and *them* are words which show the person or thing receiving the action of the verbs *covered, bring,* and *shall need.*

(2) **subjective complement:**

> He is a *newcomer*.
> His name is *Madison*.
> His hair is *grey*.
> His eyes are *blue*.

The subjective complement is either a noun (**predicate noun**) or an adjective (**predicate adjective**). Notice that the verb in each of the above sentences is a form of the verb *to be. Is, are,* and the other forms of the verb *to be,* as well as certain other verbs such as *prove, remain, grow, look, taste,* and the like, often serve as **copulas,** or **linking verbs,** and show how the subject is related to the complement.

> His advice *proved* untrustworthy.
> This soup *tastes* good.
> I *feel* fine.

63

Let us take an example of a single noun used in different sentences, each time serving a different purpose in the sentence. Note the use of the word *apple* in these four sentences:

> The *apple* is ripe.
> Give me the *apple*.
> He bit hungrily into the *apple*.
> This is an exceptionally large *apple*.

In these examples the noun *apple* is used (1) as subject of a verb, (2) as object of a verb, (3) as object of a preposition, and (4) as a predicate noun.

INDIRECT OBJECT

In addition to a direct object, a sentence may have an **indirect object.** An example of an indirect object is the word *me* in the sentence.

> He sent *me* the letter.

It is possible to present the indirect object as a prepositional phrase in which case the above sentence would read

> He sent the letter *to me*.

Note that, when there is no preposition, the indirect object precede the direct object (in this case "the letter"); and that when the indirect object is a prepositional phrase, it follows the direct object.

THE MODIFIERS

A **modifier** is a word or a group of words used to change, or "modify," the meaning of some part of the sentence. A modifier is either ADJECTIVAL or ADVERBIAL and may consist of:

> (1) a single word,
> (2) a phrase, or
> (3) a clause.

SINGLE-WORD MODIFIERS

Examples of single-word modifiers are shown in these sentences

> The *new* motor-boat is *unusually* speedy.
> It runs *very* smoothly.

New is an adjective modifying the noun *motor-boat,* and *unusually* and *very* are adverbs modifying the adjective *speedy* and the adverb *smoothly.*

> His *chattering* teeth betrayed him

contains a participle (*chattering*) used as an adjective to modify the noun *teeth.*

Words used in apposition are considered modifiers:

> We visited Denver, the *capital* of Colorado.
> The word *co-operation* is used many times in his speech.

PHRASES

Examples of phrases used as modifiers are shown in these sentences:

> Few *of the guests* were bored.
> Two *of them* played tennis *for an hour.*

Here we have three prepositional phrases: *of the guests* and *of them* are adjective-equivalents; *for an hour* is an adverb-equivalent and is used to modify the verb *played.* The sentence

> The two women *singing the song* walked away

contains a **participial phrase,** and the sentence

> His ability *to solve difficult problems* is amazing

illustrates the **infinitive phrase.** And in the sentence

> *Upon my saying I couldn't sleep,* the doctor became interested,

we have a **gerundial phrase** modifying the verb.

Absolute Phrases

Certain phrases modify the sentence or clause as a whole and are called **absolute phrases.** An absolute phrase consists of a noun (or pronoun) modified by a participle. Either part of the phrase may itself have modifiers, but the absolute phrase is distinguished from the usual participial modifier by not being a part of the basic structure of the sentence. Examples will make this clearer:

ABSOLUTE	*Marion being shy and retiring,* her friends had trouble per-
PHRASES	suading her to join them.
IN	*His tools having been left at home,* the plumber's assistant
ITALICS	had to go for them.
	Children having torn pages out of the book, it was discarded.

Do not confuse an absolute phrase with a participial phrase modifying a noun. The latter construction is illustrated in this sentence:

> Marion, *being shy and retiring,* had trouble making friends.

Here the participial phrase *being shy and retiring* modifies the noun, *Marion,* subject of the sentence.

The absolute construction has been inherited from Latin grammar and at one time was used extensively. But it is now considered pedantic and stilted to say

> Our bill having been paid, we left the restaurant

when we can say more naturally

> After paying our bill, we left the restaurant.

Certain absolute phrases have, however, become part of idiomatic English:

> We shall make the trip, *wind and weather permitting.* (= *if* wind and weather permit)
>
> *Beginning with the January issue,* the magazine will be reduced in size.
>
> *Generally speaking,* we can look for a rise in prices.

Cautions concerning Phrases

Do not confuse adjectival and adverbial phrases. The following sentences are correct:

> He was late *because of a train wreck.* (adverbial)
>
> His lateness was *due to a train wreck.* (adjectival)

Do not begin a sentence with the words *due to:*

| WRONG: | Due to the oil shortage, the building was closed for three weeks. |
| CORRECT: | Because of the oil shortage, the building was closed for three weeks. |

66

Modifiers should as a rule be placed as near as possible to the word they modify. Especial care must be taken when a sentence begins with a participial phrase:

WRONG: Rushing around the corner, the courthouse came into view.

CORRECT: Rushing around the corner, we came in sight of the courthouse.

The so-called "dangling" construction illustrated in the first sentence must be avoided in careful writing.

CLAUSES AS MODIFIERS

Examples of **clauses used as modifiers** are shown in these sentences:

She is fond of people *who think as she does.*
Los Angeles is a city *of which the Californians are proud.*

The nouns *people* and *city* are modified by adjective clauses introduced by relative pronouns. Now look at these sentences:

There is the shed *where the tools will be stored.*
They know the reason *why Sarah did it.*
It happens at a time *when you least expect it.*

Here the nouns *shed, reason,* and *time* are followed by clauses, each of which is introduced by a relative adverb (*where, why, when*) equivalent to a preposition plus a relative pronoun (*in which, for which, at which*).

Adverbial clauses used as modifiers are said to be clauses of:

TIME: It was raining heavily *when he left the house.*
PLACE: We saw him standing *where the bus usually stops.*
MANNER: He acted *as if he were extremely annoyed.*
COMPARISON: The bus was later *than it had been for weeks.*
CAUSE: He stood under a tree *because it was now raining harder than ever.*
CONDITION: *If I had been he,* I should have given up.
CONCESSION: *Although he was drenched to the skin,* he stubbornly refused to come back to the house.

67

PURPOSE:	As the bus came into sight, he stepped forward *so that he would lose no time.*
RESULT:	He had waited so long *that we could well imagine his state of mind.*

PHRASES USED AS NOUNS

In analyzing sentences, we frequently find that a **phrase** serves as the equivalent of an **adjective** or **adverb**. A phrase may also serve as a **noun**.

INFINITIVE PHRASES

Examples of **infinitive phrases** used as nouns are:

(1) SUBJECT OF A VERB:	*To mention everyone present at the dinner* is obviously impossible in this short article.
(2) OBJECT OF A VERB:	If I had more space, I should like *to give their names at least.*
(3) OBJECT OF A PREPOSITION:	As it happens, I have no choice but *to omit them.*
(4) SUBJECTIVE COMPLEMENT:	My original plan was *to include everyone.*
(5) APPOSITIVE*:	I have one main purpose: *to please my readers.*

GERUNDIAL PHRASES

Examples of **gerundial phrases** used as nouns are:

(1) SUBJECT OF A VERB:	*Writing reports on social affairs* keeps me busy.
(2) OBJECT OF A VERB:	Some reporters like *writing such things.*
(3) OBJECT OF A PREPOSITION:	They are paid well for *doing it.*
(4) SUBJECTIVE COMPLEMENT:	My main difficulty is *keeping my readers happy.*
(5) APPOSITIVE*:	That usually means one thing: *mentioning their names in my articles.*

*An appositive is a noun or its equivalent, set alongside a noun or its equivalent to name it in other words.

CLAUSES USED AS NOUNS

Clauses, like phrases, may, under certain circumstances, be considered as **adjectives,** modifying nouns or pronouns, or as **adverbs,** modifying verbs, adjectives, or adverbs. Clauses may also serve as **nouns,** as the following sentences show:

(1) *That they were doubtful about our plans* was obvious.
(2) To feel secure economically is *what many persons want.*
(3) I hope *that you are planning to join us.*
(4) Give the suitcases to *whoever meets you at the station.*
(5) They reminded him of his written agreement *that the money should be paid.*

In the first sentence, the subject of the verb *was* is the entire clause *That they were doubtful about our plans.* Neither the pronoun *they* (third person plural) nor the word *plans* (third person plural) can serve as subject of the verb *was* without violating the rule of agreement of subject and verb. *They* is the subject of *were* and *plans* is the object of the preposition *about.* The second sentence illustrates the use of a clause (*what many persons want*) as a predicate noun after the verb *is.* The third and fourth sentences show us a clause (*that you are planning to join us*) used as direct object after the verb *hope,* and a clause (*whoever meets you at the station*) used as object of the preposition *to.* The fifth sentence shows that a clause may serve as an appositive: *that the money should be paid* is in apposition with the noun *agreement.*

Clauses containing the pronouns *who, whoever, whom,* and *whomever* sometimes cause trouble for the beginning writer. Notice sentence (4) above. *Whoever* is correctly used, because the subject of the verb *meets* must be in the nominative case. Another version of the sentence requires *whomever* instead of *whoever:*

Give the suitcases to *whomever* you see first at the station.

In this sentence, the objective case of the pronoun (*whomever*) is used because the pronoun is to serve as object of the verb *see.* In analyzing such a sentence we must decide in which clause the pronoun belongs and then use *who* or *whoever* for subject or subjective complement and *whom* or *whomever* for other functions. We must not forget that an entire clause may serve as a single part of speech.

69

The following sentences are correct:

> He is the man *who* was employed here last year.
> He is the man *whom* we employed last year.
> He is the man of *whom* I was speaking.
> He is the man *who,* we think, will do the work best.
> He is the man *whom,* we think, you mentioned.
> *Whoever* he may be, we need him badly.
> *Whomever* you employ from this group will satisfy me.
> *Whoever* is employed will be kept busy.

Independent and Dependent Clauses

We have seen that clauses may be used as single parts of speech. We must now classify all clauses as either **independent** or **dependent**. Examine these sentences:

> (1) The men have arrived, and the work will begin.
> (2) When the men arrive, the work will begin.
> (3) The men who will do the work have arrived.

Observe that each of these three sentences is made up of two clauses and that structurally the sentences are unlike.

The first sentence consists of two **independent clauses**: *The men have arrived* expresses a complete thought and could stand alone as a full-fledged sentence. So also with the second clause: *the work will begin*. Although it is true that each of these clauses is complete in itself, the two are joined together by *and* because they are somewhat closely related to each other. The word *and* is a coordinating conjunction (see p. 49), the function of which is to join elements of equal grammatical value within the sentence.

A different relationship is apparent between the two clauses of the second sentence. The independent clause *the work will begin* is qualified or "modified" by the subordinate or **dependent** clause *When the men arrive*. This clause tells "when" the action suggested in the independent clause will occur and thus it may be said that the clause is equivalent to an adverb. (See pp. 45–47.)

Briefly, then, we may define an **independent clause** as one that can stand alone as a sentence; and a **dependent clause** as one that occupies a subordinate position in a sentence, that is equivalent to a single part of speech, and cannot by itself be a complete sentence.

70

SENTENCES CLASSIFIED AS TO FORM

Depending upon how it is constructed, a sentence is **simple, compound, complex,** or **compound-complex.** Analysis of sentences requires that we distinguish these four kinds of sentences from each other.

The Simple Sentence

The **simple** sentence consists of a single independent clause. Any sentence, however short or long, that contains one subject and one predicate is called a simple sentence:

> *Sparks fly* upward.

> The tired, dirty, and footsore *hikers straggled* wearily across the old bridge, up the hill, and, finally, into the camp in the pine forest.

The second sentence contains twenty-four words, but, because it has one subject (*hikers*) and one finite verb (*straggled*), it is classified as a simple sentence.

Any part of the single clause making up the "simple sentence" may, however, be compound. The compound subject, compound predicate, and compound complement are illustrated in these sentences:

COMPOUND SUBJECT	*Addison* and *Steele* wrote charming essays.
COMPOUND PREDICATE	They *were born in the same year, 1672, attended the same university,* and *contributed later to the same newspaper.*
COMPOUND COMPLEMENT	Steele was *good-natured* and *likable*.
COMPOUND PREDICATE AND COMPOUND COMPLEMENT	Addison *was quiet and retiring* but nevertheless *had many friends in London.*
COMPOUND SUBJECT, PREDICATE, AND COMPLEMENT	*Addison* and *Steele created* and *immortalized* the *country-gentleman* Sir Roger de Coverley and his *associates* in the Spectator Club.

Compound modifiers are illustrated in these sentences:

<table>
<tr><td>Compound
Adjectives</td><td>Addison became well-known because of his timely and patriotic poem about the foreign campaign of the Duke of Marlborough.</td></tr>
<tr><td></td><td>Steele wrote several brilliant and satirical comedies for the London stage.</td></tr>
<tr><td>Compound
Adverbs
and
Compound
Objects of
Prepositions</td><td>Both men tried to reform society by writing amusingly and often ironically about the faults and foibles of their contemporaries.</td></tr>
</table>

The Compound Sentence

The **compound** sentence consists of two or more independent clauses joined by a coordinating conjunction. Each clause must be itself a simple sentence. It must have a subject and a predicate and it must express a complete thought. The following are compound sentences:

Daniel Defoe was one of the earliest journalists, *and* his newspaper was extremely influential.

He is remembered today as the author of *Robinson Crusoe,* but, during his life-time, he was known principally for his political pamphlets and newspaper articles.

His life was not an easy one, *nor* was it uneventful.

Perhaps he will someday be called the first English novelist, *or* perhaps he will always be spoken of as the precursor of Fielding and Richardson.

Each independent clause forming part of a compound sentence may contain compound elements. It is important to remember, too, that the subject of each clause must be expressed.

If the coordinating conjunction joining the clauses of a compound sentence is omitted, as often happens, it must be replaced by a semicolon:

The eighteenth century begins with the Glorious Revolution of 1689; it closes with the French Revolution of 1789.

The full form of this sentence requires that the clauses be joined by a coordinating conjunction such as *and* preceded by a comma; the semicolon replaces both the conjunction and the comma. (See p. 194.)

THE COMPLEX SENTENCE

A **complex** sentence consists of one independent clause and one or more dependent clauses. We have already considered the several ways in which a dependent clause may be used in a sentence, and the following complex sentences are by way of additional illustration of clauses used as adjectives, as adverbs, or as nouns. (See also p. 69.)

ADVERBIAL   *When the century began,* there were many coffee-houses in London.

ADJECTIVAL   Men *who wanted to meet their friends or to read the news-papers* frequented one or another of these shops.

ADVERBIAL   Ship-owners and speculators used to gather at Lloyd's Coffee-house *where they could gamble on the probable safe arrival of trading vessels.*

NOUN   We know *that these gatherings led eventually to the formation of a great insurance firm.*

THE COMPOUND-COMPLEX SENTENCE

The **compound-complex** sentence consists of a compound sentence (two or more independent clauses) and at least one dependent clause. The following sentences are classified as compound-complex:

Some of the coffee-houses which were famous in their day developed later into taverns, and many of them ultimately became restaurants.

Although their influence was, for the most part, a good one, the coffee-houses sometimes fell into disrepute, and the authorities more than once complained that they were being used for seditious gatherings.

Nevertheless, the average man approved of the coffee-house; he regarded it as an important institution; to him it was the pleasantest place in which he could spend his leisure time without incurring needless expense.

73

SENTENCES CLASSIFIED AS TO MEANING

According to the traditional classification of sentences as to meaning, every sentence is either **declarative, imperative, interrogative,** or **exclamatory.**

THE DECLARATIVE SENTENCE

A **declarative** sentence is a sentence that makes a statement. The illustrative sentences in the previous section. (Sentences Classified as to Form) are all declarative sentences, as are also these sentences:

> I suggest that you do nothing about it.
> They kept very busy all summer.
> The small wagon is overloaded.

THE IMPERATIVE SENTENCE

An **imperative** sentence is a sentence that voices a command or entreaty:

> Do nothing about it.
> Keep busy.
> Don't overload the wagon.

Observe that the subject of each of these sentences is *you* (understood.

THE INTERROGATIVE SENTENCE

An **interrogative** sentence is a sentence that asks a question:

> What are you going to do about it?
> Will they manage to keep busy?
> Don't you think the wagon is overloaded?

THE EXCLAMATORY SENTENCE

An **exclamatory** sentence is a sentence that voices an exclamation, cry, or expression of strong feeling:

> They've done it!
> Gracious! they certainly are busy!
> Don't overload the wagon!

Observe that every sentence requires a mark of punctuation at the end. Declarative and imperative sentences are followed by the period; interrogative sentences, by the question mark; and exclamatory sentences, by the exclamation point.

DIAGRAMING THE SENTENCE

Many students of grammar and sentence structure have found it helpful to be able to construct a diagram, or picture, of the sentence. Especially is this true of the beginning student, who is often uncertain about the relationship of one part of a sentence to another until he can see, by means of a schematic picture, that a certain clause, let us say, must modify the subject of the sentence and not the predicate. The diagram is no substitute for a mastery of the principles of syntax, but the visual aid supplied by the diagram will often facilitate the study of the sentence structure, particularly in the early stages.

There are many different systems of diagraming. The system employed in this book is not necessarily the only workable one, but it is simple, flexible, and easy to learn. The reader should familiarize himself with it by diagraming the sentences in the exercises and should then feel free to use whatever additional devices he may decide are necessary for the analysis of other, and perhaps more complicated, sentences.

The first step in diagraming a **simple** sentence is to separate the simple subject from the simple predicate. This is also the first step if we are diagraming a **compound** sentence: the simple subject of each independent clause is separated from the simple predicate. If we are concerned with a **complex** sentence, we must first find the independent or "main" clause, and proceed to separate subject from predicate, as we did with the simple sentence. Examples will make this clearer:

SIMPLE   The men have arrived.

men | have arrived

COMPOUND   The men have arrived, and the work will begin.

INDEPENDENT CLAUSE   men | have arrived

INDEPENDENT CLAUSE   work | will begin

75

COMPLEX   The men who will do the work have arrived.

INDEPENDENT
CLAUSE

men | have arrived

DEPENDENT
CLAUSE

who | will do

The following pages parallel, to some extent, the earlier part of this chapter and treat of the proper method of diagraming subject, predicate, complement, modifiers, and phrases or clauses used as nouns.

DIAGRAMS

I. Separate the subject from the predicate thus:

subject | predicate

(1) He shouted.
(2) They listened.
(3) Sam jumped.

He | shouted

They| listened

Sam| jumped

II. If the complement is a direct object, separate it from the verb thus:

subject | verb | object

76

(4) He shouted commands.
(5) They read magazines.
(6) Johnson builds bridges.

He | shouted | commands.

They | read | magazines.

Johnson | builds | bridges

III. If the complement is a predicate noun or predicate adjective, separate it from the verb thus:

subject | verb \ subjective complement

(7) My uncle is a sailor.
(8) He has been a sailor for many years.
(9) His training was thorough.
(10) He is an excellent navigator.

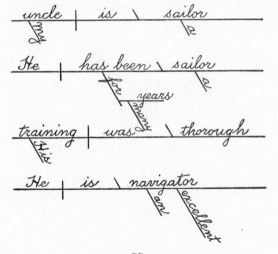

IV. If the complement consists of a direct object and an objective complement (predicate noun or adjective referring to the direct object), use this scheme:

subject | verb / objective complement \ direct object

    (11) We appointed him leader.
    (12) They named their house "The Pines."
    (13) I thought the chair uncomfortable.
    (14) Joan let the dogs loose.

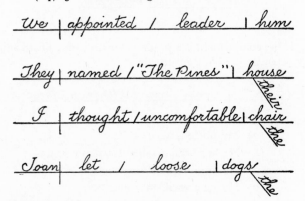

V. Modifiers are represented according to this pattern:

A. Single-word modifiers:

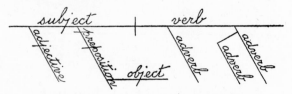

    (15) Yesterday I bought ten eggs.

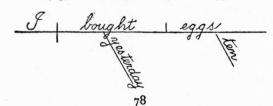

78

B. Prepositional phrase:

> (16) Few of the guests were bored.
> > (adjectival)
>
> (17) They played tennis for an hour.
> > (adverbial)

C. Participle:

> (18) The two women singing the song walked away.
> (19) He can do it with his eyes closed.

D. Infinitive:

(20) His ability to solve difficult problems was amazing.

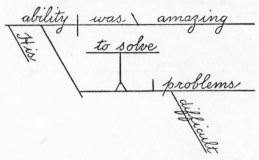

E. Gerund:

(21) Upon my saying that, the doctor became interested.

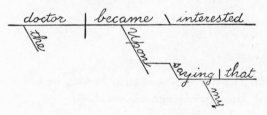

F. Indirect object:

(22) He sent me the letter.
(23) He will send the letter to me.

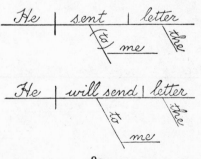

G. Adjectival clause:

(24) This is the house that Jack built.

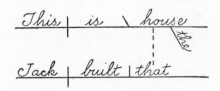

H. Adverbial clause:

(25) Since he went away, his parents have received three letters from him.

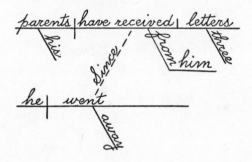

VI. Absolute phrases modify the sentence or clause as a whole and are diagramed separately:

(26) John being absent, the game was postponed.

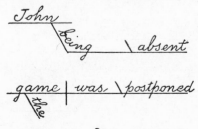

81

VII. Infinitive or gerundial phrases used as nouns are enclosed in parentheses and placed above the base line:

A. Infinitive phrase used as subject:

(27) To mention everyone is obviously impossible in this short article.

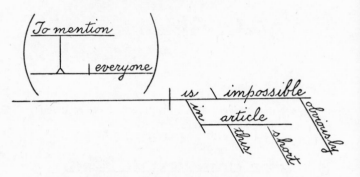

B. Infinitive phrase used as direct object:

(28) I should like at least to give their names.

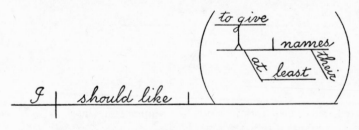

C. Infinitive phrase used as object of a preposition:

(29) I have no choice but to omit them.

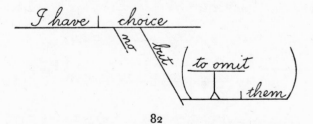

D. Infinitive phrase used as subjective complement:

(30) My original plan was to include everyone.

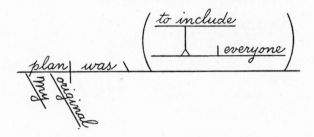

E. Infinitive phrase used as an appositive:

(31) I have one main purpose: to please my readers.

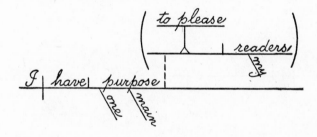

F. Gerundial phrase used as subject, direct object, object of a preposition, subjective complement, or appositive:

(32) Writing reports on social affairs keeps me busy.

(33) Some reporters like writing such things.

(34) They are well paid for doing it.

(35) My greatest difficulty is keeping all my readers happy.

(36) That usually means one thing: mentioning their names in my article.

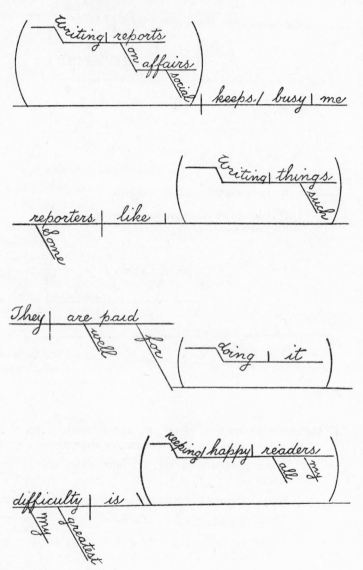

84

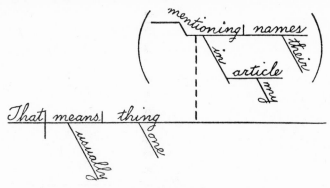

VIII. Clauses used as nouns are represented thus:

(37) That they were doubtful about our plans was obvious.

(38) To feel secure economically is what many persons want.

(39) I hope that you are planning to join us.

(40) The reason is that they are timid.

(41) Give the suitcases to whoever meets you at the station.

(42) They reminded him of his written agreement that the money should be paid.

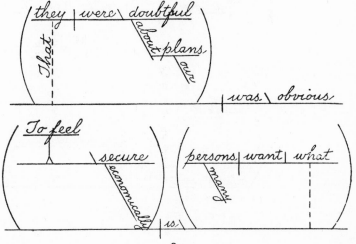

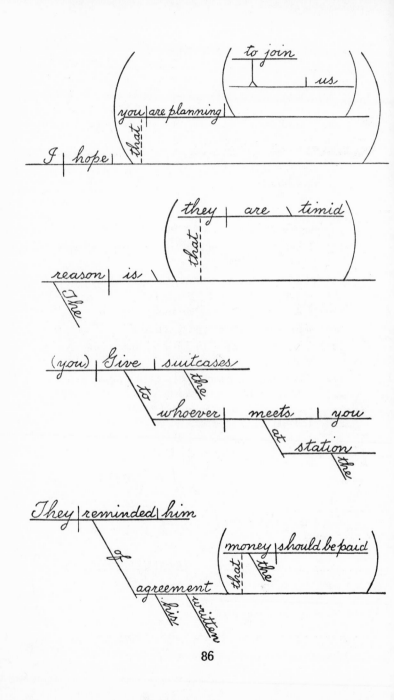

86

IX. Compound elements are represented thus:

A. Compound subject:

(43) Addison and Steele wrote charming essays.

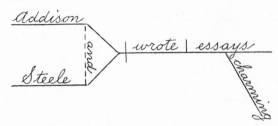

B. Compound predicate:

(44) They were born in the same year, attended the same university, and later contributed to the same newspaper.

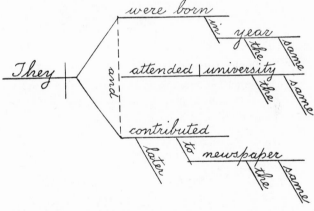

C. Compound complement:

(45) Steele was good-natured and likable.

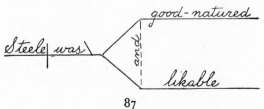

D. Compound adjectives:

(46) Steele wrote several brilliant and satirical comedies.

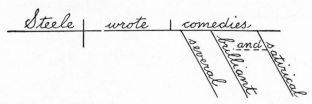

E. Compound adverbs:

(47) Both men wrote amusingly and often ironically.

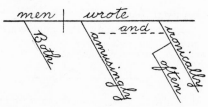

X. The compound sentence is diagramed thus:

(48) Daniel Defoe was one of the earliest journalists, and his newspaper was extremely influential.

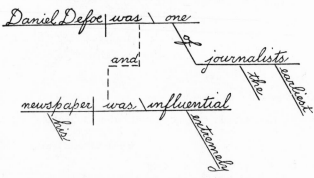

XI. Parenthetical elements such as interjections or words of direct address are diagramed like appositives:

88

(49) Pshaw! I knew he could not do it.

(50) Father, may I borrow the car?

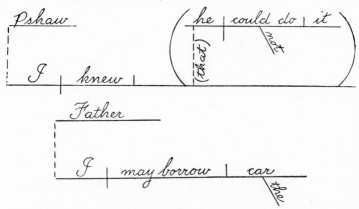

XII. The reader should now be ready for more-involved sentences and should study these concluding examples carefully before proceeding to the exercises:

A. Complex sentence containing an objective infinitive and an adjectival clause:

(51) The elderly man who was standing near the entrance of the theater told him to return on Thursday at the same time.

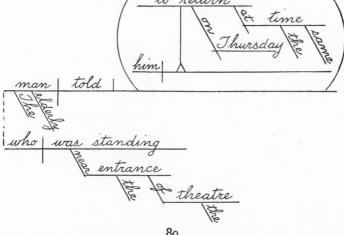

B. A sentence beginning with the expletive *it:*

> (52) It is clear that nobody has lived in this house
>   for many years.

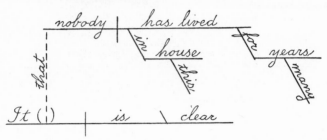

C. A simple sentence with compound subject and predicate
   and with several modifiers:

> (53) In the early months of the war, a young
>   farmer from New Hampshire, a rancher
>   from Colorado, a bank clerk from Chicago,
>   and the nephew of the commanding officer
>   met at camp, became friends, and have been
>   inseparable since that time.

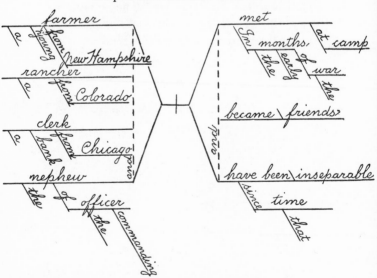

D. A compound-complex sentence:

(54) The crowd of workmen had been standing patiently in the rain for two hours, and a great shout of relief arose when the rescuers finally appeared.

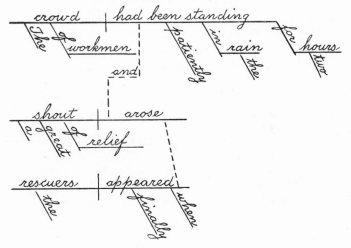

E. Direct quotation:

(55) "I can't (can not) read this letter without my glasses," said Mr. Alexander, plaintively.

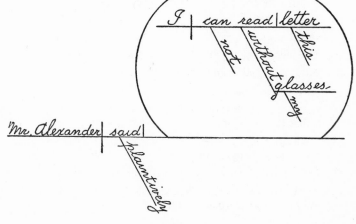

EXERCISES

A. State whether the italicized phrases and clauses are used as adjectives, as adverbs, or as nouns:

(1) *Although he had never been out of New York before,* Martin decided that he was going to enjoy himself.

(2) The bus was a large one and was more comfortable *than he had expected it to be.*

(3) The man *driving the bus* looked experienced.

(4) *Rushing across New Jersey,* the bus soon approached the Pennsylvania line.

(5) Many *of the passengers* left the bus at Trenton.

(6) Martin planned *to make a two-day stop at Philadelphia.*

(7) He hoped *that he could do the same at Pittsburgh.*

(8) He wondered if he would recognize David, *because after all he had not seen him in ten years.*

(9) *When the bus reached Philadelphia,* it was beginning to get dark.

(10) Martin felt that he would be glad to see *whoever came to meet the bus.*

B. In some of these sentences, the verb does not agree with the subject in person and number. Copy the sentences and make any necessary changes in the verbs:

(1) Martin, together with his friend David, have been seeing the sights of Pittsburgh.

(2) The part that interested them most were the two colleges they visited.

(3) The junction of the three rivers were an impressive sight, too.

(4) There is, in and around Pittsburgh, a great many steel mills.

(5) Each seems larger than the next.

(6) In order to reach David's home, it is usual to travel on one of the inclined railways that runs to the top of the cliff.

(7) From the top, the visitor enjoys one of the most interesting sights that is to be found in the state.

(8) Neither David nor his parents were anxious for Martin to leave.

(9) At the bus station, there was an elderly couple and four soldiers waiting to start for Chicago.

(10) The bus for Chicago, like the other long-distance busses, were large and roomy.

C. Each of these sentences contains a complement (in italics). For each sentence, decide whether the complement is a direct object (DO), a predicate noun (PN), or a predicate adjective (PA):

(1) Martin's bus soon crossed *the state line.*

(2) He was *tired* by the time Columbus, Ohio, was reached.

(3) The man across the aisle was *a travelling salesman.*

(4) He told Martin *several interesting stories about his* trips through the Middle West.

(5) He said that his name was *Carl Miller.*

(6) One of the soldiers played *tunes* on a harmonica.

(7) The noise bothered *the elderly couple,* who were trying to sleep.

(8) Mr. Miller recommended *a hotel* in Chicago.

(9) Martin decided *to go there.*

(10) He hoped that it would not prove *too expensive.*

D. State whether the italicized portions of these sentences are independent (IND) or dependent (DEP) clauses:

(1) The hotel *that Mr. Miller recommended* proved to be large and impressive.

(2) Because he knew of no other, *Martin decided to ask for a room.*

(3) His room, *which was a small one on the eighteenth floor,* overlooked the lake.

(4) The bed looked comfortable, and *there was a radio on the table beside it.*

(5) *The bathroom was small,* but it contained both a tub and a shower.

E. Study the following sentences and decide which are simple sentences (S), which are compound (CD), which are complex (CX), and which are compound-complex (CC):

(1) Martin went to the phone and called his cousin's number.

(2) His cousin, who was surprised to hear Martin's voice, suggested that they meet for lunch the next day.

(3) Martin was glad to agree, and his cousin told him that he would be at the hotel at twelve-thirty.

(4) For several hours Martin was unable to sleep.

(5) Finally, he dozed off and did not wake until eleven in the morning.

(6) After lunch, Martin and his cousin did some sightseeing, made a stop at a large department store, bought theater tickets for the evening.

(7) The Loop was impressive, but Martin thought that Lake Shore Drive was really more beautiful than any other street he had ever seen.

(8) When his cousin asked about his itinerary, Martin said that he intended to go on as far as Denver.

(9) His cousin was suitably impressed.

(10) Martin said that he hoped to visit Yellowstone Park also, but that he wasn't sure he would have time.

F. The word *hand* is used variously in these sentences. Decide whether *hand* is used as subject, direct object, verb, predicate noun, object of preposition, or adjective:

(1) The hand is quicker than the eye.

(2) Lend a hand, will you?

(3) The house I spoke of is near at hand.

(4) These portraits are both by the same hand.

(5) The hand grenade was widely used during the war.

(6) Billy is really getting out of hand these days.

(7) Shall we hand him over to the police?

(8) Mike Sellars is the hired hand on my uncle's farm.

(9) Please deal me a new hand.

(10) He asked for her hand in marriage.

EXERCISE ON DIAGRAMING

I. Diagram these sentences by separating the **simple subject** from the **simple predicate.** Do not diagram modifiers.

(1) Frank chuckles.

(2) His mother looks up.

(3) She is knitting and listening to the radio.

(4) "Why are you laughing?"

(5) "This letter from Uncle Louis is very funny."

(6) "His letters do not usually amuse you."

(7) "Uncle Louis writes about his experiences on the way home last week."

(8) "Open the door, Frank."

(9) "Do you find it warm in here?"

(10) "Knitting can be warm work, sometimes."

II. Construct complete diagrams of the following sentences.

(1) His long search finally ended.

(2) That tall, white building must be the one.

(3) It was obvious that the place was prosperous and well-kept.

(4) He walked to the main entrance and talked to the doorman.

(5) The latter's uniform was resplendent with brass buttons and gold braid.

(6) Walter asked for the Smiths' apartment.

(7) The doorman and Walter discussed the number of Smiths in the city.

(8) Finally, the buzzer sounded and the door opened.

(9) A ferocious sound of dogs barking greeted him on the third floor.

(10) The Smiths were undoubtedly at home.

(11) Come in, Walter!

(12) Let me take your coat.

(13) Thank you very much.

(14) Excuse me for a moment.

(15) Living with four dogs is no joke.

(16) Bill, put these dogs in the kitchen.

(17) You've (you have) grown since I saw you.

(18) You're (you are) taller than I.

(19) Sit here; this chair is less shaky than that.

(20) Do you like our place?

(21) Bill and I like it, but Dad and Mother object to the noise.

(22) They prefer the peace and quiet of Brooklyn Heights.

(23) When they visit us, they notice strange and wonderful sounds.

(24) Mother thinks that the rooms are too small, the walls too thin, the neighbors' radio too loud.

(25) Dad believes that the dogs should have more space.

(26) To be near Bill's office makes it worthwhile for us.

(27) He can sleep until the last minute, have his breakfast with me, and get there without hurrying.

(28) Fred and Miriam are coming later to play bridge.

(29) When they arrive, ask Fred about his trip to Albany and Syracuse.

(30) If you don't (do not) ask about it, he will be disappointed and will probably be grouchy during the whole evening.

CHAPTER IV

EFFECTIVE SENTENCES

"EFFECTIVENESS" in writing depends upon more than grammatical correctness. Sentences, paragraphs, and longer compositions may follow the rules of grammar accurately and still not be "effective." The three essential requirements of effective writing are: Unity, Coherence, and Emphasis.

By **unity** we mean that every part of a sentence or composition must contribute to one principal, unifying thought.

By **coherence** we mean that the various parts of a sentence or composition must follow one another in an order which makes their relationship clear.

By **emphasis** we mean that the most important parts of a sentence or composition must be so placed that attention is directed toward them rather than toward less important parts.

We shall now consider these three requirements as illustrated in the writing of effective sentences.

UNITY

A sentence has "unity" when every part contributes to one principal, unifying thought.

> Hubbard sprang from his chair, and the startled dog began to bark furiously.

But we must not combine unrelated ideas:

> The students at State College use a great deal of slang and they are from all parts of the country.

Too many ideas or details in a single sentence will violate unity by distracting the reader from the main thought of the sentence:

> Reading his letter that morning, standing on the crowded platform waiting for the downtown train, the morning sun just lighting up the tops of the nearby buildings and making the sleepy-eyed commuters blink or shade their eyes, made a profound impression on me.

Failure to complete an idea or a grammatical construction will destroy sentence unity. Sentences like the following are the result of carelessness on the part of the writer, who apparently thinks that the reader will not object to filling in gaps in the thought or completing comparisons.

> This is such a thick book.
> I was so pleased about the letter.
> The news is too wonderful.

The expressions just given are not complete. They can be improved by adding a clause or substituting another word for *such, so,* and *too*.

> This is a very thick book indeed.
> This is such a thick book that it is uncomfortable to handle.
> I was extremely pleased.
> I was so pleased about the letter that I ran to tell Bill.
> The news is indeed wonderful.
> The news is too wonderful to be true.

SUBORDINATION

In the last chapter, we learned something about sentence structure. We considered the several units making up a single sentence word, phrase, clause. We learned that some clauses express complete thoughts and that others do not. The former we called independent or main clauses; the latter we called dependent or subordinate clauses. If a sentence contains, as it well may, not merely one single, simple thought but rather a complete thought containing a number of constituent thoughts, we are faced with our first problem. We must decide which of the several ideas is the main idea and which ideas are subordinate, and we must then so construct our sentence that the subordinate thoughts will give emphasis to the main thought.

Our thoughts have a tendency to consist of a sequence of simple sentences.

> Here is the door. It is closed. Probably it is locked. Paul usually locks the door. He is very careful. He puts the key under the doormat. Perhaps it is there now. I will look. I hope it is.

However, if we are to write effectively, we must do more than put down our thoughts in this monotonous fashion. Perhaps our first attempt at grouping ideas will result in compound sentences:

Here is the door, but it is closed. Probably it is locked, for Paul usually locks the door. He is very careful, and he puts the key under the doormat.

If we are telling someone what happened, we may write something like this:

I was waiting on the platform for the train and I suddenly remembered about Paul's package, but there was still time, and I decided to go back for it. So I looked at my wrist watch and it was ten minutes to five, and I dashed back down the street towards Paul's house. I ran up the steps and I tried the door but it was locked and I was ready to give up. But then I remembered something about Paul and that was his habit of leaving the key under the doormat and I kicked the mat aside and there was the key.

We have succeeded in grouping our ideas somewhat, although the result is still amateurish. Each thought is treated as though it were as important as the next. Of the fifteen separate ideas, some are obviously less important than others. By reducing some clauses to phrases (a process known as "reduction of predication") we may achieve something like this:

Waiting on the station platform I suddenly remembered the package. With a quick glance at my wrist watch, which told me that there was just enough time to go back and get it, off I went down the street, towards Paul's house. Dashing up the steps, I tried the door, only to find it locked. Just as I was ready to give up in despair, I remembered Paul's habits, kicked the doormat aside, and pounced upon—the key!

This may not be great prose, but it is a definite improvement. Fifteen separate thoughts have been reduced to four principal and eleven subordinate thoughts. Subordinate ideas may be related to the main idea of the sentence in a number of ways. In Chapter III we learned something about the connectives used to link various clauses to the main clause. (See p. 70.)

Suppose we have two statements:

He has many friends.
He is a gloomy person.

99

Obviously, it will not do to regard these two statements as of equal value in a single sentence.

> He has many friends and he is a gloomy person

is correct enough grammatically, but most readers will find it ridiculous. We may point a contrast and write

> He has many friends *but* he is a gloomy person,

or we may, (and probably should) write

> Although he is a gloomy person, he has many friends,

or,

> Although he has many friends, he is a gloomy person.

We place one idea rather than another in the main clause, depending upon how we wish the sentence to be read.

Three special cautions may be given here:

1. Do not place the principal thought in a subordinate position:

FAULTY: The fullback crossed the goal-line, when the game was definitely lost.

IMPROVED: When the fullback crossed the goal-line, the game was definitely lost.

FAULTY: We read the headlines, a feeling of utter despair overwhelming us.

IMPROVED: As we read the headlines, a feeling of utter despair overwhelmed us.

2. Do not nullify subordination by inserting a coordinating conjunction:

FAULTY: Compound interest is a complicated subject, *and* which some people can't grasp.

IMPROVED: Compound interest is a complicated subject which some people can't grasp.

FAULTY: I want several new books, *but* which are too expensive for me to buy.

IMPROVED: I want several new books which are too expensive for me to buy.

3. Do not use the wrong subordinating connective:

WRONG: They are not positive *as* they can do it.
RIGHT: They are not positive *that* they can do it.

WRONG: The reason he was late getting to work was *because* he overslept.
RIGHT: The reason he was late getting to work was *that* he overslept.

WRONG: Because he speaks softly is no proof that he is kind.
RIGHT: That he speaks softly is no proof that he is kind.
RIGHT: His gentle speech is no proof that he is kind.

PARALLELISM

We have seen that less-important ideas must be made subordinate to the main idea of a sentence. If, however, two ideas are coordinate, they must be given equal rank in the sentence. Suppose we have these two statements:

> Charles is my brother.
> James is my cousin.

If these two statements are to form a single sentence, it is clear that the result will be:

> Charles is my brother and James is my cousin,

for it would be absurd to attempt to subordinate one statement to the other as in this sentence:

> Charles is my brother, James being my cousin.

If we have three statements instead of two, our problem is the same:

> He was born in 1905.
> He attended school at Watertown.
> He entered Union College in 1925.

The three thoughts are logically coordinate and must be made parallel in the completed sentence:

> He was born in 1905, he attended school at Watertown, and he entered Union College in 1925.

Observe that we have written a compound sentence. We may also reduce predication and write:

> He was born in 1905, attended school at Watertown, and entered Union College in 1925.

In this, three independent clauses have been reduced to one simple sentence with a compound predicate, without violating the principle of parallelism. But if we attempt subordination, we shall succeed only in giving a distorted thought as in this:

> Born in 1905, he attended school at Watertown, entering Union College in 1925.

Consider these statements:

> He was born of poor parents.
> He was obliged to work his way through high school.
> He graduated at the head of his class.

Two of these may readily be subordinated to the third:

> Although he was born of poor parents and was obliged to work his way through high school, he graduated at the head of his class.

Great care must be exercised in this matter of parallel structure. Nouns must be parallel to nouns, verbs to verbs, subordinate clauses to subordinate clauses, gerunds to gerunds, and so on. The following illustrative sentences will call attention to certain dangers:

> WRONG: She told us *to look* on the mantel and *that we should tell* her what we found.
> RIGHT: She told us to look on the mantel and to tell her what we found.

> WRONG: Phil's job is *reading* books and *to write* book reviews.
> RIGHT: Phil's job is reading books and writing book reviews.

> WRONG: We want *to travel* extensively and *new experiences.*
> RIGHT: We want to travel extensively and to have new experiences.

> WRONG: He was *sympathetic, tolerant,* and *people respected him.*
> RIGHT: He was sympathetic, tolerant, and respected by people.
> RIGHT: Because he was sympathetic and tolerant, most people respected him.

WRONG: The lecturer called attention to the *beginning* of the movement and *how it ended.*

RIGHT: The lecturer called attention to the beginning and end of the movement.

It is often necessary to repeat prepositions or other words in order to make the parallelism clear:

FAULTY: For dessert I had an apple and plum.

BETTER: For dessert I had an apple and *a* plum.

FAULTY: They were sure that the attendance would be large, interest would be keen, and the affair would be a success.

BETTER: They were sure that the attendance would be large, *that* interest would be keen, and *that* the affair would be a success.

MISLEADING: He wrote to his uncle and employer.

IMPROVED: He wrote to his uncle and *to* his employer.

Correlatives (see pp. 51–52) should be used only with parallel elements:

WRONG: He *not only* likes tennis *but also* golf.

IMPROVED: He likes not only tennis but also golf.

WRONG: We were uncertain whether *we should turn* to the right or *to go* straight ahead.

IMPROVED: We were uncertain whether to turn to the right or to go straight ahead.

WRONG: Frank neither *looked hurt* nor *discouraged.*

IMPROVED: Frank looked neither hurt nor discouraged.

The beginning writer must bear in mind that faulty parallelism is worse than no parallelism at all. He should use parallelism freely in his sentences, but he should equally resist all temptation to force into parallel structure clauses not parallel in thought.

COHERENCE

A sentence has "coherence" when the various parts follow one another in an order which makes their relationship clear. Correct handling of matters of unity, parallelism, and subordination contributes to coherence. There are four special problems which must be borne in mind in working for coherence, namely: reference of pronouns, split constructions, mixed constructions and mixed figures, and point of view. In the discussion of these four problems, the sentences marked "Improved" or "Better" are good examples of coherence.

REFERENCE OF PRONOUNS

In Chapter II, we learned that a pronoun must have an antecedent and that it must agree with that antecedent in person, number, and gender. The careful writer avoids weak, vague, general, or ambiguous reference:

POOR: Henry saw Albert and Frank yesterday and *he* said that *he* had the money.

IMPROVED: Henry saw Albert and Frank yesterday, and Frank told him he had the money.

POOR: My uncle's dog was crippled, and *he* was never the same again.

IMPROVED: My uncle was never the same again after his dog was crippled.

POOR: In France, *they* eat truffles, frogs' legs, snails, and other strange things.

IMPROVED: The French eat truffles, frogs' legs, snails, and other strange things.

POOR: Shakespeare's hero Hamlet is one of *his* finest creations, although *he* is a melancholy man.

IMPROVED: In Hamlet, Shakespeare has given us one of his finest creations, although Hamlet is a melancholy man.

POOR: Mr. Barnes calls himself a mortician. *This* is a profession I have no intention of entering.

IMPROVED: Although Mr. Barnes calls himself by the striking name of "mortician," undertaking is a profession I have no intention of entering.

POOR: Do not start across the street unless you are sure that the lights have changed. *This* is dangerous.

IMPROVED: Do not start across the street until you are sure that the lights have changed. Jaywalking is dangerous.

POOR: He put the typewriter on the table, *which* his sister had bought.

IMPROVED: He put the typewriter which his sister had bought upon the table.

Do not treat an antecedent first as singular and then as plural:

POOR: The Ajax Company *is* now using gas as fuel for *their* furnaces instead of oil.

IMPROVED: The Ajax Company is now using gas as fuel for *its* furnaces instead of oil.

POOR: The club *has* done *their* best to raise the money.

IMPROVED: The club has done *its* best to raise the money.

Avoid remote reference:

The Library occupies a commanding position on the college campus. From the steps, one can look down a long path bordered by flower-beds and trees, with a spacious lawn extending to right and left of it. *It* is built of gray stone.

(WRITE: *The Library* is built of gray stone.)

SPLIT CONSTRUCTIONS

Do not separate words that are closely related to each other. The Split Infinitive—

No student is *to* ever under any circumstances *chew* gum in class—

is perhaps the most notorious of the split constructions. Beginning writers will do well to avoid it, despite the fact that its use has been sanctioned by some authorities. Usually a slight change in word order will be sufficient to eliminate the split infinitive. If the re-worded sentence is unnatural or too formal, the entire sentence should be recast:

DOUBTFUL: The player started *to* viciously *hit* the ball.

BETTER: The player started to hit the ball viciously.

DOUBTFUL: I am going *to* privately *discuss* the matter with him.

BETTER: I am going to discuss the matter with him privately.

NOTE: Over-anxious writers often confuse the following construction, which is permissible, with the split infinitive:

I am not going *to be* really *satisfied* until I have a signed statement from him.

In general, do not separate closely related sentence elements unless there is a resultant gain in emphasis:

AWKWARD: *We,* having finished our work earlier than we expected, found ourselves watching the clock.

BETTER: Having finished our work earlier than we expected, we found ourselves watching the clock.

AWKWARD: He began to feel the effects of the medicine which he *had* earlier that morning *taken* in his coffee.

BETTER: He began to feel the effects of the medicine which, earlier that morning, he had taken in his coffee.

AWKWARD: If we had the time, we could make some changes, if we wanted to.

BETTER: If we had the time and if we wanted to, we could make some changes.

MIXED CONSTRUCTIONS AND MIXED FIGURES

Beginning writers sometimes get their sentences badly tangled. The trouble may be a matter of syntax:

CARELESS: This is the page *to* which I was referring *to.*

IMPROVED: This is the page to which I was referring.

CARELESS: The author gives the *best* idea of the South *than* any other I have read.

IMPROVED: The author gives a *better* idea of the South *than* any other I have read.

ALSO PERMISSIBLE: The author gives the *best* idea of the South *of* any I have read.

CARELESS: The cowboy walks up to the bronco, which he mounts and rides it around the corral.

BETTER: The cowboy walks up to the bronco, mounts it, and rides it around the corral.

POOR: The officer ordered him to keep up with the others as well as he can.

IMPROVED: The officer ordered him to keep up with the others as well as he could.

POOR: They can and have made mistakes.

BETTER: They can make mistakes and they have made them in the past.

POOR: I can't help but notice how pale he is.

IMPROVED: I can't help noticing how pale he is.

The trouble may be a matter of inappropriate figures of speech crowded together without regard for consistency:

The bone of contention seized upon by Carlyle had come to a head, inasmuch as the Industrial Revolution was in full swing.

My castles in air came tumbling down into a bottomless heap.

His rapier-like wit will help him weather the legal storm.

POINT OF VIEW

Aimless shifting from one point of view to another will destroy coherence in a sentence.

Do not shift needlessly from active to passive:

He ran to the station and the train was taken by him.

(He ran to the station and took the train.)

Do not shift suddenly from singular to plural:

If *one* tries hard, *they* can accomplish much.

(If one tries hard, one can accomplish much. Or: If people try hard, they can accomplish much.)

Try hard, and one can accomplish much.

(Try hard and you can accomplish much.)

Do not shift from past tense to present tense:

> The only words that we were able to distinguish *are* "house" and "barn."

> (The only words that we were able to distinguish *were* "house" and "barn.")

EMPHASIS

Making a sentence emphatic means giving most space to the most important ideas and placing them in the most effective positions. Such mechanical aids as italics, capital letters, dashes, exclamation points, and the like are, of course, helpful in promoting emphasis. But, in the final analysis, the arrangement of words determines the emphasis or lack of emphasis in the sentence. Because most coherent sentences are also emphatic sentences, the student of composition should concentrate his energy first upon the problem of coherence. The following suggestions may then prove helpful for handling certain special problems, if the writer bears in mind that overworking any one of the devices discussed here will probably result, not in emphatic sentences and paragraphs, but in strained, unnatural writing.

POSITION

Put important words in important positions. In English sentences, the middle is less important than either the beginning or the end; the end is unquestionably the most important of all. It is frequently advisable, therefore, to put less-important phrases and words in the middle of the sentence, if this can be done without violating English idiom, and to reserve the final position for the idea felt to be the most important.

Study the following sentences:

> WEAK: Simon graduated with highest honors, we were told.
> IMPROVED: Simon, we were told, graduated with highest honors.

> UNEMPHATIC: I shall be called a liar, in all probability.
> IMPROVED: I shall, in all probability, be called a liar.

> UNEMPHATIC: She flatly refused to see him, for some unknown reason.
> IMPROVED: For some unknown reason, she flatly refused to see him.

UNEMPHATIC: Nevertheless, we have made up our minds to go, no matter what they say.

BETTER: No matter what they say, we have made up our minds to go.

UNEMPHATIC: Jonathan was the only one to agree with me, however.

BETTER: Jonathan was, however, the only one to agree with me.

Prepositions are seldom emphatic words. As a rule, therefore, it is well to avoid placing them at the end of a sentence:

UNEMPHATIC: Dr. Adams is a man we can rely on.

BETTER: Dr. Adams is a man on whom we can rely.

UNEMPHATIC: What are you reading that magazine for?

BETTER: Why are you reading that magazine?

But observe that the following sentences will become stilted or unnatural if the word order is changed:

Where on earth did that cat come from?

We can't understand what the boy is talking about.

It is an ideal he is willing to die for.

What are you looking at?

PERIODIC SENTENCES

Emphasis can sometimes be gained by changing a loose sentence into a periodic sentence. If a sentence is not really complete until the end, we call it a periodic sentence. A sentence in which the principal idea is not reserved for the end we call a loose sentence. Both kinds of sentences may be good:

LOOSE: It was really an education to watch the faces of the crowd during the final minutes of the game.

PERIODIC: To watch the faces of the crowd during the final minutes of the game was really an education.

The writer must remember that most English sentences are loose, not periodic. Too many periodic sentences one after the other will make the paragraph ridiculous, for no reader enjoys being kept constantly in suspense.

The following loose sentences gain in emphasis when they are changed into periodic sentences:

Loose: The car tipped over, just as it reached the intersection.

Periodic: Just as it reached the intersection, the car tipped over.

Loose: Read your book, if you are not interested in what I am saying.

Periodic: If you are not interested in what I am saying, read your book.

Loose: It is of course stupid to think that she will appreciate our help or even thank us for it.

Periodic: To think that she will appreciate our help or even thank us for it is, of course, stupid.

Loose: The things that he really considers important are sports, dancing, and movies.

Periodic: Sports, dancing, and movies—these are the things that he really considers important.

Loose: He never seemed quite the same after he returned from his trip to Washington last Friday.

Periodic: After he returned from his trip to Washington last Friday, he never seemed quite the same.

ORDER OF CLIMAX

Ideas may be arranged in the order of climax but only if the ideas are of varying importance. It is unemphatic to write

During his long career he served as President, as Secretary of the Treasury, and as Vice-President,

when we can gain emphasis by the simple device of arranging the three ideas in the order of increasing importance:

During his long career, he served as Secretary of the Treasury, as Vice-President, and as President.

If the parallel ideas in a sentence do not lend themselves to such arrangement, it is of course unwise to suggest a developing importance which does not exist:

Lillian paused at the dressing-table and picked up a pair of gloves, an emerald necklace, a small mirror, and a lipstick.

Do not allow the emeralds to obscure the fact that the objects mentioned were probably not picked up in the order of increasing monetary value. The device of climax must be used only with great care.

REPETITION

Repetition of important words will sometimes give desirable emphasis. Thoughtless or careless repetition of words or sounds is, of course, something quite different from deliberate repetition designed to make the sentence clear and forceful.

WEAK: They believe that most of us believe they are lazy.

BETTER: They believe that most of us consider them lazy.

Do not, however, weaken your sentences by resorting to what is known as "Elegant Variation." The amateur writer is afraid to repeat himself and searches feverishly for synonyms. He uses *the writer, the author,* and *we* when he means *I*. Instead of mentioning Shakespeare again and again, he speaks of *that great poet* or *the man of Avon* or *the creator of Hamlet* or *the Bard*. He is apparently afraid to call a spade a spade, and the reader soon becomes more interested in the writer's search for equivalents than in what the writer is trying to say.

WEAK: We gazed out upon a wet world: the trees were damp; the streets were moist; the roof tops were rain-soaked; the pedestrians were dripping.

EMPHATIC: We gazed out upon a wet world: the trees were wet; the streets were wet; the roof tops were wet; the pedestrians were wet.

WEAK: They never were friendly, they are not now amicable, and they never will be cordial.

EMPHATIC: They never were friendly, they are not now friendly, and they never will be friendly.

WEAK: To be, or the contrary—that is the question.

EMPHATIC: "To be or not to be—that is the question."

INVERSION

Reversing the normal order of the English sentence will sometimes give emphasis. Like other devices, inversion must be used sparingly.

NORMAL ORDER: I have never seen anything like it in my life.

EMPHATIC: Never in my life have I seen anything like it.

NORMAL ORDER: You cannot convince him.

EMPHATIC: Convince him you cannot.

Whenever possible, use the active voice instead of the passiv voice. Some sentences, however, require the passive:

> Fifty-eight persons were killed in street accidents last month.

But we should, as a rule, avoid the passive:

> WEAK: I was told by Father to try again.
> BETTER: Father told me to try again.

> WEAK: The prize is announced by the committee to be awarded ne week.
> BETTER: The committee announces that it will award the prize ne week.

> WEAK: The package was obtained, which she opened in great excit ment.
> BETTER: She obtained the package and opened it in great excitemen

> WEAK: I was congratulated by most of them.
> BETTER: Most of them congratulated me.

> WEAK: On his head a curious green hat ornamented with a r feather was worn.
> BETTER: On his head he wore a curious green hat ornamented wi a red feather.

SENTENCE ERRORS TO BE AVOIDED

Having considered the general elements which make for effectiv ness in sentences, we shall now take up four errors in sentence co struction which all writers must be careful to avoid. These four se tence errors are: The Fragment, The Comma Splice, The Fuse Sentence, and The Dangling Modifier.

THE FRAGMENT

A sentence is a group of words expressing one complete though Therefore, a number of different ideas should not be huddled t gether in a single unit; similarly, no phrase or subordinate clause w e able to satisfy the requirement that a sentence express a complete hought. The following are fragments:

> The partner being a typical big business executive who prides himself on his efficiency.
>
> As he comes in each morning, glancing keenly about at the clerks in the outer office.
>
> Because there are two telephones on his desk.
>
> Making his visitors wait outside while he pretends to be busy.

The writer of these incomplete statements apparently forgot that sentence must express a complete thought. Perhaps he intended to rite:

> I am frequently made aware these days of my own shiftlessness and inefficiency, *my partner being a typical big business executive who prides himself on his efficiency.*
>
> *As he comes in each morning, glancing keenly at the clerks in the outer office,* he struts like a turkey-cock.

It is true, of course, that professional writers do use incomplete ntences, but observe that the fragments in the selection which fol- ws convey complete thoughts and convey them immediately.

London. Implacable November weather. As much mud in the streets as the waters had been but newly retired from the face of the earth and it ould not be wonderful to meet a Megalosaurus, forty feet long or so, addling like an elephantine lizard up Holborn Hill. Smoke lowering own from chimney-pots, making a soft black drizzle, with flakes of soot a it as big as full-grown snowflakes—gone into mourning, one might nagine, for the death of the sun. Dogs, undistinguishable in mire. Horses, arcely better; splashed to their very blinkers. Foot passengers, jostling ne another's umbrellas, in a general infection of ill-temper, and losing heir foothold at street-corners, where tens of thousands of other foot- assengers have been slipping and sliding since the day broke (if the day ver broke), adding new deposits to the crust upon crust of mud, sticking at ose points tenaciously to the pavement, and accumulating compound terest.—DICKENS: *Bleak House*

The following suggestions will serve as warnings:

1. Do not write a dependent clause as though it were a complete ntence.

> WRONG: Harriet was trembling with excitement. As it was her first airplane ride.

RIGHT: Harriet was trembling with excitement, as it was her first airplane ride.

RIGHT: As it was her first airplane ride, Harriet was trembling with excitement.

2. Do not write an appositive (introduced by such expressions as *that is, for example,* or *namely*) as though it were a complete sentence.

WRONG: He made a hobby of collecting unusual things. For example, match-boxes.

RIGHT: He made a hobby of collecting unusual things, for example, match-boxes.

RIGHT: He made a hobby of collecting unusual things, such things, for example, as match-boxes.

3. Do not write a participial phrase as though it were a complete sentence.

WRONG: Terry wandered about for two hours. Eventually losing himself in the business section of the city.

RIGHT: Terry wandered about for two hours, eventually losing himself completely in the business section of the city.

Ellipitical constructions (in which there is an omission that can be readily supplied) are not considered as violating the rule of completeness:

"Georgiana?"
"Yes?"
"Coming with us?"
"No."
"Why not?"
"Too busy."

THE COMMA SPLICE

The second basic error results from an attempt to use a separating mark (the comma) to join two clauses in a compound sentence:

Four of us were in the taxi, I was looking out the rear window when the truck side-swiped us.

The Comma Splice illustrated here may be corrected by construct-
ing two sentences:

> Four of us were in the taxi. I was looking out the rear window when
> the truck side-swiped us.

Or we may use a coordinating conjunction:

> Four of us were in the taxi, and I was looking out the rear window
> when the truck side-swiped us.

Or we may use a semicolon to show that the coordinating conjunction has been omitted:

> Four of us were in the taxi; I was looking out the rear window when
> the truck side-swiped us.

If the reader has studied Chapter III, he need only be reminded
at this point of two situations in which the inexperienced writer is
likely to fall into the error called the Comma Splice:

1. When a direct quotation is interrupted by such words as *he
said* or *she replied,* do not use a comma after the interruption if
what follows is an independent clause:

> WRONG: "I was never more surprised in my life," replied Pauline,
> "there he was, calmly reading a book."

> RIGHT: "I was never more surprised in my life," replied Pauline.
> "There he was, calmly reading a book."

2. Except in the most informal writing, use a semicolon before
conjunctive adverbs such as *so, however, moreover,* and the like
(see also p. 53).

> CORRECT: We find we save money living in Pleasantville; moreover,
> we like it here.

> PERMISSIBLE IN A PERSONAL LETTER: Ruth didn't know his last name,
> so she asked her brother.

THE FUSED SENTENCE

Two or more sentences run together with no mark of punctuation between them are said to be "fused." The writer guilty of
such a blunder is either extremely careless or is ignorant of the most
elementary facts about sentence structure. Correct such fused

sentences as the following by separating them and punctuating them
appropriately:

WRONG: They didn't say that they merely spoke of what fun they
were having.

INTELLIGIBLE: They didn't say that. They merely spoke of what fun
they were having.

WRONG: Our club raised some money for the Red Cross an organiza
tion like this is a wonderful thing.

INTELLIGIBLE: Our club raised some money for the Red Cross. An
organization like this is a wonderful thing.

BETTER: Our club raised some money for that wonderful organization
the Red Cross.

WRONG: He left early he said he had a toothache.

IMPROVED: He left early. He said he had a toothache.

THE DANGLING MODIFIER

In Chapter II we learned that a modifier should be so placed in a
sentence that it will be related immediately and unmistakably to the
word it modifies. If a participle, for example, cannot be thus con
nected with its antecedent in the sentence, it is said to "dangle."
Usually, a dangling modifier makes the sentence ridiculous at once:

WRONG: Puffing and panting, the top of the hill was reached at last

IMPROVED: Puffing and panting, we reached the top of the hill.

WRONG: Gazing out the window, the church steeple was clearly visi
ble.

IMPROVED: Gazing out the window, we could see the church steeple

Dangling infinitives, dangling phrases and clauses, and dangling
gerunds are illustrated in the following sentences. Correct them by
so rewriting them that the connection between modifier and ante
cedent is grasped at once:

To slice the bread, the knife must be held firmly.

To avoid squeaking, the user should lubricate the sewing machine.

While on a visit to Europe, the Stock Exchange closed for a week

Although only seven years old, my grandfather gave me a bicycle.

He was gazing up at the tree, when a squirrel ran along one branch
laughing quietly.

Being adequately boiled, I took the stew from the stove.

EXERCISES

A. Re-write the following sentences, correcting any errors in parallelism:

(1) He taught grammar and how to spell.

(2) Swimming and to go fishing are summer sports.

(3) If we have packed and should we get up early enough, we should get to the beach by ten.

(4) Not only were they disappointed but also angry.

(5) I both want exercise and to be amused.

(6) He offered either to pay for it now or tomorrow.

(7) As we were unfamiliar with the route and because of approaching darkness, we decided to ask for advice.

(8) Not only had he attended a great many weddings but had been best man twice.

(9) When he first tried to enlist and when we remember that he was only thirteen, we ought not to be surprised at what happened.

(10) He had spent his previous summers travelling in Europe, sailing on Lake Erie, and had visited Mexico.

(11) Michael has brought his little girl a doll and Easter egg.

(12) Sam wants to buy a motorcycle with a sidecar and two horns and trade-in his bicycle.

(13) Billy's face was streaked with dirt and his feet muddy.

(14) The critics praised McAdam for his short-stories dealing with the war and his poems.

(15) He was neither willing to pay nor was he able.

B. Re-write the following sentences, correcting any dangling modifiers you may find in them:

(1) Dashing to the front window, the parade came into view.

(2) Missing on two cylinders and backfiring badly, the driver stopped his car at the filling station.

(3) Having diagnosed my case and given me a prescription, I paid Dr. Robins and left.

(4) Opening one eye a fraction, the room appeared empty.

(5) Taking our great Dane for his morning walk, the neighbors' cat is a nuisance.

(6) Being nicely browned on both sides, I removed the pancake from the griddle.

(7) At the tender age of three my parents moved to New Jersey.

(8) I went to a dance last night, thus causing me to be late at the office this morning.

(9) Two months ago, after graduating from high school, my grandfather gave me a gold watch.

(10) To open this door, it must be given a sudden push.

(11) Being unaccustomed to smoking, the pipe made him ill.

(12) To learn French well, it must be spoken regularly.

(13) When neatly typewritten and folded correctly, hand the essay to the teacher.

(14) Swimming half a mile out into the bay, the shore seemed distant indeed.

(15) We had just started the third rubber of bridge when, looking up, there was Mrs. Green.

(16) While talking about his experiences in New Orleans, Stephen's excitement often makes him stutter.

(17) After much frantic searching in my desk, the missing fountain pen was discovered.

(18) I had forgotten to change my shirt, thus causing me much embarrassment.

(19) When properly sprinkled, roll the tablecloths up and put them aside.

(20) Not being used to the water, the small boat looked dangerous to her.

C. Improve the following sentences. Pay especial attention to subordination and the use of connectives:

(1) He had made that speech so many times that he was so accustomed to it that he couldn't understand the lack of applause.

(2) I was reaching down to pick up my hat just as I saw the two rattlesnakes.

(3) We came within sight of the village when our car suddenly caught fire.

(4) Because he has been to college is no sign he is cultured.

(5) She felt like she was walking on air.

(6) I am not sure as we ought to let him have that gun.

(7) The main reason I left early was because I was bored.

(8) Mr. Samuelson is the vice-president while Mr. Daniels is the sec·retary.

(9) Due to illness, he was obliged to postpone his vacation.

(10) My cousin was recovering normally just as she had a relapse.

D. Re-write the following. Correct any fragments:

(1) We go to camp during the summer. Whenever we can, of course.

(2) Everyone appeared pleased about the outcome. Especially the out-of-town visitors.

(3) The small boy was always active. Running, jumping, climbing on chairs, dashing in and out of rooms.

(4) Our literary club has only two officers. Mr. Dawson being president and Miss Gaines being secretary-treasurer.

(5) Living in the city is not always pleasant. During the summer months particularly.

(6) "We'll have to wait here," said Bill, disgustedly. "Since they haven't left the door unlocked."

(7) His new clothes giving him a feeling of confidence such as he had never had before.

(8) There was one thing he couldn't tolerate. Namely, neighbors who give noisy parties late at night.

(9) To live in New York, to feel that she was in the very center of things, to get away once and for all from small-town pettiness. This was her ambition.

(10) He hated foreign languages. Latin, French, and German especially.

E. Improve the following. Pay especial attention to the Comma Splice:

(1) Talking to the mayor gave Elizabeth a new feeling of confidence, she felt it had done wonders for her.

(2) I walked confidently down the street, I was sure I'd get there on time.

(3) "I've never done any skiing before," Melvin whispered to me, "I'm rather disturbed at the idea. "

(4) The sand was beginning to blow. we headed for shelter.

(5) She saved money by making her own clothes, moreover she enjoyed designing them.

(6) My brother was obviously disconcerted by Mr. Simpson's flat refusal, so he turned away abruptly.

(7) Spending forty minutes on the subway every morning is no joke, it's a fearful nuisance, to tell the truth.

(8) They are still quite young, therefore, they can afford to wait a year or two.

(9) "I was back in my hotel room by ten o'clock," stated the witness, "I did not go out again until the following morning."

(10) We saw her fall, we never want to see a sight like that again.

F. Re-write the following as complete sentences:

(1) It wasn't his idea he should have known better than to do it.

(2) I can't quite picture him as a teacher he isn't the type somehow.

(3) We were tired and hungry in fact we were almost exhausted.

(4) We hesitated a moment or two but then decided to go in anyway if worst came to worst we could always mention Jack's name.

(5) Joan had never read any novels by Sinclair Lewis so she bought a copy of *Arrowsmith*.

(6) The room looked wonderful the rugs had just been vacuumed.

(7) I don't think it's his fault he hasn't played tennis for three years he's out of practice.

(8) He is taking a pre-medical course to enter medical school is his greatest ambition.

(9) Kenneth may be able to tell you on the other hand you may have to ask Mr. Edwardson.

(10) Come inside at once I'm tired of having to reprimand you.

G. The following sentences are lacking in unity. Re-write them, adding details and changing words wherever necessary:

(1) The librarian was so discouraged about the lack of funds.

(2) Our situation is too wonderful.

(3) Trying to work when my roommate is playing his accordion is such a problem.

(4) The young girls wore ankle-socks and were kind-hearted.

(5) She is so talented.

(6) Courses in science have more appeal for the college student today.

(7) From my boyish days I had always felt a great perplexity on one point in *Macbeth* and it was this: the knocking at the gate which succeeds to the murder of Duncan produced to my feelings an effect for which I never could account because the effect was that it reflected back upon the murderer a peculiar awfulness and a depth of solemnity; yet, however obstinately I endeavoured with my understanding to comprehend this, for many years I never could see *why* it should produce such an effect.

H. Re-write the following sentences, paying especial attention to coherence:

(1) He was apparently content to patiently wait outside the door.

(2) I wrote and asked my nephew to let me know about the horses as soon as he can.

(3) The membership committee are trying to make up its mind about Sidney's application.

(4) Sally and her sister both saw the play, but she was disappointed in it.

(5) He took an oath to never, no matter what happened, reveal the secrets of the organization.

(6) She lifted her eyes from the floor and cast them out the window.

(7) I informed the policeman I am always anxious to be of service.

(8) We went on a trip to Mexico. They are very hospitable people.

(9) I have been reading Thackeray's *Henry Esmond,* who is one of the best authors of the nineteenth century.

(10) She, having worked steadily at the sewing-machine for three hours and having finished stitching five dresses, sat down wearily in the armchair.

(11) She is as old if not older than Marion.

(12) We have and will again talk to him about his plans.

(13) The icy finger of Winter smothered the broad fields.

(14) She told us it was difficult for her to easily follow the doctor's advice.

(15) I heard Wagner's *Die Meistersinger.* He was a great composer, undoubtedly.

I. Make the following sentences more emphatic:

(1) My sister is happy in her new home, on the other hand.

(2) The guests left early, for some reason or other.

(3) His teacher is one person he can confide in.

(4) The rain began to fall, just as we came out of the house.

(5) Go away, if you don't like it here.

(6) It is unlikely, to say the least, that they will put much faith in his words.

(7) He testified that he had attended college, grammar school, and high school.

(8) Lincoln's speech at Gettysburg was not appreciated at the time, but the Great Emancipator's short oration will live forever.

(9) We were informed by the policeman that Edith had been told of her mother's death by him.

(10) It is a worthy cause, we think.

CHAPTER V

EFFECTIVE PARAGRAPHS

A GOOD paragraph is a sentence or a group of sentences expressing and developing a complete thought. The paragraph is like the sentence and the longer units in that it must concern itself with one thought. It must have unity. But whereas some ideas can be adequately treated in a single sentence, others require the fuller treatment afforded by a group of sentences (paragraph) or a group of paragraphs (chapter, section, or book).

PARAGRAPH STRUCTURE

There is no fixed length for a paragraph. In general, informal material is presented in shorter paragraphs than is formal material. Newspapers, for various technical reasons, use short paragraphs; scholarly articles are usually made up of longer paragraphs. Few modern paragraphs contain more than five hundred words, and perhaps it is safe to say that the average paragraph is about one hundred words in length.

The student of paragraph structure finds himself concerned with the following problems:

(1) The Topic Sentence
(2) The Substance of the Paragraph
(3) The Orderly Arrangement of Material
(4) Transition within the Paragraph

We shall consider these problems in order and study certain illustrative paragraphs from the works of professional writers.

The Topic Sentence

In most paragraphs it is possible to say of one of the sentences that it expresses the principal idea of the paragraph. Such a sentence is called the **topic sentence.** Most expository paragraphs begin, logically enough, with a topic sentence. The reader wants to be told, and is told, what, in general, is to be the subject-matter of the paragraph. If the topic sentence is omitted, as it sometimes is for one reason or another in narratives or essays, it is always implied or understood and can be reconstructed.

The beginning writer will do well to write paragraphs in which the topic sentence comes at or near the beginning. There is no fixed rule, of course, about the position of the topic sentence. In some paragraphs it comes in the middle; in others it is reserved for the end in order that what precedes may lead up to a statement of the topic. But most readers, whether they are aware of it or not, like to be informed promptly, when they begin a new paragraph, as to the material to be treated. And it is the duty of the careful writer to help the reader.

The following series consists of the first sentences of eight consecutive paragraphs from Sir James G. Frazer's *The Golden Bough* (Vol. I, 247 ff.), forming a complete outline of the material contained in those paragraphs:

(1) Of the things which the public magician sets himself to do for the good of the tribe, one of the chief is to control the weather and especially to ensure an adequate fall of rain.

(2) Thus, for example, in a village near Dorpat, in Russia, when rain was much wanted, three men used to climb up the fir-trees of an old sacred grove.

(3) Other people besides the Arabs have used fire as a means of stopping rain.

(4) In the torrid climate of Queensland the ceremonies necessary for wringing showers from the cloudless heaven are naturally somewhat elaborate.

(5) The Dieri of Central Australia enact a somewhat similar pantomime for the same purpose.

(6) The Kaitish tribe of Central Australia believe that the rainbow is the son of the rain, and with filial regard is always anxious to prevent his father from falling down.

(7) Among the Arunta tribe of Central Australia a celebrated rain-maker resides at the present day in what is called by the natives the Rain Country (*Kartwia quatcha*), a district about fifty miles to the east of Alice Springs.

(8) Although we cannot, perhaps, divine the meaning of all the details of this curious ceremony, the analogy of the Queensland and the Dieri ceremonies, described above, suggests that we have here a rude attempt to represent the gathering of rainclouds and the other accompaniments of a rising storm.

Except in paragraphs of one sentence, the topic sentence never does the work of a paragraph. It points out or states the topic and may even suggest how the topic will be developed. It is, however, at best only a statement of the topic. Such sentences as the following could serve as topic sentences but would need to be developed:

(1) Commuters have special problems of their own.

(2) The educational value of the moving picture has been exaggerated.

(3) Francis Bacon uses two distinct prose styles in his work.

(4) Writing is either a pleasure or a form of slave labor.

To the problem of enlarging upon, or developing, such statements as these we may now turn our attention.

Substance and Arrangement

If the writer is interested in saying something in his paragraph, his problem will not be one of padding out his topic sentence but rather one of selecting certain kinds of **substance** and rejecting others. There are several kinds of substance: details, examples, comparisons, contrasts, typical instances. The writer must decide which to use in his paragraph, or, if more than one kind is to be used, which combination will be most effective. The problem of substance is closely linked with the problem of arrangement, and it may be well, before turning to other matters, to study a few paragraphs in which effective use has been made of one or another of the kinds of substance mentioned.

The following sentence contains a good deal of information in compressed form:

> Monsters such as the Sphinx, the Chimaera, and the giants were beings of unnatural proportions or parts, usually regarded with terror, as possessing immense strength and ferocity, which they employed for the injury and annoyance of men.

Under certain circumstances, the author may wish to extend this information into a paragraph. How does he do it? Dr. Bulfinch, author of *The Age of Fable,* decided to draw a distinction between monsters like the Sphinx and those monsters called Giants. He decided also to show that two chief kinds of giants are mentioned in mythology: human giants and superhuman giants. The original paragraph shows us how he arranged his material. Observe that the paragraph is not "padded out" with extraneous matter. Observe, too, that each sentence helps reinforce the thought of the first or topic sentence:

From Thomas Bulfinch, *The Age of Fable*

Monsters, in the language of mythology, were beings of unnatural proportions or parts, usually regarded with terror, as possessing immense strength and ferocity, which they employed for the injury and annoyance of men. Some of them were supposed to combine the members of different animals; such were the Sphinx and Chimaera; and to these all the terrible qualities of wild beasts were attributed, together with human sagacity and faculties. Others, as the giants, differed from men chiefly in their size; and in this particular we must recognize a wide distinction among them. The human giants, if so they may be called, such as the Cyclops, Antaeus, Orion, and others, must be supposed not to be altogether disproportioned to human beings, for they mingled in love and strife with them. But the superhuman giants, who warred with the gods, were of vastly larger dimensions. Tityus, we are told, when stretched on the plain, covered nine acres, and Enceladus required the whole of Mount Aetna to be laid upon him to keep him down.

Taine, writing about Macaulay's *Essays,* might have said merely:

I confess that I am fond of books such as these, for they may be read haphazardly, they have variety, and they reveal much about the author.

But instead Taine expanded each of these three points slightly and wrote the following paragraph:

From H. A. Taine, *History of English Literature*

His essays are an assemblage of articles: I confess that I am fond of books such as these. In the first place, we can throw down the volume after a score of pages, begin at the end, or in the middle; we are not its slave, but its master; we can treat it like a newspaper: in fact it is a journal of a mind. In the second place, it is varied; in turning over a page, we pass from the Renaissance to the nineteenth century, from England to India: this diversity surprises and pleases. Lastly, involuntarily, the author is indiscreet; he displays himself to us, keeping back nothing; it is a familiar conversation, and no conversation is worth so much as that of England's greatest historian. We are pleased to mark the origin of this generous and powerful mind, to discover what faculties have nourished his talent, what researches have shaped his knowledge; what opinions he has formed on philosophy, religion, the state, literature; what he was, and what he has become; what he wishes, and what he believes.

Thomas De Quincey tells us that he has often been asked how he came to be a user of opium. He then proceeds to enumerate his reasons in a well-developed paragraph from the essay *Confessions of an English Opium-Eater:*

I have often been asked how I came to be a regular opium-eater; and have suffered, very unjustly, in the opinion of my acquaintance, from being reputed to have brought upon myself all the sufferings which I shall have to record, by a long course of indulgence in this practice purely for the sake of creating an artificial state of pleasurable excitement. This, however, is a misrepresentation of my case. True it is, that for nearly ten years I did occasionally take opium for the sake of the exquisite pleasure it gave me; but, so long as I took it with this view, I was effectually protected from all material bad consequences by the necessity of interposing long intervals between the several acts of indulgence, in order to renew the pleasurable sensations. It was not for the purpose of creating pleasure, but of mitigating pain in the severest degree, that I first began to use opium as an article of daily diet. In the twenty-eighth year of my age, a most painful affection of the stomach, which I had first experienced about ten years before, attacked me in great strength. This affection had originally been caused by extremities of hunger, suffered in my boyish days. During the season of hope and redundant happiness which succeeded (that is, from eighteen to twenty-four) it had slumbered: for the three following years it had revived at intervals; and now, under unfavorable circumstances, from depression of spirits, it attacked me with a violence that yielded to no remedies but opium. As the youthful sufferings which first produced this derangement of the stomach were interesting in themselves and in the circumstances that attended them, I shall here briefly retrace them.

Comparison is a useful device in developing topic sentences into paragraphs. Professor Breasted, in his book *Ancient Times,* tells us that the Aegean Sea is "like a large lake" and concludes his paragraph by drawing an analogy specifically with Lake Michigan:

The Aegean Sea is like a large lake, almost completely encircled by the surrounding lands. Around its west and north sides stretches the mainland of Europe, on the east is Asia Minor, while the long island of Crete on the south lies like a breakwater, shutting off the Mediterranean from the Aegean Sea. From north to south this sea is at no point more than four hundred miles in length, while its width varies greatly. It is a good deal longer than Lake Michigan, and in places over twice as wide. Its coast is deeply indented with many bays and harbors, and it is so thickly sprinkled with hundreds of islands that it is often possible to sail from one island to another in an hour or two. Indeed it is almost impossible to cross the Aegean without seeing land all the way, and in a number of directions at the same time. Just as Chicago, Milwaukee, and other towns around Lake Michigan are linked together by modern steamboats, so we shall see incoming civilization connecting the shores of the Aegean by sailing ships. This sea, therefore, with its islands and the fringe of shores around it, formed a region by itself, which we may call the Aegean world.

A topic sentence can often be developed by the use of details. Mark Twain, recalling his early days, writes:

I can see the farm yet, with perfect clearness,

and goes on to give us a selection of details so that we too may see it. He decides to concentrate, in this paragraph, on the "family room of the house," and he tells us enough to help us understand why it was an important room at every hour of the day.

I can see the farm yet, with perfect clearness. I can see all its belongings, all its details; the family room of the house, with a "trundle" bed in one corner and a spinning-wheel in another—a wheel whose rising and falling wail, heard from a distance, was the mournfullest of all sounds to me, and made me homesick and low spirited, and filled my atmosphere with the wandering spirits of the dead; the vast fireplace, piled high, on winter nights, with flaming hickory logs from whose ends a sugary sap bubbled out, but did not go to waste, for we scraped it off and ate it; the lazy cat spread out on the rough hearthstones; the drowsy dogs braced against the jambs and blinking; my aunt in one chimney corner, knitting; my uncle in the other, smoking his corn-cob pipe; the slick and carpetless oak floor faintly mirroring the dancing flame tongues and freckled with black indentations where the fire coals had popped out and died a leisurely death; half a dozen children romping in the background twilight; "split"-bottomed chairs here and there, some with rockers; a cradle—out of service, but waiting, with confidence; in the early cold mornings a snuggle of children, in shirts and chemises, occupying the hearthstone and procrastinating—they could not bear to leave that comfortable place and go out on the wind-swept floorspace between the house and kitchen where the general tin basin stood, and wash.

G. K. Chesterton writes an orderly paragraph in which he enumerates the four principal points he wishes to make in his second chapter, called "The Age of Chaucer." The paragraph is complete in itself and at the same time provides the reader with an admirable introduction to the more detailed discussion to follow:

There are four facts about Chaucer, which are the four corners of the world he lived in; the four conditions of Christendom at the end of the fourteenth century. In themselves they can be stated very simply. Chaucer was English; at a time when the full national identity was still near its beginning. Chaucer was Catholic; at a time when the full Catholic unity of Europe was near the beginning of its end. Chaucer was chivalric, in the sense that he belonged, if only by adoption, to the world of chivalry and armorial blazonry, broadly French, when that world was in its gorgeous autumn, glorious with decay. Finally, Chaucer was none the less *bourgeois,* as our dear comrades say, in the sense that he himself was born and bred of burgesses, of tradesmen working under the old Guild system, also already rather too grand for its own good, but fresher and stronger than the fading feudal system. His figure bestrides the gap between these two last systems. It is as if he had the Trade Guild for a mother and the Order of Knighthood for a father.—CHESTERTON, *Chaucer*

TRANSITION WITHIN THE PARAGRAPH

A unified, orderly paragraph is probably also a coherent paragraph. In some paragraphs, each sentence seems to grow easily and naturally out of the previous sentence. In others, the several sentences are deliberately related by means of such devices as transitional expressions and connective or reference words. When they are skillfully and unobtrusively used, such terms are of great assistance to the reader. They guide him through the paragraph and make it easy for him to follow the writer as he passes from one phase of the subject to another. The problem of transition cannot, of course, be reduced to a simple rule of thumb. But we may say in general that coherence is usually achieved by one or another of three methods or by a combination:

(1) **Linking expressions** such as the following:

therefore	for example
moreover	for instance
consequently	as a result
in addition to	nevertheless
furthermore	obviously

first	clearly
next	that is
finally	that is to say
in conclusion	of course
meanwhile	naturally
at length	at any rate
yet	no doubt
however	on the whole

(2) **Pronouns** to call attention to antecedents:

Were Dickens dead, his biography might be written. On the day after the burial of a celebrated man, his friends and enemies apply themselves to the work; his schoolfellows relate in the newspapers his boyish pranks; another man recalls exactly, and word for word, the conversations he had with him a score of years ago. The lawyer, who manages the affairs of the deceased, draws up a list of the different offices he has filled, his titles, dates and figures, and reveals to the matter-of-fact readers how the money left has been invested, and how the fortune has been made; the grand-nephews and second cousins publish an account of his acts of humanity, and the catalogue of his domestic virtues.

—Taine, *History of English Literature*

(3) **Repetition** of words or phrases or the **use of synonyms:**

A quibble is to Shakespeare, what luminous vapours are to the traveller; he follows it at all adventures: it is sure to lead him out of his way, and sure to engulf him in the mire. It has some malignant power over his mind, and its fascinations are irresistible. Whatever be the dignity or profundity of his disquisition, whether he be enlarging knowledge or exalting affection, whether he be amusing attention with incidents, or enchaining it in suspense, let but a quibble spring up before him, and he leaves his work unfinished. A quibble is the golden apple for which he will always turn aside from his career, or stoop from his elevation. A quibble, poor and barren as it is, gave him such delight, that he was content to purchase it, by the sacrifice of reason, propriety, and truth. A quibble was to him the fatal Cleopatra for which he lost the world, and was content to lose it.

—Johnson, *Preface to Shakespeare*

THE PARAGRAPH AS PART OF THE WHOLE COMPOSITION

The paragraphs we have examined in this chapter were never intended to stand alone. Each was designed to serve as part of a longer composition. Since this is true, we may well ask not only if it is unified, orderly, and coherent but also if it performs some useful function in the chapter or essay of which it is a part. Moreover, we shall want to know whether or not the paragraph we are studying is carefully related to the surrounding paragraphs. In skillful writing, each paragraph has its proper place, just as each word has its proper place in a coherent, emphatic sentence. And just as there is a problem of transition from one sentence to another within the paragraph, so there is a similar problem when we are dealing with a group of paragraphs.

We shall treat the longer forms of composition in the next chapter. For the moment we shall merely consider three special kinds of paragraphs:

Introductory
Transitional
Concluding.

THE INTRODUCTORY PARAGRAPH

A short essay needs no introductory paragraph. If the beginning writer finds, upon re-reading his essay, that he has written a rambling preliminary paragraph, he should discard it and plunge immediately into his subject. Notice how Francis Bacon begins four of his essays:

He that hath wife and children hath given hostages to fortune; for they are impediments to great enterprises, either of virtue or mischief.

—"Of Marriage and Single Life"

Men in great places are thrice servants: servants of the sovereign or state; servants of fame; and servants of business.

—"Of Great Place"

Studies serve for delight, for ornament, and for ability.

—"Of Studies"

Men fear Death as children fear to go in the dark; and as that natural fear in children is increased with tales, so is the other.

—"Of Death"

The longer essay, especially if the subject is complicated, may well begin, however, with an introductory paragraph. In fact, several such paragraphs may be required, in some compositions, to prepare the reader for what is to follow. Here are passages from two of William Hazlitt's essays, illustrating both the long and the short introductory paragraph:

> There are people who have but one idea: at least, if they have more, they keep it a secret, for they never talk but of one subject.
> —"On People with One Idea"

> The two chief points which Sir Joshua aims at in his Discourses are to shew that excellence in the Fine Arts is the result of pains and study, rather than of genius, and that all beauty, grace, and grandeur are to be found, not in actual nature, but in an idea existing in the mind. On both these points he appears to have fallen into considerable inconsistencies, or very great latitude of expression, so as to make it difficult to know what conclusion to draw from his various reasonings. I shall attempt little more in this Essay than to bring together several passages, that from their contradictory import seem to imply some radical defect in Sir Joshua's theory, and a doubt as to the possibility of placing an implicit reliance on his authority.
> —"On Certain Inconsistencies in Sir Joshua Reynolds's Discourses"

Charles Lamb begins his essay "The Two Races of Men" with this introductory paragraph:

> The human species, according to the best theory I can form of it, is composed of two distinct races, *the men who borrow,* and *the men who lend.* To these two original diversities may be reduced all those impertinent classifications of Gothic and Celtic tribes, white men, black men, red men. All the dwellers upon earth, "Parthians, and Medes, and Elamites," flock hither, and do naturally fall in with one or other of these primary distinctions. The infinite superiority of the former, which I choose to designate as the *great race,* is discernible in their figure, port, and a certain instinctive sovereignty. The latter are born degraded. "He shall serve his brethren." There is something in the air of one of this cast, lean and suspicious; contrasting with the open, trusting, generous manners of the other.

THE TRANSITIONAL PARAGRAPH

The transitional paragraph is usually short. It serves very often to mark a turning point in the discussion and to bridge the gap between what has just been said and what is to be said next. Professor James Harvey Robinson provides an interesting example of the transitional paragraph:

> We have now considered briefly the three main hopes that have been hitherto entertained of bettering things, (1) by changing the rules of the

game, (II) by urging men to be good, and to love their neighbor as themselves, and (III) by education for citizenship. It may be that these hopes are not wholly unfounded, but it must be admitted that so far they have been grievously disappointed. Doubtless they will continue to be cherished on account of their assured respectability. Mere lack of success does not discredit a method, for there are many things that determine and perpetuate our sanctified ways of doing things besides their success in reaching their proposed ends. Had this not always been so, our life to-day would be far less stupidly conducted than it is. But let us agree to assume for the moment that the approved schemes of reform enumerated above have, to say the least, shown themselves inadequate to meet the crisis in which civilized society now finds itself. Have we any other hope?

—Robinson, *The Mind in the Making*

The Concluding Paragraph

A short essay requires no formal concluding paragraph. If the essay is close-knit and emphatic, we who read it know when the end is approaching. The careful writer will not add a superfluous word when he has once reached his goal; certainly he will not add a "concluding" paragraph. But often we need to be reminded of the several points made during the course of a long exposition. We need, not so much a mere recapitulation of the headings treated, as a reminder of their relation to each other. We need, perhaps, to be shown how each point has reinforced each other point and produced some special result. Professor Breasted concludes his *Ancient Times* with the following brief paragraph:

Today, marking the various stages of that long career, the stone fist-hatchets lie deep in the river gravels of France; the furniture of the pile-villages sleeps at the bottom of the Swiss lakes; the majestic pyramids and temples announcing the dawn of civilization rise along the Nile; the silent and deserted city-mounds by the Tigris and Euphrates shelter their myriads of clay tablets; the palaces of Crete look out toward the sea they once ruled; the noble temples and sculptures of Greece still proclaim the new world of beauty and freedom first revealed by the Greeks; the splendid Roman roads and aqueducts assert the supremacy and organized control of Rome; and the Christian churches proclaim the new ideal of human brotherhood. These things still reveal the fascinating trail along which our ancestors came, and in following that trail we have recovered the earliest chapters in the wonderful human story which we call Ancient History.

—Breasted, *Ancient Times*

PARAGRAPHS FOR FURTHER STUDY

In the paragraphs that follow, the authors have made use of a variety of methods to secure coherence and emphasis. In studying these paragraphs, we must bear in mind that they were written as parts of longer compositions and especially that they were not composed by their authors for the purpose of providing us with models of paragraph structure. Yet we can, if we will make the effort, learn much from these paragraphs.

From SAMUEL JOHNSON, *Preface to Shakespeare*

Every man's performance, to be rightly estimated, must be compared with the state of the age in which he lived, and with his own particular opportunities; and though to the reader a book be not worse or better for the circumstances of the author, yet as there is always a silent reference of human works to human abilities, and as the inquiry how far man may extend his designs, or how high he may rate his native force, is of far greater dignity than in what rank we shall place any particular performance, curiosity is always busy to discover the instruments, as well as to survey the workmanship, to know how much is to be ascribed to origina powers, and how much to casual and adventitious help. The palaces of Peru or Mexico were certainly mean and incommodious habitations, if compared to the houses of European monarchs; yet who could forbear to view them with astonishment, who remembered that they were built without the use of iron?

From THOMAS CARLYLE, *Heroes and Hero-Worship*

But I will say of Shakespeare's works generally that we have no ful impress of him there—even as full as we have of many men. His works are so many windows through which we see a glimpse of the world that was in him. All his works seem, comparatively speaking, cursory, imperfect, written under cramping circumstances, giving only here and there a note of the full utterance of the man. Passages there are that come upon you like splendor out of Heaven, bursts of radiance, illuminating the very heart of the thing; you say, "That is true, spoken once and forever; wheresoever and whensoever there is an open human soul, that will be recognized as true!" Such bursts, however, make us feel that the surrounding matter is not radiant, that it is, in part, temporary, conventional. Alas, Shakespeare had to write for the Globe Playhouse; his great soul had to crush itself, as it could, into that and no other mold. It was with him, then, as it is with us all. No man works save under conditions. The sculptor cannot set his own free thought before us, but his thought as he could translate it into the stone that was given, with the tools that were given. *Disjecta membra* are all that we find of any poet, or of any man.

From Holmes, *Poet at the Breakfast Table*

That poets are treated as privileged persons by their admirers and the educated public can hardly be disputed. That they consider themselves so there is no doubt whatever. On the whole, I do not know so easy a way of shirking all the civic and social and domestic duties, as to settle it in one's mind that one is a poet. I have, therefore, taken great pains to advise other persons laboring under the impression that they were gifted beings, destined to soar in the atmosphere of song above the vulgar realities of earth, not to neglect any homely duty under the influence of that impression. The number of these persons is so great that if they were suffered to indulge their prejudice against every-day duties and labors, it would be a serious loss to the productive industry of the country. My skirts are clear (so far as other people are concerned) of countenancing that form of intellectual opium-eating in which rhyme takes the place of the narcotic. But what are you going to do when you find John Keats an apprentice to a surgeon or apothecary? Isn't it rather better to get another boy to sweep out the shop and shake out the powders and stir up the mixtures, and leave him undisturbed to write his Ode on a Grecian Urn or to a Nightingale? Oh yes, the critic I have referred to would say, if he is John Keats; but not if he is of a much lower grade, even though he be genuine, what there is of him. But the trouble is, the sensitive persons who belong to the lower grades of the poetical hierarchy do not know their own poetical limitations, while they do feel a natural unfitness and disinclination for many pursuits which young persons of the average balance of faculties take to pleasantly enough. What is forgotten is this, that every real poet, even of the humblest grade, is an *artist*. Now I venture to say that any painter or sculptor of real genius, though he may do nothing more than paint flowers and fruit, or carve cameos, is considered a privileged person. It is recognized perfectly that to get his best work he must be insured the freedom from disturbances which the creative power absolutely demands, more absolutely perhaps in these slighter artists than in the great masters. His nerves must be steady for him to finish a rose-leaf or the fold of a nymph's drapery in his best manner; and they will be unsteadied if he has to perform the honest drudgery which another can do for him quite as well. And it is just so with the poet, though he were only finishing an epigram; you must no more meddle roughly with him than you would shake a bottle of Chambertin and expect the "sunset glow" to redden your glass unclouded. On the other hand, it may be said that poetry is not an article of prime necessity, and potatoes are. There is a disposition in many persons just now to deny the poet his benefit of clergy, and to hold him no better than other people. Perhaps he is not, perhaps he is not so good, half the time;

but he is a luxury, and if you want him you must pay for him, by not trying to make a drudge of him while he is all his lifetime struggling with the chills and heats of his artistic intermittent fever.

From THOREAU, *Week on the Concord and Merrimac Rivers*

A perfectly healthy sentence, it is true, is extremely rare. For the most part we miss the hue and fragrance of the thought, as if we could be satisfied with the dews of the morning or evening without their colors, or the heavens without their azure. The most attractive sentences are, perhaps, not the wisest, but the surest and roundest. They are spoken firmly and conclusively, as if the speaker had a right to know what he says, and, if not wise, they have at least been well learned. Sir Walter Raleigh might well be studied, if only for the excellence of his style, for he is remarkable in the midst of so many masters. There is a natural emphasis in his style, like a man's tread, and a breathing space between the sentences, which the best of modern writing does not furnish. His chapters are like English parks, or say rather like a western forest, where the larger growth keeps down the underwood, and one may ride on horseback through the openings. All the distinguished writers of that period possess a greater vigor and naturalness than the more modern—for it is allowed to slander our own time—and when we read a quotation from one of them in the midst of a modern author, we seem to have come suddenly upon a greener ground, a greater depth and strength of soil. It is as if a green bough were laid across the page, and we are refreshed as by the sight of fresh grass in midwinter or early spring. You have constantly the warrant of life and experience in what you read. The little that is said is eked out by implication of the much that was done. The sentences are verdurous and blooming as evergreen and flowers because they are rooted in fact and experience, but our false and florid sentences have only the tints of flowers without their sap or roots. All men are really most attracted by the beauty of plain speech, and they even write in a florid style in imitation of this. They prefer to be misunderstood rather than to come short of its exuberance. Hussein Effendi praised the epistolary style of Ibrahim Pasha to the French traveler Botta, because of "the difficulty of understanding it." "There was," he said, "but one person at Jidda who was capable of understanding and explaining the Pasha's correspondence." A man's whole life is taxed for the least thing well done. It is its net result. Every sentence is the result of a long probation. Where shall we look for standard English but to the words of a standard man? The word which is best said came nearest to not being spoken at all, for it is cousin to a deed which the speaker could have better done. Nay, almost it must have taken the place of a deed by some urgent necessity, even by some misfortune, so that the truest writer will be some captive knight after all. And perhaps the fates had such a design, when, having stored Raleigh so richly with the substance of life and experience, they made him a fast prisoner and compelled him to make his words his deeds and transfer to his expression the emphasis and sincerity of his action.

From EMERSON, *On Friendship*

Our intellectual and active powers increase with our affection. The scholar sits down to write, and all his years of meditation do not furnish him with one good thought or happy expression; but it is necessary to write a letter to a friend, and, forthwith, troops of gentle thoughts invest themselves, on every hand, with chosen words. See in any house where virtue and self-respect abide the palpitation which the approach of a stranger causes. A commended stranger is expected and announced, and an uneasiness between pleasure and pain invades all the hearts of a household. His arrival almost brings fear to the good hearts that would welcome him. The house is dusted, all things fly into their places, the old coat is exchanged for the new, and they must get up a dinner if they can. Of a commended stranger, only the good report is told by others, only the good and new is heard by us. He stands to us for humanity. He is what we wish. Having imagined and invested him, we ask how we should stand related in conversation and action with such a man, and are uneasy with fear. The same idea exalts conversation with him. We talk better than we are wont. We have the nimblest fancy, a richer memory, and our dumb devil has taken leave for the time. For long hours we can continue a series of sincere, graceful, rich communications, drawn from the oldest, secretest experience, so that they who sit by, of our own kinsfolk and acquaintance, shall feel a lively surprise at our unusual powers. But as soon as the stranger begins to intrude his partialities, his definitions, his defects, into the conversation, it is all over. He has heard the first, the last and best, he will ever hear from us. He is no stranger now. Vulgarity, ignorance, misapprehension are old acquaintances. Now, when he comes, he may get the order, the dress, and the dinner, but the throbbing of the heart, and the communications of the soul, no more.

From GREENOUGH AND KITTREDGE, *Words and Their Ways*

Now certain facts in the history of our language have made it peculiarly inclined to borrow from French and Latin. The Norman Conquest in the eleventh century made French the language of polite society in England; and, long after the contact between Norman French and English had ceased to be of direct significance in our linguistic development, the reading and speaking of French and the study of French literature formed an important part of the education of English-speaking men and women. When literary English was in process of formation in the fourteenth and fifteenth centuries, the authors whose works determined the cultivated vocabulary were almost as familiar with French as with their mother tongue, and it was therefore natural that they should borrow a good many French words. But these same writers were also familiar with Latin, which, though called a dead language, has always been the professional dialect of ecclesiastics and a *lingua franca* for educated men. Thus the borrowing from French and from Latin went on side by side, and it is often impossible to say from which of the two languages a particular English word is taken. The practice of naturalizing French and Latin words was, then, firmly established in the fourteenth century, and when in the sixteenth century there was a great revival of Greek studies in England, the close literary relations between Greece and Rome facilitated the adoption of a considerable number of words from the Greek. Linguistic processes are cumulative; one does not stop when another begins. Hence we find all of these influences active in increasing the modern vocabulary. In particular, the language of science has looked to Greece for its terms as the language of abstract thought has drawn its nomenclature from Latin.

From RUSKIN, *Crown of Wild Olive*

In all my past work my endeavor has been to show that good architecture is essentially religious—the production of a faithful and virtuous, not of an infidel and corrupted people. But, in the course of doing this, I have had also to show that good architecture is not ecclesiastical. People are so apt to look upon religion as the business of the clergy, not their own, that the moment they hear of anything depending on "religion" they think it must also have depended on the priesthood; and I have had to take what place was to be occupied between these two errors, and fight both, often with seeming contradiction. Good architecture is the work of good and believing men; therefore, you say, at least some people say, "Good architecture must essentially have been the work of the clergy, not of the laity." No—a thousand times no; good architecture has always been the work of the commonalty, not of the clergy. "What," you say, "those glorious cathedrals—the pride of Europe—did their builders not form Gothic architecture?" No; they corrupted Gothic architecture. Gothic was formed in the baron's castle, and the burgher's street. It was formed by the thoughts, and hands, and powers of laboring citizens and warrior kings. By the monk it was used as an instrument for the aid of his superstition; when that superstition became a beautiful madness, and the best hearts of Europe vainly dreamed and pined in the cloister, and vainly raged and perished in the crusade, through that fury of perverted faith and wasted war the Gothic rose also to its loveliest, most fantastic, and, finally, most foolish dreams; and in those dreams was lost.

From JAMES FENIMORE COOPER, *The American Democrat*

All that democracy means, is as equal a participation in rights as is practicable; and to pretend that social equality is a condition of popular institutions, is to assume that the latter are destructive of civilization, for, as nothing is more self-evident than the impossibility of raising all men to the highest standard of tastes and refinement, the alternative would be to reduce the entire community to the lowest. The whole embarrassment on this point exists in the difficulty of making men comprehend qualities they do not themselves possess. We can all perceive the difference between ourselves and our inferiors, but when it comes to a question of the difference between us and our superiors, we fail to appreciate merits of which we have no proper conceptions. In face of this obvious difficulty, there is the safe and just governing rule, already mentioned, or that of permitting everyone to be the undisturbed judge of his own habits and associations, so long as they are innocent, and do not impair the rights of others to be equally judges for themselves. It follows, that social intercourse must regulate itself, independently of institutions, with the exception that the latter, while they withhold no natural, bestow no factitious advantages beyond those which are inseparable from the rights of property, and general civilization.

From THOMAS H. HUXLEY, *Essays: On Science and Art in Relation to Education*

Then we come to the subject-matter, whether scientific or aesthetic, of education, and I should naturally have no question at all about teaching the elements of physical science of the kind I have sketched, in a practical manner; but among scientific topics, using the word scientific in the broadest sense, I would also include the elements of the theory of morals and of that of political and social life, which, strangely enough, it never seems to occur to anybody to teach a child. I would have the history of our own country, and of all the influences which have been brought to bear upon it, with incidental geography, not as a mere chronicle of reigns and battles, but as a chapter in the development of the race, and the history of civilization.

Then with respect to aesthetic knowledge and discipline, we have happily in the English language one of the most magnificent storehouses of artistic beauty and models of literary excellence which exists in the world at the present time. I have said before, and I repeat it here, that if a man cannot get literary culture of the highest kind out of his Bible, and Chaucer, and Shakespeare, and Milton, and Hobbes, and Bishop Berkeley, to mention only a few of our illustrious writers, he cannot get it out of anything; and I would assuredly devote a very large portion of the time of every English child to the careful study of the models of English writing of such varied and wonderful kind as we possess, and, what is still more important and still more neglected, the habit of using that language with precision, with force, and with art. I fancy we are almost the only nation in the world who seem to think that composition comes by nature. The

French attend to their own language, the Germans study theirs; but Englishmen do not seem to think it is worth their while. Nor would I fail to include, in the course of study I am sketching, translations of all the best works of antiquity, or of the modern world. It is a very desirable thing to read Homer in Greek; but if you don't happen to know Greek, the next best thing we can do is to read as good a translation of it as we have recently been furnished with in prose. You won't get all you would get from the original, but you may get a great deal; and to refuse to know this great deal because you cannot get all, seems to be as sensible as for a young man to refuse bread because he cannot get partridge. Finally, I would add instruction in either music or painting, or, if the child should be so unhappy, as sometimes happens, as to have no faculty for either of those, and no possibility of doing anything in an artistic sense with them, then I would see what could be done with literature alone; but I would provide, in the fullest sense, for the development of the aesthetic side of the mind. In my judgment, those are all the essentials of education for an English child. With that outfit, such as it might be made in the time given to education which is within the reach of nine-tenths of the population— with that outfit, an Englishman, within the limits of English life, is fitted to go anywhere, to occupy the highest positions, to fill the highest offices of the State, and to become distinguished in practical pursuits, in science, or in art. For, if he have the opportunity to learn all those things, and have his mind disciplined in the various directions the teaching of those topics would have necessitated, then, assuredly, he would be able to pick up, on his road through life, all the rest of the intellectual baggage he wants.

If the educational time at our disposal were sufficient there are one or two things I would add to those I have just now called the essentials; and perhaps you will be surprised to hear, though I hope you will not, that I should add, not more science, but one, or, if possible, two languages. The knowledge of some other language than one's own is, in fact, of singular intellectual value. Many of the faults and mistakes of the ancient philosophers are traceable to the fact that they knew no language but their own, and were often led into confusing the symbol with the thought which it embodied. I think it is Locke who says that one-half of the mistakes of philosophers have arisen from questions about words; and one of the safest ways of delivering yourself from the bondage of words is, to know how ideas look in words to which you are not accustomed. That is one reason for the study of language; another reason is that it opens new fields in art and science. Another is the practical value of such knowledge; and yet another is this, that if your languages are properly chosen, from the time of learning the additional languages you will know your own language better than ever you did. So, I say, if the time given to education permits, add Latin and German. Latin, because it is the key to nearly one-half of English and to all the Romance languages; and German, because it is the key to almost all the remainder of English, and helps you to understand a race from whom most of us have sprung, and who have a character and a literature of a fateful force in the history of the world, such as probably has been allotted to those of no other people, except the Jews, the Greeks, and ourselves. Beyond these, the essential and the eminently desirable elements of all education, let each man take up his special line—the historian devote himself to his history, the man of science to his science, the man of letters to his culture of that kind, and the artist to his special pursuit.

CHAPTER VI

THE WHOLE COMPOSITION

FUNDAMENTAL PROBLEMS

THE problems we have considered in our discussion of the sentence and the paragraph are the fundamental problems also of the whole composition: unity, coherence, emphasis—and interest. Some topics can be treated in a single paragraph; others require more elaborate development. Problems of arrangement arise and must be solved. Our composition divides itself usually into a number of parts. In what order shall we present them? More important still, how much emphasis shall we give to each? The answers to these and other questions will depend fundamentally upon the kind of effect we hope to create.

THREE KINDS OF COMPOSITION

If we are writing primarily to give information, we shall be as exact as possible in the interest of clear, logical presentation of fact. If we are writing primarily to conjure up an image—to paint a picture, as it were—we shall perhaps put less emphasis upon accurate measurement and more upon suggestive and revealing details. If we are writing primarily to tell a story, we shall decide upon the point of highest interest and arrange our material carefully to give our reader the illusion of participating in the action. A moment's thought will show that usually all three purposes are present to some extent in a single composition. Explanation cast in story-form is often highly effective. Stories require actors and a setting, and the reader must have some picture in his mind of these actors and the scene of their activity. We may wish to stress explanation or picture-making or story-telling, but the chances are that we shall use the methods of all three at once.

142

For the purposes of discussion we may, however, disregard this inevitable mingling, for the moment, and examine each purpose separately. Teachers of composition speak of **exposition** instead of explanation, of **description** instead of picture-making, and of **narration** instead of story-telling. We shall adopt these traditional names in this chapter.

EXPOSITION

Exposition is explanation. Exposition answers questions. Someone may ask: "What is this thing?" Our answer: "A slide rule" may or may not satisfy him. He may ask further: "How does it work?" Our answer to this question will be perhaps a single paragraph or a series of paragraphs, depending on how full an explanation we wish to give. Practical advice on how a slide rule works can best be given with the slide rule itself. Our substitute explanation in words will (or should) be accompanied by diagrams or pictures.

How do you change a tire? How do you load a gun? a camera? What does the word *vitamin* mean? Many of these questions can be answered by definition of the term or terms involved. What is a dictionary? What is a thesaurus? How are they different? How do you bake angel's food cake? What equipment should I take with me on a pack-trip into the mountains? What is dynamite?

EXPOSITION BY DEFINITION

An expository essay may define *dynamite*. It may begin with some such logical definition as this:

> "Dynamite is an explosive made of nitroglycerin absorbed in a porous material."

A concise statement of this sort suggests other questions. What do you mean by "an explosive"? What is nitroglycerin? Which materials are porous? Which porous materials are used especially? Why one rather than another?

Our expository paragraph or paragraphs will be based upon definition. We will begin with a brief statement of the *genus* ("Dynamite is an *explosive*") to show the general class to which dynamite belongs. Next we will show how dynamite differs from other members of this class—from other "explosives." This we do by indicating the *differentia* ("made of nitroglycerin absorbed in a porous material"). The single expository sentence will serve for an abridged dictionary. But our reader may want more. Using the single sentence as a topic sentence, we may then proceed to develop it by expanding the *differentia*.

We may often explain something by showing its effects upon something else. The word *vitamin* may be defined as:

> Any of a group of constituents of most foods in their natural state, of which very small quantities are essential for the normal nutrition of animals, and possibly of plants.

This may be immediately clear to a biochemist. But the general reader wants to know more. He wants, perhaps, to know something about the **origin** of vitamins or about their **effects.** How many different vitamins are recognized? Where do they occur? What happens if they are absent from the diet? Answering such questions as these will make the exposition meaningful to the average reader, who may or may not grasp the full implications of the concise dictionary definition, but who will perhaps be interested to learn that six distinct vitamins are recognized, that lack of Vitamin A causes failure of young animals to grow, that lack of Vitamin B causes loss of weight and appetite, and that lack of Vitamin C causes scurvy.

In planning an expository paper on vitamins, we may decide to limit ourselves to such effects. We may begin with a general statement and then proceed to show the effects upon the human body of the absence of the several vitamins from the diet, following some such plan as this:

(1) Absence of Vitamin A causes . . . .
(2) Absence of Vitamin B causes . . . .
(3) Absence of Vitamin C causes . . . .

EXPOSITION BY COMPARISON

Let us consider the word *thesaurus* as a possible subject for an expository essay. We ask first: How does a thesaurus differ from a dictionary? and we write down definitions of the two terms:

> A dictionary is a work of reference in which the words of a language or of any system or province of knowledge are entered alphabetically and defined.

> A thesaurus is a treasury or storehouse; hence, a repository, especially of words.

We observe that there are resemblances as well as differences between a dictionary and a thesaurus. Each is a collection of words. In
the dictionary, words are "entered alphabetically and defined." No
such arrangement, apparently, characterizes a thesaurus. But we
know that a thesaurus must have some plan. What is it? If we examine a typical thesaurus we quickly discover that in it words are
grouped according to the ideas which they express. The dictionary,
then, gives the ideas conveyed by certain words; the thesaurus gives
the words by which the ideas may be conveyed.

Is this important? To whom is it important? Answers to these and
other questions will provide material for our essay. Dr. Roget, author
of *Roget's Thesaurus of English Words and Phrases,* answers some
of these questions in his Introduction:

The present Work is intended to supply, with respect to the English
language, a desideratum hitherto unsupplied in any language; namely, a
collection of the words it contains and of the idiomatic combinations
peculiar to it, arranged, not in alphabetical order as they are in a Dictionary, but according to the *ideas* which they express. The purpose of an
ordinary dictionary is simply to explain the meaning of words; and the
problem of which it professes to furnish the solution may be stated thus:—
The word being given, to find its signification, or the idea it is intended
to convey. The object aimed at in the present undertaking is exactly the
converse of this: namely,—The idea being given, to find the word, or
words, by which that idea may be most fitly and aptly expressed. For this
purpose, the words and phrases of the language are here classed, not
according to their sound or their orthography, but strictly according to
their *signification.*

The communication of our thoughts by means of language, whether
spoken or written, like every other object of mental exertion, constitutes
a peculiar art, which, like other arts, cannot be acquired in any perfection
but by long and continued practice. Some, indeed, there are more highly
gifted than others with a facility of expression, and naturally endowed
with the power of eloquence; but to none is it at all times an easy process
to embody, in exact and appropriate language, the various trains of ideas
that are passing through the mind, or to depict in their true colours and
proportions, the diversified and nicer shades of feeling which accompany
them. To those unpractised in the art of composition, or unused to ex-
tempore speaking, these difficulties present themselves in their most for-
midable aspect. However distinct may be our views, however vivid our
conceptions, or however fervent our emotions, we cannot but be often
conscious that the phraseology we have at our command is inadequate to
do them justice. We seek in vain the words we need, and strive ineffectually
to devise forms of expression which shall faithfully portray our thoughts

145

and sentiments. The appropriate terms, notwithstanding our utmost effort cannot be conjured up at will. Like "spirits from the vasty deep," they come not when we call; and we are driven to the employment of a set of words and phrases either too general or too limited, too strong or too feeble, which suit not the occasion, which hit not the mark we aim at; and the result of our prolonged exertion is a style at once laboured and obscure, vapid and redundant, or vitiated by the still graver faults of affectation or ambiguity.

It is to those who are thus painfully groping their way and struggling with the difficulties of composition, that this Work professes to hold out a helping hand. The assistance it gives is that of furnishing on every topic a copious store of words and phrases, adapted to express all the recognizable shades and modifications of the general idea under which those words and phrases are arranged. The inquirer can readily select, out of the ample collection spread out before his eyes in the following pages, those expressions which are best suited to his purpose, and which might not have occurred to him without such assistance. In order to make this selection, he scarcely ever need engage in any critical or elaborate study of the subtle distinctions existing between synonymous terms; for if the materials set before him be sufficiently abundant, an instinctive tact will rarely fail to lead him to the proper choice. Even while glancing over the columns of this Work, his eye may chance to light upon a particular term which may save the cost of a clumsy paraphrase, or spare the labour of a tortuous circumlocution. Some felicitous turn of expression thus introduced will frequently open to the mind of the reader a whole vista of collateral ideas, which could not, without an extended and obtrusive episode, have been unfolded to his view; and often will the judicious insertion of a happy epithet, like a beam of sunshine in a landscape, illumine and adorn the subject which it touches, imparting new grace and giving life and spirit to the picture.

Every workman in the exercise of his art should be provided with proper instruments. For the fabrication of complicated and curious pieces of mechanism, the artisan requires a corresponding assortment of various tools and instruments. For giving proper effect to the fictions of the drama, the actor should have at his disposal a well-furnished wardrobe, supplying the costumes best suited to the personages he is to represent. For the perfect delineation of the beauties of nature, the painter should have within reach of his pencil every variety and combination of hues and tints. Now, the writer, as well as the orator, employs for the accomplishment of his purposes the instrumentality of words; it is in words that he clothes his thoughts; it is by means of words that he depicts his feelings. It is therefore essential to his success that he be provided with a copious vocabulary, and that he possess an entire command of all the resources and appliances of his language. To the acquisition of this power no procedure appears more directly conducive than the study of a methodized system such as that now offered to his use.

EXPOSITION BY DIVISION OR ENUMERATION

Many subjects lend themselves readily to division into a number of parts. We may, for example, state in the opening sentence that we are about to discuss four steps in planting a garden, or we may enumerate three main reasons for going to college, or we may say that we will describe first the outside and then the inside of a church. Exposition by division or enumeration has certain distinct advantages: the reader knows at once what to expect; the writer is obliged to keep to his announced plan.

The Book of Exodus in the Bible contains much exposition, much of it detailed instructions for the building of certain sacred objects:

And thou shalt make the breastplate of the judgment with cunning work; after the work of the ephod thou shalt make it; of gold, of blue, and of purple, and of scarlet, and of fine twined linen, shalt thou make it. Foursquare it shall be being doubled; a span shall be the length thereof, and a span shall be the breadth thereof. And thou shalt set in it settings of stones, even four rows of stones: the first row shall be a sardius, a topaz, and a carbuncle: this shall be the first row. And the second row shall be an emerald, a sapphire, and a diamond. And the third row a ligure, an agate, and an amethyst. And the fourth row a beryl, and an onyx, and a jasper: they shall be set in gold in their inclosings. And the stones shall be with the names of the children of Israel, twelve, according to their names, like the engravings of a signet; every one with his name shall they be according to the twelve tribes. (Exodus xxviii: 15–21)

An essay called "How to Use a Simple Slide Rule" might begin with a statement that the user must

(1) learn to use the C and D scales,
(2) learn to use the A and B scales, and
(3) learn to use the S and T scales.

Learning to use the C and D scales involves

(1) learning to read the scale until he can locate numbers quickly and easily,
(2) learning how to multiply,
(3) learning how to approximate the position of the decimal,
(4) learning how to divide,
(5) learning how to solve problems involving both multiplication and division, and
(6) learning how to solve problems in proportion.

Learning to use the A and B scales involves

    (1) finding squares, and
    (2) finding square roots.

Learning to use the S and T scales involves

    (1) finding natural sines, and
    (2) finding natural tangents.

This rough outline indicates the normal division into paragraphs. Such an essay, to be useful, is generally accompanied by diagrams or pictures. Its aim is clearness. The reader wants to know how to use the slide rule and naturally expects the writer to proceed from simple to complex or from what is easy to what is difficult or, in other words, to treat first things first.

In writing practical descriptive exposition we must remember that orderly development is of the utmost importance. We must announce our plan and follow it consistently. Point of view is important. Needless shifting from one point of view to another is a source of irritation to the reader, who rightly expects that an explanation begun in the third person will not suddenly change to the first person or the second person.

Do not do this:

    A. The first step in baking a cake is . . .
    B. Next, you should . . .
    C. Finally, we must . . .

Do one of the following:

  I. Use the first person:

    A. First, I prepare . . .
    B. Next, I take . . .
    C. Finally, I put . . .

  II. Use the second person:

    A. First, prepare . . .
    B. Next, take . . .
    C. Finally, put . . .

III. Use the third person:

A. The first thing to do is to prepare . . .
B. The next step is to take . . .
C. The final step is to put . . .

An article on mythology may well be divided into two parts, the first, and more extensive, being devoted to southern mythology, and the second to northern mythology. Before retelling the stories of Thor and the other northern deities, Dr. Bulfinch gives his readers a general account of the creation as it is explained in Scandinavian myths:

NORTHERN MYTHOLOGY

The stories which have engaged our attention thus far relate to the mythology of southern regions. But there is another branch of ancient superstitions which ought not to be entirely overlooked, especially as it belongs to the nations from which we, through our English ancestors, derive our origin. It is that of the northern nations, called Scandinavians, who inhabited the countries now known as Sweden, Denmark, Norway, and Iceland. These mythological records are contained in two collections called the *Eddas,* of which the oldest is in poetry and dates back to the year 1056, the more modern or prose *Edda* being of the date of 1640.

According to the *Eddas* there was once no heaven above nor earth beneath, but only a bottomless deep, and a world of mist in which flowed a fountain. Twelve rivers issued from this fountain, and when they had flowed far from their source, they froze into ice, and one layer accumulating over another, the great deep was filled up.

Southward from the world of mist was the world of light. From this flowed a warm wind upon the ice and melted it. The vapours rose in the air and formed clouds, from which sprang Ymir, the Frost giant and his progeny, and the cow Audhumbla, whose milk afforded nourishment and food to the giant. The cow got nourishment by licking the hoar frost and salt from the ice. While she was one day licking the salt stones there appeared at first the hair of a man, on the second day the whole head, and on the third the entire form endowed with beauty, agility, and power. This new being was a god, from whom and his wife, a daughter of the giant race, sprang the three brothers Odin, Vili, and Ve. They slew the giant Ymir, and out of his body formed the earth, of his blood the seas, of his bones the mountains, of his hair the trees, of his skull the heavens, and of his brain the clouds, charged with hail and snow. Of Ymir's eyebrows the gods formed Midgard (mid earth), destined to become the abode of man.

Odin then regulated the periods of day and night and the seasons by placing in the heavens the sun and moon, and appointing to them their respective courses. As soon as the sun began to shed its rays upon the earth, it caused the vegetable world to bud and sprout. Shortly after the gods had created the world they walked by the side of the sea, pleased with their new work, but found that it was still incomplete, for it was without human beings. They therefore took an ash tree and made a man out of it, and they made a woman out of an alder, and called the man Aske and the woman Embla. Odin then gave them life and soul, Vili reason and motion, and Ve bestowed upon them the senses, expressive features, and speech. Midgard was then given them as their residence, and they became the progenitors of the human race.

The mighty ash tree Ygdrasill was supposed to support the whole universe. It sprang from the body of Ymir, and had three immense roots, extending one into Asgard (the dwelling of the gods), the other into Jotunheim (the abode of the giants), and the third to Niffleheim (the regions of darkness and cold). By the side of each of these roots is a spring, from which it is watered. The root that extends into Asgard is carefully tended by the three Norns, goddesses, who are regarded as the dispensers of fate. They are Urdur (the past), Verdandi (the present), Skuld (the future). The spring at the Jotunheim side is Ymir's well, in which wisdom and wit lie hidden, but that of Niffleheim feeds the adder Nidhogge (darkness), which perpetually gnaws at the root. Four harts run across the branches of the tree and bite the buds; they represent the four winds. Under the tree lies Ymir, and when he tries to shake off its weight the earth quakes.

Asgard is the name of the abode of the gods, access to which is only gained by crossing the bridge Bifrost (the rainbow). Asgard consists of golden and silver palaces, the dwellings of the gods, but the most beautiful of these is Valhalla, the residence of Odin. When seated on his throne he overlooks all heaven and earth. Upon his shoulders are the ravens Hugin and Munin, who fly every day over the whole world, and on their return report to him all they have seen and heard. At his feet lie his two wolves, Geri and Freki, to whom Odin gives all the meat that is set before him, for he himself stands in no need of food. Mead is for him both food and drink. He invented the Runic characters, and it is the business of the Norns to engrave the runes of fate upon a metal shield. From Odin's name, spelt Woden, as it sometimes is, came Wednesday, the name of the fourth day of the week.

Odin is frequently called Alfadur (All-father), but this name is sometimes used in a way that shows that the Scandinavians had an idea of a deity superior to Odin, uncreated and eternal.

—*Age of Fable,* Chapter xxxviii.

In the following expository essay, observe the arrangement of details and the orderly progress from a discussion of conditions before
1914, to conditions during the First World War, and finally to conditions in 1941. The author's general thesis is given in the opening
sentence:

> There has never been a time in the existence of the American nation
> when the people as a whole have been so well informed as they
> are at present as to the history of the European states which are at
> grips with one another.

The reader is willing to be convinced of the truth of this assertion
and reads on through the author's comments on foreign news reporting during the First World War. The third paragraph marks a
turning point with the reminder that radio has entered the field
of journalism. The author shows the importance of radio broadcasts to listeners during the Second World War and to historians
and concludes with the hope that "radio companies are preserving
these invaluable records in such form as to make them usable."

NEW DIMENSIONS IN INFORMATION

There has never been a time in the existence of the American nation
when the people as a whole have been so well informed as they are at
present as to the history of the European states which are at grips with
one another. When the world conflict broke out in 1914, Americans as a
body were lamentably ignorant of the long train of events which had
antedated and led up to the holocaust and hardly less so of the politics
and policies which immediately preceded the catastrophe. Newspaper
coverage of foreign affairs outside New York and a few of the largest cities
was practically non-existent and even the most important metropolitan
dailies devoted only a meager few columns or often paragraphs to European happenings except when they flared into sudden dramatic crises. If
the German Kaiser rattled his saber the papers reported it with ominous
forecasts, but in between a telegram to Kruger and an Agadir incident important events could follow one another in the Reich, or, for that matter,
in any other country, with nothing more than brief items tucked modestly
away on inside pages to record them. There were foreign correspondents,
of course, and there was a small fringe of travelled Americans who brought
back from their journeyings abroad an uneasy sense of complications in
European foreign relations, but on the whole the United States lived in
an uninformed indifference to the strains in the European body politic.

When war in the Balkans broke out in 1912 Americans probably saw in it more a fulfillment of the pessimism of Kipling's correspondent in "The Light That Failed" than of their own forebodings.

The World War changed all that. As one country after another went into the conflict, literature about the belligerent nations poured from the presses to be eagerly snatched by the public. The newspapers, in addition to printing thousands of columns upon immediate events, carried long historical surveys; colleges and schools laid increased stress on readings in European history; lecturers wove back and forth through the land delivering travelogues combining history with description, and books galore appeared upon all phases of Europe's past and present. The habit of European news formed by the newspapers between 1914 and 1918 has never since been broken, not even during the period of the false dawn which followed upon the Treaty of Paris. Ever since the war European news has maintained the position of importance it won during the struggle. And what has been true of journalism has been true of publishing in general.

But there has entered into the coverage of foreign news during the present conflict a new factor as important as it is excellent. No single agency has been more effective in the education of the public to the course and significance of events than the radio which, through its brief resumé put forth almost hourly and the lengthier interpretative comments which supplement them, has kept the world informed of the march of events almost as they happen. These rapid summaries are not hastily assembled announcements but painstakingly prepared surveys into which have gone hours of labor and the most scrupulous efforts for correctness. They are history, and accurate history even as they are written, a part, like newspaper correspondence, of the quarry out of which the standard histories of the future will be hewn. The scholar of tomorrow, like the listener of today, will find in these reports written close to the scene but put through a careful sieve of checking, not only the happenings of the war years but the hopes, the fears, the conjectures, the determination, the heroic resolve of the peoples whose daily agony is being retailed. That even out of the propaganda-ridden countries neutral broadcasters can send reliable reports is proved by the work of such men as William Shirer and others in the Axis nations. And how vivid and accurate a portrayal the radio can present at its best such a book as the recent one by Edward Murrow, CBS correspondent in London, makes amply evident. Compiled from broadcasts delivered almost as they now appear in print, this volume is history in the best sense of the word, accurate, revealing, and discriminating. Radio reporting, under the stress of a strict allotment of time, has become an art in which economy of language is the highest desideratum, and selection and compression of news a necessity. Stripped of all save significant fact as these broadcasts are, they should furnish the research scholar of the future with what is virtually a syllabus for any extensive work on which he may launch. It is to be hoped that the radio companies are preserving

these invaluable records in such form as to make them usable when that happy day comes when their chronicles will not be news but history.
—AMY LOVEMAN (*Saturday Review of Literature,* May 17, 1941, p. 10.)

Much has been written about the English language and especially about the differences between British English and American English. The author of the following essay has limited himself to a consideration of the question of change. He is struck by the fact that "language alters much more slowly than we are led to think." With this as his central idea, he writes an interesting and timely piece of exposition:

Language is the oldest and dearest possession of men. Language is the last feature in the established order which the revolutionist will tamper with. George Bernard Shaw, who has found nothing in English life to revere or even approve, says he will leave part of his fortune to a foundation for the defense of the English language.

The builders of Soviet Russia brought in with them, along with much useful housecleaning in the overladen Russian alphabet, a new revolutionary dialect of the kind we over here have learned to call alphabet soup. They were new words made up of telescoped letters and syllables, but the fashion did not last. Its excesses have been frowned upon by Mr. Stalin, who has strongly recommended his proletarian young writers to go back to good old Pushkin and Gogol and Tolstoy, both for content and language.

We are all the time being reminded that language is always changing; and as a challenge to the pedants this is true enough. But, on the other hand, language alters much more slowly than we are led to think. It is arguable that in six hundred years since Chaucer the English language has changed less than the English climate or even than English geography, if we exclude the main natural features. The cliffs around Dover and the course of the Thames and the Tweed are, presumably, very much what they were at the time of the Canterbury Pilgrims; and, presumably, the hours for sunrise and sunset for the different British seasons are the same as when Shakespeare commented on them. But climate, in the sense of rainfall, and a landscape changed with the felling of the forests and the draining of the swamps, has altered with the centuries. Social and economic transformation since Chaucer's time has certainly been more startling than changes in Chaucer's language.

American geography has undergone greater change since 1776 than has the language in which the Declaration of Independence is written. Take that first paragraph of seventy-odd words. There is just one word that requires modernization to make the style quite good enough for our own time. Where Thomas Jefferson said a decent respect "to" the opinions of mankind we would say respect "for" the opinions of mankind. An exceptionally sensitive ear might insist on dissolving political "ties" where Jefferson proposed to dissolve political "bands." But compare with this very modest revision of perhaps two or three per cent in Jefferson's language by time the changes wrought in the face of an American continent which in Jefferson's time was overwhelmingly forest and fen.

Winston Churchill said in his speech before Congress that the Allies must "take the most earnest counsel one with another" in order to speed the fulfillment of their war aims. Here is a distinctly archaic flavor in the mouth of a man speaking in 1943 and concerned with issues that certainly are not archaic. It is like the music of a Rachmaninoff which some judges find outdated. But if old-fashioned words or music can set men's hearts beating in 1943, how can they be out of date?

—New York *Times,* "Topics of the Times," May 23, 1943

THE INFORMAL ESSAY

Essays are more often informal than formal, for the purpose of the essay is usually to give the writer's personal reaction to the subject in hand. He may, of course, wish to give us a solemn treatise on child care, full of important and sound advice. But, again, he may wish to humanize his material by approaching his subject from an unexpected direction and treating playfully of his experiences with babies. How effective such an essay will be will depend largely upon the author's personality. If he is clearly enjoying himself, the chances are his readers will share his enjoyment; if he is harassed by safety-pins and infant's formulas and two-o'clock feedings and the advice of friends and relatives—by all those ordinary problems of the new parent—his readers may be willing to sympathize and to understand. The practising light-essayist often gives the impression that he is talking in an offhand way, but we know, of course, that even the most casual piece of writing requires a plan and much careful thought if it is to be a success.

Study of the essays of Lamb, Hazlitt, Stevenson, and others is the best way to learn to write the personal or informal essay. Heywood Broun not too long ago and James Thurber and E. B. White more recently have shown the continuing aptness and appeal of this form.

HOLDING A BABY

By HEYWOOD BROUN

When Adam delved and Eve span, the fiction that man is incapable of housework was first established. It would be interesting to figure out just

154

how many foot-pounds of energy men have saved themselves, since the creation of the world, by keeping up the pretense that a special knack is required for washing dishes and for dusting, and that the knack is wholly feminine. The pretense of incapacity is impudent in its audacity, and yet it works.

Men build bridges and throw railroads across deserts, and yet they contend successfully that the job of sewing on a button is beyond them. Accordingly, they don't have to sew buttons.

It might be said, of course, that the safety of suspension bridges is so much more important than that of suspenders that the division of labor is only fair, but there are many of us who have never thrown a railroad in our lives, and yet swagger in all the glory of masculine achievement without undertaking any of the drudgery of odd jobs.

Probably men alone could never have maintained the fallacy of masculine incapacity without the aid of women. As soon as that rather limited sphere, once known as woman's place, was established, women began to glorify and exaggerate its importance, by the pretense that it was all so special and difficult that no other sex could possibly begin to accomplish the tasks entailed. To this declaration men gave immediate and eager assent and they have kept it up. The most casual examination will reveal the fact that all the jokes about the horrible results of masculine cooking and sewing are written by men. It is all part of a great scheme of sex propaganda.

Naturally there are other factors. Biology has been unscrupulous enough to discriminate markedly against women, and men have seized upon this advantage to press the belief that, since the bearing of children is exclusively the province of women, it must be that all the caring of them belongs properly to the same sex. Yet how ridiculous this is.

Most things which have to be done for children are of the simplest sort. They should tax the intelligence of no one. Men profess a total lack of ability to wash baby's face simply because they believe there's no great fun in the business, at either end of the sponge. Protectively, man must go the whole distance and pretend that there is not one single thing which he can do for baby. He must even maintain that he doesn't know how to hold one. From this pretense has grown the shockingly transparent fallacy that holding a baby correctly is one of the fine arts; or, perhaps even more fearsome than that, a wonderful intuition, which has come down after centuries of effort to women only.

"The thing that surprised Richard most," says a recent woman novelist, "was the ease and the efficiency with which Eleanor handled Annabel. . . . She seemed to know, by instinct, things that Richard could not understand and that he could not understand how she came by. If she reached out her hands to take Annabel, her fingers seemed, of themselves, to curve into the places where they would fit the spineless bundle and give it support."

155

At this point interruption is inevitable. Places indeed! There are one hundred and fifty-two distinctly different ways of holding a baby—and all are right! At least all will do. There is no need of seeking out special places for the hands. A baby is so soft that anybody with a firm grip can make places for an effective hold wherever he chooses. But to return to our quotation: "If Richard tried to take up the bundle, his fingers fell away like the legs of the brittle crab and the bundle collapsed, incalculable and helpless. 'How do you do it?' he would say. And he would right Annabel and try to still her protests. And Eleanor would only smile gently and send him on some masculine errand, while she soothed Annabel's feelings in the proper way."

You may depend upon it that Richard also smiled as soon as he was safely out of the house and embarked upon some masculine errand, such as playing eighteen holes of golf. Probably, by the time he reached the tenth green, he was too intent upon his game to remember how guile had won him freedom. Otherwise, he would have laughed again, when he holed a twenty-foot putt over a rolling green and recollected that he had escaped an afternoon of carrying Annabel because he was too awkward. I once knew the wife of the greatest billiard player in the world, and she informed me with much pride that her husband was incapable of carrying the baby. "He doesn't seem to have the proper touch," she explained.

As a matter of fact, even if men in general were as awkward as they pretend to be at home, there would still be small reason for their shirking the task of carrying a baby. Except that right side up is best, there is not much to learn. As I ventured to suggest before, almost any firm grip will do. Of course the child may cry, but that is simply because he has become over-particular through too much coddling. Nature herself is a cavalier. Young rabbits don't even whimper when picked up by the ears, and kittens are quite contented to be lifted by the scruff of the neck.

This same Nature has been used as the principal argument for woman's exclusive ability to take care of the young. It is pretty generally held that all a woman needs to do to know all about children is to have some. This wisdom is attributed to instinct. Again and again we have been told by rapturous grandmothers that: "It isn't something which can be read in a book or taught in a school. Nature is the great teacher." This simply isn't true. There are many mothers in America who have learned far more from the manuals of Dr. Holt than instinct ever taught them—and Dr. Holt is a man. I have seen mothers give beer and spaghetti and Neapolitan ice-cream to children in arms, and, if they got that from instinct, the only conclusion possible is that instinct did not know what it was talking about. Instinct is not what it used to be.

I have no feeling of being a traitor to my sex, when I say that I believe in at least a rough equality of parenthood. In shirking all the business of caring for children we have escaped much hard labor. It has been convenient. If we have avoided arduous tasks, we have also missed much fun of a very special kind. Like children in a toy shop, we have chosen to live with the most amusing of talking-and-walking dolls, without ever attempting to tear down the sign which says, "Do not touch." In fact we have helped to set it in place. That is a pity.

Children mean nothing at long range. For our own sake we ought to throw off the pretense of incapacity and ask that we be given a half share in them. I hope that this can be done without its being necessary for us to share the responsibility of dishes also. I don't think there are any concealed joys in washing dishes. Washing children is quite a different matter. After you have washed somebody else's face you feel that you know him better. This may be the reason why so many trained nurses marry their patients—but that is another story. A dish is an unresponsive thing. It gives back nothing. A child's face offers competitive possibilities. It is interesting to see just how high a polish can be achieved without making it cry.

There is also a distinct sense of elation in doing trifling practical things for children. They are so small and so helpless that they contribute vastly to a comforting glow in the ego of the grown-up. When you have completed the rather difficult task of preparing a child for bed and actually getting him there, you have a sense of importance almost divine in its extent. This is to feel at one with Fate, to be the master of another's destiny, of his waking and his sleeping and his going out into the world. It is a brand-new world for the child. He is a veritable Adam and you loom up in his life as more than mortal. Golf is well enough for a Sunday sport, but it is a trifling thing beside the privilege of taking a small son to the zoo and letting him see his first lion, his first tiger and, best of all, his first elephant. Probably he will think that they are part of your own handiwork turned out for his pleasure.

To a child, at least, even the meanest of us may seem glamorous with magic and wisdom. It seems a pity not to take the fullest advantage of his chance before the opportunity is lost. There must come a day when even the most nimblewitted father has to reply, "I don't know." On that day the child comes out of Eden and you are only a man again. Cortes on his lonely peak in Darien was a pigmy discoverer beside the child eating his first spoonful of ice-cream. There is the immediate frightened and angry rebellion against the coldness of it, and then the amazing sensation as the strange substance melts into magic of pleasant sweetness. The child will go on to high adventure, but I doubt whether the world holds for anyone more soul-stirring surprise than the first adventure with ice-cream. No, there is nothing dull in feeding a child.

There is less to be said for dressing a child, from the point of view of recreation. This seems to us laborious and rather tiresome, both for father and child. Still I know one man who managed to make an advantage of it. He boasted that he had broken all the records of the world for changing all or any part of a child's clothing. He was a skilled automobile mechanic,

157

much in demand in races, where tires are whisked on and off. He brought his technic into the home. I saw several of his demonstrations. He was a silent man who habitually carried a mouthful of safety pins. Once the required youngster had been pointed out, he wasted no time in preliminary wheedlings but tossed her on the floor without more ado. Even before her head had bumped, he would be hard at work. With him the thrill lay in the inspiration of the competitive spirit. He endeavored always to have his task completed before the child could begin to cry. He never lost. Often the child cried afterward, but by that time my friend felt that his part of the job was completed—and would turn the youngster over to her mother.

The personal essay is to be classified as exposition. It explains something—usually the writer's oft-times unconventional way of looking at the world. Like all good exposition it deals with the relationships of ideas and, however light or humorous or even flippant it may be, the personal essay always does something more than tell a story. It is a search for something fundamental—for some general truth. When it does succeed in moving unobtrusively from particular opinions and experiences to something greater, the personal essay yields to few other forms of composition in effectiveness and genuine importance.

DESCRIPTION

We recognize two chief kinds of description: explanatory description and creative description. The purpose of the first is, as its name suggests, to inform. The purpose of the second is to create a picture or image. Both deal with concrete experience. Both aim to make something visible to the reader or hearer through the medium of words. *Explanatory description* of a table, a bed, a house, a machine, and the like uses the orderly methods of exposition. Exact measurements are expected in such description. *Creative description* is written primarily to entertain. It uses details carefully selected in order to conjure up a picture. Thus, as is true of all careful writing, the problem is again one of careful planning, selection, and arrangement.

CREATIVE DESCRIPTION

Our study of expository methods has made us aware of the problems of explanatory description. Creative description may be dealt with briefly at this point.

A composition today is almost never pure description. Modern writers strive to get along with fewer and fewer set pieces of description and to secure their effects with fewer and fewer details. With the triumph of the modern short story there is more emphasis upon characters in action and less emphasis upon static portraits. Readers today become impatient with long descriptive passages and as often as not "skip over" them in their anxiety to "get on with the story." But the fact remains that descriptive writing is still important. In even the most rapidly moving narrative we must be able to visualize the characters and the setting, for action does not take place in a vacuum and actors must be flesh and blood. All of which means that the modern writer, instead of writing description as such, uses description to reinforce his expository and narrative writing, with the result that he is faced with some special problems.

Point of View

A football game may be described from many different points of view. The referee may describe it, a spectator in the top row of the bleachers may tell us what he sees, or one of the players may give us a picture of the game. The important thing to remember is this: the reader sees only what we see. His view is our view, to the exclusion, for the moment at least, of all other points of view. In writing creative description, then, we must adopt a useful point of view and maintain it until there is good reason to change. We must tell the reader what we see—not what we know we should see. The best description is written with the eye on the object. Description may be written from memory by a trained writer, but the amateur is likely to include details not visible from the point of view he has adopted, simply because he knows that they exist.

In some descriptive passages we may adopt a stationary point of view. We take up a position at a street corner, for example, and describe what we see. Other passages may require successive views of the scene. We may cross the street, enter a building, climb the stairs, and look out of a window at the traffic flowing along beneath us. Whenever it becomes expedient to shift from one physical point of view to another, we must of course mark the transition carefully, so that the reader can follow us. Thomas Hardy shows how this can be done. Having described a solitary figure on the hill called Rainbarrow, as seen from the road in the valley, and having remarked that the figure disappeared from view at the approach of certain other figures, he wishes to change his position. Chapter III of *The Return of the Native,* therefore, begins:

Had a looker-on been posted in the immediate vicinity of the barrow, he would have learned that these persons were boys and men of the neighbouring hamlets. Each, as he ascended the barrow, had been heavily laden with furze-faggots, carried upon the shoulder by means of a long stake sharpened at each end for impaling them easily—two in front and two behind. They came from a part of the heath a quarter of a mile to the rear, where furze almost exclusively prevailed as a product.

Every individual was so involved in furze by his method of carrying the faggots that he appeared like a bush on legs till he had thrown them down. The party had marched in trail, like a travelling flock of sheep that is to say, the strongest first, the weak and young behind.

In the next chapter, Hardy wishes us to accompany two of his characters on their trip from the top of Rainbarrow to the inn in the valley. He begins:

Down, downward they went, and yet further down—their descent at each step seeming to outmeasure their advance. Their skirts were scratched noisily by the furze, their shoulders brushed by the ferns, which, though dead and dry, stood erect as when alive, no sufficient winter weather having as yet arrived to beat them down. Their Tartarean situation might by some have been called an imprudent one for two unattended women. But these shaggy recesses were at all seasons a familiar surrounding to Olly and Mrs. Yeobright; and the addition of darkness lends no frightfulness to the face of a friend.

And he marks the several turning-points by such expressions as:

"The besom-maker turned to the left . . ."
"Mrs. Yeobright followed the straight track . . ."
"She first reached Wildeve's Patch . . ."
"When Mrs. Yeobright had drawn near to the inn . . ."
"Instead of entering the inn at once, she walked by it and towards the van . . ."

Such expressions are sometimes called directive terms. Their utility is obvious, for without them the reader easily becomes confused. Distances and directions are given approximately:

"some two hundred yards beyond it . . ."
"a few yards aside . . ."

Hardy need not be more precise, for his object is to give us a picture and not a map. Then, too, the emphasis in the chapter is on the story of Thomasin's return and not upon a description of this part of Egdon Heath.

Fundamental Image

Words, coming as they do one at a time, are less efficient for description than is paint. The completed portrait in oils we take in all at once. We get a general image at a glance, and, upon closer inspection, strengthen it by noticing details. But the difficulty is that words must be read one after the other. Consequently, the problem of selection and arrangement is one of the chief problems in description. Teachers of composition suggest that a descriptive passage begin, if possible, with a general statement of the whole scene or object or person. If we are describing something of standard size such as an armchair or a kitchen table, we need merely mention the fact and give the reader credit for having seen one before. Our chair may be an especially luxurious one or an especially shabby one. A well-chosen adjective used with the noun will convey the fundamental image to the reader. Perhaps our subject lends itself to comparison with something else: a triangle, a halfmoon, a circle. Such a simile provides us with a fundamental image. In the last chapter, we observed that Professor Breasted made use of this device when he began by saying that the Aegean Sea is "like a large lake."

Often, however, we shall want to do more than suggest a fundamental physical image. We may want to make the reader aware of what is called the fundamental quality or dominant impression. A room may give the immediate impression of cheerfulness or gloom, of neatness or of disorder, of beauty or of ugliness. A face may strike us as especially lovely because it is seen against a contrasting background. Hardy gives us a glimpse of Thomasin Yeobright asleep on a make-shift couch in the reddleman's cart:

A fair, sweet, and honest country face was revealed, reposing in a nest of wavy chestnut hair. It was between pretty and beautiful. Though her eyes were closed, one could easily imagine the light necessarily shining in them as the culmination of the luminous workmanship around. The groundwork of the face was hopefulness; but over it now lay like a foreign substance a film of anxiety and grief. The grief had been there so shortly as to have abstracted nothing of the bloom which had as yet but given a dignity to what it might eventually undermine. The scarlet of her lips had not had time to abate, and just now it appeared still more intense by the absence of the neighbouring and more transient colour of her cheek. The lips frequently parted, with a murmur of words. She seemed to belong rightly to a madrigal—to require viewing through rhyme and harmony.

Hardy has built this description around the dominant impression given in the words:

The groundwork of the face was hopefulness; but over it now lay like a foreign substance a film of anxiety and grief.

To strengthen this impression, Hardy shows the effect upon the other characters when he goes on to say:

One thing at least was obvious: she was not made to be looked at thus. The reddleman had appeared conscious of as much, and, while Mrs. Yeobright looked in upon her, he cast his eyes aside with a delicacy which well became him.

DESCRIPTIVE WORDS AND PHRASES

The problem of description finally comes to this: what is the right word or phrase to summon up in the mind of the reader the scene or person or object being described. The writer of good description is highly sensitive to the connotations of words. (See Chapter IX: Diction.) In writing explanatory description he seeks the exact word. If he is describing a machine he has no occasion to indulge in subtle nuances. The writer of creative description, on the other hand, must concern himself with nice shades of meaning. To him, nuances are all-important, for creative description appeals not simply to the mind but more especially to the emotions—to the imagination. Such a writer, if asked how he achieves his effects, will probably say that he uses specific and concrete words wherever possible, that he does not shun adjectives but rather tends to put more emphasis upon verbs and adverbs, and that he finds it important to use figures of speech.

Here are two descriptions of persons:

Mr. Slope is tall, and not ill made. His feet and hands are large, as has ever been the case with all his family, but he has a broad chest and wide shoulders to carry off these excrescences, and on the whole his figure is good. His countenance, however, is not specially prepossessing. His hair is lank, and of a dull pale reddish hue. It is always formed into three straight lumpy masses, each brushed with admirable precision, and cemented with much grease; two of them adhere closely to the sides of his face, and the other lies at right angles above them. He wears no whiskers, and is always punctiliously shaven. His face is nearly of the same colour as his hair, though perhaps a little redder: it is not unlike beef—beef, however, one would say, of a bad quality. His forehead is capacious and high, but square and heavy, and unpleasantly shining. His mouth is large, though his lips are thin and bloodless; and his big, prominent, pale brown eyes inspire anything but confidence. His nose, however, is his redeeming feature: it is pronounced straight and well-formed; though I myself should have liked it better did it not possess a somewhat spongy, porous appearance, as though it had been cleverly formed out of a red coloured cork.

I never could endure to shake hands with Mr. Slope. A cold, clammy perspiration always exudes from him, the small drops are ever to be seen standing on his brow, and his friendly grasp is unpleasant.

—TROLLOPE, *Barchester Towers*

Much of the effectiveness of the preceding passage depends upon the personal reaction of the narrator. Henry Fielding does not depend upon this device in the following description of parson Trulliber:

Parson Adams came to the house of parson Trulliber, whom he found stript into his waistcoat, with an apron on, and a pail in his hand, just come from serving his hogs; for Mr. Trulliber was a parson on Sundays, but all the other six might more properly be called a farmer. He occupied a small piece of land of his own, besides which he rented a considerable deal more. His wife milked his cows, managed his dairy, and followed the markets with butter and eggs. The hogs fell chiefly to his care, which he carefully waited on at home, and attended to fairs; on which occasion he was liable to many jokes, his own size being, with much ale, rendered little inferior to that of the beasts he sold. He was indeed one of the largest men you should see, and could act the part of Sir John Falstaff without stuffing. Add to this that the rotundity of his belly was considerably increased by the shortness of his stature, his shadow ascending very near as far in height, when he lay on his back, as when he stood on his legs. His voice was loud and hoarse, and his accents extremely broad. To complete the whole, he had a stateliness in his gait, when he walked, not unlike that of a goose, only he walked slower.—FIELDING, *Joseph Andrews*

The next description grows naturally out of a preliminary picture of a scene, but, like the two just given, is concerned primarily with a person:

The afternoon sun was warm on the five workmen there, busy upon doors and window-frames and wainscoting. A scent of pine-wood from a tent-like pile of planks outside the open door mingled itself with the scent of the elderbushes which were spreading their summer snow close to the open window opposite; the slanting sunbeams shone through the transparent shavings that flew before the steady plane, and lit up the fine grain of the oak panelling which stood propped against the wall. On a heap of those soft shavings a rough grey shepherd-dog had made himself a pleasant bed, and was lying with his nose between his fore-paws, occasionally wrinkling his brows to cast a glance at the tallest of the five workmen, who was carving a shield in the centre of a wooden mantelpiece. It was to this workman that the strong baritone belonged which was heard above the sound of plane and hammer singing—

> "Awake my soul, and with the sun
> Thy daily stage of duty run;
> Shake off dull sloth . . . ."

Here some measurement was to be taken which required more concen-trated attention, and the sonorous voice subsided into a low whistle; but it presently broke out again with renewed vigour—

> "Let all thy converse be sincere,
> Thy conscience as the noonday clear."

Such a voice could only come from a broad chest, and the broad chest belonged to a large-boned muscular man nearly six feet high, with a back so flat and a head so well poised that when he drew himself up to take a more distant survey of his work, he had the air of a soldier standing at ease. The sleeve rolled up above the elbow showed an arm that was likely to win the prize for feats of strength; yet the long supple hand, with its broad finger-tips, looked ready for works of skill. In his tall stalwartness Adam Bede was a Saxon, and justified his name; but the jet-black hair, made the more noticeable by its contrast with the light paper cap, and the keen glance of the dark eyes that shone from under strongly marked, prominent and mobile eyebrows, indicated a mixture of Celtic blood. The face was large and roughly hewn, and when in repose had no other beauty than such as belongs to an expression of good-humoured honest intelligence.

—GEORGE ELIOT, *Adam Bede*

The swift characterization of Spandrell in Aldous Huxley's *Point Counter Point* shows the effectiveness of concrete imagery and the usefulness of analogy:

Spandrell uttered a brief and snorting laugh and, letting his chair fall back on to its four legs, leaned forward across the table. Pushing aside his coffee cup and his half-emptied liqueur glass, he planted his elbows on the table and his chin in his hands. His face came into the light of the rosy lamp. Like a gargoyle, Mary thought—a gargoyle in a pink boudoir. There was one on Notre Dame in just that attitude, leaning forward with his daemon's face between his claws. Only the gargoyle was a comic devil, so extravagantly diabolical that you couldn't take his devilishness very seri-ously. Spandrell was a real person, not a caricature; that was why his face was so much more sinister and tragical. It was a gaunt face. Cheekbone and jaw showed in hard outline through the tight skin. The gray eyes were deeply set. In the cadaverous mask only the mouth was fleshy—a wide mouth, with lips that stood out from the skin like two thick weals.

When Mr. Pickwick and Sam Weller call at the premises of Messrs. Dodson and Fogg, Dickens gives us a brief but characteristic sketch of the setting:

The clerk's office of Messrs. Dodson and Fogg was a dark, mouldy, earthy-smelling room, with a high wainscotted partition to screen the clerks from the vulgar gaze: a couple of old wooden chairs: a very loud-ticking clock: an almanack, an umbrella-stand, a row of hat-pegs, and a few shelves, on which were deposited several ticketed bundles of dirty papers, some old deal boxes with paper labels, and sundry decayed stone ink bottles of various shapes and sizes. There was a glass door leading into the passage which formed the entrance to the court, and on the outer side of this glass door, Mr. Pickwick, closely followed by Sam Weller, presented himself on the Friday morning succeeding the occurrence, of which a faithful narration is given in the last chapter.

Aldous Huxley inserts at one point a brief description of an interior:

The dining room at Philip's club was enormous. A double row of stucco Corinthian pillars supported a gilded ceiling. From the pale chocolate-brown walls the portraits of distinguished members, now deceased, glared down. Curtains of claret-coloured velvet were looped up at either side of the six windows, a claret-coloured carpet muffled the floor, and in their claret-coloured liveries the waiters darted about almost invisibly, like leaf-insects in a forest.—ALDOUS HUXLEY, *Point Counter Point*

Notice especially the verb *glared,* the adverb *invisibly,* and the figure of speech: "like leaf-insects in a forest."

W. D. Howells makes skillful use in his description of the castle of Ferrara of the fact that the feudal edifice is now used for modern offices:

The castle of the Dukes of Ferrara, about which cluster so many sad and splendid memories, stands in the heart of the city. I think that the moonlight which, on the night of our arrival, showed me its massive walls rising from the shadowy moat that surrounds them, and its four great towers, heavily buttressed, and expanding at the top into bulging cornices of cavernous brickwork, could have fallen on nothing else in all Italy so picturesque, and so full of the proper dread charm of feudal times, as this pile of gloomy and majestic strength. The daylight took nothing of this charm from it; for the castle stands isolated in the midst of the city, as

165

its founder meant that it should, and modern civilization has not crossed the castle moat, to undignify its exterior with any visible touch of the present. To be sure, when you enter it, the magnificent life is gone òut of the old edifice; it is no stately halberdier who stands on guard at the gate of the drawbridge, but a stumpy Italian soldier in baggy trousers. The castle is full of public offices, and one sees in its courts and on its stairways, not brilliant men-at-arms, nor gay squires and pages, but whistling messengers going from one office to another with docketed papers, and slipshod serving-men carrying the clerks their coffee in very dirty little pots. Dreary-looking suitors, slowly grinding through the mills of law, or passing in the routine of the offices, are the guests encountered in the corridors; and all that bright-colored throng of the old days, ladies and lords, is passed from the scene. The melodrama is over, friends, and now we have a play of real life, founded on fact and inculcating a moral.

—WILLIAM DEAN HOWELLS, *Italian Journeys*

Finally, let us read Hardy's description of Mrs. Yeobright's view from the Devil's Bellows on a stifling thirty-first of August. Notice how careful the author is to indicate his point of view and the transition from a distant to a closer view, and with what skill he chooses details for the picture of the scene in front of the cottage:

From her elevated position the exhausted woman could perceive the back roof of the house below, and the garden and the whole enclosure of the little domicile. And now, at the moment of rising, she saw a second man approaching the gate. His manner was peculiar, hesitating, and not that of a person come on business or by invitation. He surveyed the house with interest, and then walked round and scanned the outer boundary of the garden, as one might have done had it been the birthplace of Shakespeare, the prison of Mary Stuart, or the Château of Hougomont. After passing round and again reaching the gate he went in. Mrs. Yeobright was vexed at this, having reckoned on finding her son and his wife by themselves; but a moment's thought showed her that the presence of an acquaintance would take off the awkwardness of her first appearance in the house, by confining the talk to general matters until she had begun to feel comfortable with them. She came down the hill to the gate, and looked into the hot garden.

There lay the cat asleep on the bare gravel of the path, as if beds, rugs, and carpets were unendurable. The leaves of the hollyhocks hung like half-closed umbrellas, the sap almost simmered in the stems, and foliage with a smooth surface glared like metallic mirrors. A small apple tree, of the sort called Ratheripe, grew just inside the gate, the only one which thrived in the garden, by reason of the lightness of the soil; and among the fallen apples on the ground beneath were wasps rolling drunk with the juice, or creeping about the little caves in each fruit which they had eaten out before stupefied by its sweetness. By the door lay Clym's furze-hook and the last handful of faggot-bonds she had seen him gather; they had plainly been thrown down there as he entered the house.

NARRATION

Narration is the expression of action in words. It is story-telling. We read in the newspaper that the police have raided a nightclub, that the President has made a surprise trip to the West Coast, that a ship has been launched. We are reading narrative. A friend tells us about the experiences of two visiting English sailors in downtown New York. He sketches the situation for us briefly, identifies the characters involved, plunges them into the action, and lets us follow them from one experience to another through the day. A letter arrives from a boy at camp, and we experience with him his first two days in an unfamiliar and perhaps bewildering environment. Depending upon the writer's natural sense for story-telling or his lack of it, the letter will be good narrative or an incoherent series of episodes. In narration, selection of details is all important.

ESSENTIALS

What are the essentials of narration? Assuming that we are to deal with a connected succession of happenings, we must create first of all a sense of movement. The actions we are relating may require an illusion of rapid movement or of slow, painful, deliberate, or laborious movement. But movement there must be—movement toward a goal—if our narrative is to have unity. The second requirement is a sense of reality. To make our reader see our characters as vividly as we ourselves see them, experience their emotions in the various situations in which we place them, we must be concrete. Our characters must be individualized. The third requirement is truth. Like other artists, the writer of narrative must select. He must not simply record. His goal is not a photographic copy of life, but an illusion of life.

Biography, autobiography, and history are to be classified usually as narration rather than as exposition or description. Good biography will also contain both exposition and description, of course, but the emphasis will be primarily upon a series of happenings, more often than not told in chronological order. Travel books and diaries are narratives as a rule. And of course the factual reports of current events found in newspapers are predominantly narrative.

167

We may distinguish two kinds of narration: simple narration, or narration without plot, and creative narration, or narration with plot.

THE INCIDENT

One kind of simple narration is the incident: the brief narration of a subordinate event which serves to illustrate some idea or principle. It is often helpful to begin an essay with an incident. The reader's interest is gained at once and, if the incident is skillfully phrased, he discovers for himself the author's purpose in using the short narrative. Alexander Woollcott begins one of his essays with the following incident:

When my godchild was six, a bevy of the younger set was invited in her name to occupy a box at the circus. In the week preceding this social event her mother grew haggard under the strain of the arrangements. Finally the last reassuring telephone call had been put in, the last touch given to the vitamins of the aseptic luncheon, the last exquisite guest, piloted by a skeptical nursemaid, had been delivered. The impresario of the occasion was exhausted, but her reward, she knew, would be the sweet soprano pleasure of the little ones at all the marvels in Madison Square Garden. It took these pretty innocents some time to unbend, but finally they did vouchsafe a quite gratifying, if somewhat special, delight. It was when a dejected fox-terrier, accompanying one of the lesser clowns along the sawdust trail, paused for a moment in front of them and stood sadly on his head. At this modest achievement the children were beside themselves with excitement. Oh, look at the dear little dog! Oh, look! Oh, look! They gesticulated. They shrieked. They beat one another in their common ecstasy, and almost fell from the box in a moist heap in their effort to see the last of the pensive terrier as he trotted out of sight around the curve. And all this time the rest of the Garden was holding its breath because just then twenty-five elephants, all unnoticed by these infuriating young *flâneurs,* were standing on *their* heads.

Mr. Woollcott has given the reader a charming little story, but his real purpose in telling it becomes apparent when he goes on to say:

I have an uneasy feeling that if I were honestly to assess my delights at the Fair it would be discovered that, whereas the treasure chests of the earth were ransacked for my pleasure . . . what really ensures my enjoyment of the Fair is the little fox-terrier who stands on his head. Or, at least, it is a detail as minor, as casual, and as clearly an afterthought.

And he goes on to devote his essay to "that gentle conveyance which combines the maximum of view with the maximum of comfort, the rickshaw"—used at the 1933 Fair in Chicago.

The anecdote, like the short story and the novel, is intended primarily to entertain. The anecdote may, like the incident, be used in a longer work to arouse interest, but more often than not it is independent.

The anecdote is short. It is often biographical and may be interesting because it shows us some well-known person in an unusual situation. The biographers of men like Lincoln and Dr. Johnson make excellent use of anecdote to give flavor to their writing. The story of Washington and the cherry tree is a classic. Boswell's *Life of Johnson* is a vast quarry of anecdotal material about the great doctor and his friends. The best anecdotes are those that reveal some hitherto unsuspected trait of character or that tell of an unconventional method of handling some everyday problem.

The following anecdote from the *New Yorker* shows how effective short narration can be:

A girl we've just heard of, name of Grace, is hereby cited for her bold and creative interpretation of the rules and regulations of the National Gallery of Art, in Washington. Having finished a hearty breakfast one morning in the capital, she put on her most comfortable pair of shoes and went to the gallery. After a certain length of time, she succumbed, inevitably, to the museum droops. She retired to the powder room for a cigarette and there noticed a pamphlet containing general information about the gallery. One paragraph in particular engaged her attention: "Wheel chairs are made available, without charge, for those desiring them. Application should be made at the Information Desk." Grace was struck by the fact that it didn't say "those needing them" or even "those deserving them" —just "those desiring them." Acting on the theory that a museum certainly wouldn't say anything it didn't mean, she went out to the information desk and said she desired a wheel chair. Without question, the attendant trotted out a chromium-plated, de-luxe model with fat rubber tires, gave Grace a few pointers on how to operate it, and sent her off with his good wishes. She had a fine time.

In this little story, we have the essentials of narrative writing: actors (Grace and the attendant), setting (the museum), and action (the securing of a wheel chair by a footsore visitor). We are told no more than necessary about the characters involved. The girl is called Grace; the attendant is nameless. General experience enables anyone who has visited an art gallery or museum to fill in the details of the setting. We need be told nothing about the previous life of Grace. We are told, as the story proceeds, that she "finished a hearty breakfast" and "put on her most comfortable pair of shoes," that she "succumbed, inevitably, to the museum droops" and "retired to the powder room for a cigarette" and we can ourselves expand these hints. But the anecdote is designed, not to give us a portrait of Grace, but rather to show Grace in action. We move swiftly along to the climax. Grace asks for a wheel chair and gets one promptly from an attendant who explains how it is operated and who sends her off with his good wishes. At this point the story ends. Any further details would destroy the effect.

This anecdote strikes us as unified because there are no irrelevant details to impede the movement of the action toward its inevitable end. It is concrete. The paragraph from the pamphlet is quoted directly and not paraphrased. Although, as we have remarked, Grace herself is not described directly, the wheel chair is—a "chromium-plated, de-luxe model with fat rubber tires" for the fact that the wheel chair is a luxurious one and not just any wheel chair gives added point to the story.

Anecdotes, like all narratives, can be told from many different points of view. Grace might have told her story in the first person. The story might have been related by a less-resourceful friend who watched Grace do what she lacked the courage to do. It might have been told from the point of view of the attendant at the information desk.

The anecdote presents a character at an interesting moment. The short story is concerned with how a character arrives at an interesting moment, how he meets the obstacle or hindrance, and how he behaves afterward. The anecdote, in other words, lacks something that the short story has—plot.

HOW TO PLAN A SHORT STORY

It has often been pointed out that plots do not "happen"—they must be constructed or made to order by the author. A plot is a scheme constructed by the author as an outline of the action. Because the same series of events will provide material for half a dozen different plots, it is clear that the plot must be thought through in advance in order that every detail will be related logically to every other detail. A straightforward, chronological narrative of a succession of happenings may or may not be interesting; the short story must be interesting. The short story presents a moment in the life of the principal character—a moment carefully worked up to and satisfyingly disposed of. Since all art is a simplification and in-tensification of life, the author of the short story must select and arrange his material with great care if he is to succeed in making his interpretation of the events that of his reader. The following suggestions may be helpful:

I. Select one main person and one main event.

The plot "germ" may be found in an action, a person, a location, or a mood. Many stories are predominantly stories of character. Perhaps you have met someone who, you feel, would react strangely to a sudden shock. Perhaps he has often spoken of his ability to adjust himself quickly to unexpected changes. Place him in a complicated situation and see what happens. Perhaps you have been struck by a certain place as one "in which something might happen." Perhaps you saw something happen there. Re-arrange the details and concentrate the reader's attention on the setting of your story. But remember that you must tell one story at a time. Fix attention on one principal person—make it *his* story—and on one principal event.

II. Begin at the "right" point and begin with action rather than explanation.

You will be faced with an endless chain of events, one growing out of the other. You must decide where in the series to begin your narrative. Simple stories begin "at the beginning" and proceed in chronological order. Plotted narrative usually begins shortly before the principal crisis or climax. Detective stories and a few others begin at the end and work backward. Do not begin too far back. The story of Samson in the Bible gains in intensity if we begin not with his early history—important as that may be to the author of the Book of Judges—but with his betrayal to the Philistines:

And she [Delilah] said unto him [Samson], How canst thou say, I love thee, when thine heart is not with me? Thou hast mocked me these three times, and hast not told me wherein thy great strength lieth. And it came to pass, when she pressed him daily with her words, and urged him, so that his soul was vexed unto death; that he told her all his heart, and said unto her, There hath not come a razor upon mine head; for I have been a Nazarite unto God from my mother's womb: If I be shaven, then my strength will go from me, and I shall become weak, and be like any other man. And when Delilah saw that he had told her all his heart, she sent .and called for the lords of the Philistines, saying, Come up this once, for he hath showed me all his heart. Then the lords of the Philistines came up unto her, and brought money in their hand. And she made him sleep upon her knees; and she called for a man, and she caused him to shave off the seven locks of his head; and she began to afflict him, and his strength went from him. And she said, The Philistines be upon thee, Samson. And he awoke out of his sleep, and said, I will go out as at other times before, and shake myself. And he wist not that the Lord was departed from him.

But the Philistines took him, and put out his eyes, and brought him down to Gaza, and bound him with fetters of brass; and he did grind in the prison house. Howbeit the hair of his head began to grow again after he was shaven. Then the lords of the Philistines gathered them together for to offer a great sacrifice unto Dagon their god, and to rejoice: for they said, Our god hath delivered Samson our enemy into our hand. And when the people saw him, they praised their god: for they said, Our god hath delivered into our hands our enemy, and the destroyer of our country, which slew many of us. And it came to pass, when their hearts were merry, that they said, Call for Samson, that he may make us sport. And they called for Samson out of the prison house; and he made them sport: and they set him between the pillars. And Samson said unto the lad that held him by the hand, Suffer me that I may feel the pillars whereupon the house standeth, that I may lean upon them. Now the house was full of men and women; and all the lords of the Philistines were there; and there were upon the roof about three thousand men and women, that beheld while Samson made sport. And Samson called unto the Lord, and said, O Lord God, remember me, I pray thee, and strengthen me, I pray thee, only this once, O God, that I may be at once avenged of the Philistines for my two eyes. And Samson took hold of the two middle pillars upon which the house stood, and on which it was borne up, of the one with his right hand, and of the other with his left. And Samson said, Let me die with the Philistines. And he bowed himself with all his might; and the house fell upon the lords, and upon all the people that were therein. So the dead which he slew at his death were more than they which he slew in his life.

The "right" point for the author of the Book of Judges to begin was, of course, with the birth of Samson. Our excerpt is not a short story, but if a short story were to be written about the death of Samson, the action would have to be limited somewhat as it is limited in the passage above. When John Milton put the story in dramatic form in his *Samson Agonistes,* he narrowed the action, restricted the number of speaking characters, and limited the time of the drama to a single day. He began even further along in the series than we have begun: with Samson "eyeless in Gaza, in the mill with slaves."

Begin as Bret Harte begins his *Outcasts of Poker Flat*—with action, with something happening:

As Mr. John Oakhurst, gambler, stepped into the main street of Poker Flat on the morning of the 23rd of November, 1850, he was conscious of a change in its moral atmosphere since the preceding night. Two or three men, conversing earnestly together, ceased as he approached, and exchanged significant glances. There was a Sabbath lull in the air, which, in a settlement unused to Sabbath influences, looked ominous.

Explanation can (and does) come later. Mr. Oakhurst is the major character and we need to know more about his past. But the author rightly begins with action instead of explanation.

III. Carry the action along through a series of minor crises leading to one major crisis and then conclude.

Out of the welter of episodic material you will select certain incidents and reject others. You will do well to draw up an outline or scenario of your story—a plan with subheads as follows:

A. Opening situation
B. Generating circumstance
C. Rising action
D. Climax
E. Denouement
F. Aftermath (optional)

Let us look again at the story of Samson. The **opening situation** introduces the characters: Samson and Delilah. Delilah's reproachful words to her lover indicate the antecedent action: "Thou hast mocked me these three times, and hast not told me wherein thy great strength lieth." The **generating circumstance** is that inciting force which starts the action on its way upwards toward the point of highest interest: "he told her all his heart, and said unto her . . . If I be shaven, then my strength will go from me." The **rising action** consists of those episodes which lead to the climax: "she called for a man . . . she caused him to shave off the seven locks of his head . . . the Philistines took him . . . he did grind in the prison house . . . and they called for Samson out of the prison house . . . and they set him between the pillars . . ." The **climax** is reached when Samson, having breathed a prayer to God for help, "took hold of the two middle pillars upon which the house stood." We know that we have reached a major turning-point in the story. Everything has led up to this moment. The **denouement** (or "untying" of the knot) is the completion of the action: "the house fell upon the lords, and upon all the people that were therein." In longer stories, the **aftermath** follows the denouement. Thomas Hardy's *Return of the Native* concludes with an entire Book entitled "Aftercourses." But the short story, as a rule, ends more or less abruptly after the denouement. Our story of Samson concludes with a brief statement of his burial.

DIALOGUE

It is the aim of good narration to make the reader or listener experience character, emotion, and scenery directly. The hero and the villain must express themselves; their personalities must be felt without the author's having to comment on them. By his own actions and words, by the attitude of other persons toward him, the character comes to life for the reader. On the stage, this revelation comes readily. In narration, dialogue is constantly used also, and for two chief purposes: (1) to distinguish one character from another, and (2) to carry the plot forward.

Good dialogue must sound like natural speech. The writer here as elsewhere is obliged to select, for he knows that a dictaphone recording of actual conversation will not give the illusion he needs; but since he must achieve this illusion, he does so by careful arrangement.

In the following passage from *Martin Chuzzlewit,* observe the method of the author. Dickens combines straightforward description of Tom Pinch with revealing dialogue—dialogue that advances the plot at the same time that it suggests more than a little about the characters of Tom, of Mr. Pecksniff, of his daughters, and even of John Westlock:

"Come in!" cried Mr. Pecksniff—not severely; only virtuously. "Come in!"

An ungainly, awkward-looking man, extremely short-sighted and prematurely bald, availed himself of this permission; and seeing that Mr. Pecksniff sat with his back towards him, gazing at the fire, stood hesitating, with the door in his hand. He was far from handsome, certainly; and was drest in a snuff-coloured suit, of an uncouth make at the best, which, being shrunk with long wear, was twisted and tortured into all kinds of odd shapes; but notwithstanding his attire, and his clumsy figure, which a great stoop in his shoulders, and a ludicrous habit he had of thrusting his head forward, by no means redeemed, one would not have been disposed (unless Mr. Pecksniff said so) to consider him a bad fellow by any means.

174

He was perhaps about thirty, but he might have been almost any age between sixteen and sixty: being one of those strange creatures who never decline into an ancient appearance, but look their oldest when they are very young, and get it over at once.

Keeping his hand upon the lock of the door, he glanced from Mr. Pecksniff to Mercy, from Mercy to Charity, and from Charity to Mr. Pecksniff again, several times; but the young ladies being as intent upon the fire as their father was, and neither of the three taking any notice of him, he was fain to say, at last,

"Oh! I beg your pardon, Mr. Pecksniff: I beg your pardon for intruding; but——"

"No intrusion, Mr. Pinch," said that gentleman very sweetly, but without looking round. "Pray be seated, Mr. Pinch. Have the goodness to shut the door, Mr. Pinch, if you please."

"Certainly, sir," said Pinch; not doing so, however, but holding it rather wider open than before, and beckoning nervously to somebody without: "Mr. Westlock, sir, hearing that you were come home——"

"Mr. Pinch, Mr. Pinch!" said Pecksniff, wheeling his chair about, and looking at him with an aspect of the deepest melancholy, "I did not expect this from you. I have not deserved this from you!"

"No, but upon my word, sir——" urged Pinch.

"The less you say, Mr. Pinch," interposed the other, "the better. I utter no complaint. Make no defence."

"No, but do have the goodness, sir," cried Pinch, with great earnestness, "if you please. Mr. Westlock, sir, going away for good and all, wishes to leave none but friends behind him. Mr. Westlock and you, sir, had a little difference the other day; you have had many little differences."

"Little differences!" cried Charity.

"Little differences!" echoed Mercy.

"My loves!" said Mr. Pecksniff, with the same serene upraising of his hand; "My dears!" After a solemn pause he meekly bowed to Mr. Pinch, as who should say, "Proceed;" but Mr. Pinch was so very much at a loss how to resume, and looked so helplessly at the two Miss Pecksniffs, that the conversation would most probably have terminated there, if a good-looking youth, newly arrived at man's estate, had not stepped forward from the doorway and taken up the thread of the discourse.

"Come, Mr. Pecksniff," he said, with a smile, "don't let there be any ill-blood between us, pray. I am sorry we have ever differed, and extremely sorry I have ever given you offence. Bear me no ill-will at parting, sir."

"I bear," answered Mr. Pecksniff, mildly, "no ill-will to any man on earth."

"I told you he didn't," said Pinch, in an undertone; "I knew he didn't! He always says he don't."

"Then you will shake hands, sir?" cried Westlock, advancing a step or two, and bespeaking Mr. Pinch's close attention by a glance.

"Umph!" said Mr. Pecksniff, in his most winning tone.

"You will shake hands, sir."

"No, John," said Mr. Pecksniff, with a calmness quite ethereal; "no, I will not shake hands, John. I have forgiven you. I had already forgiven you, even before you ceased to reproach and taunt me. I have embraced you in the spirit, John, which is better than shaking hands."

"Pinch," said the youth, turning towards him, with a hearty disgust of his late master, "what did I tell you?"

Good dialogue preserves the individual rhythms of speech and he who would write good dialogue must give careful thought not only to his character's vocabulary but especially to his speech mannerisms —to all those tricks of expression that combine to give flavor to a person's conversation.

Dialect

This brings us to a consideration of dialect. Careful reading of dialectal passages in modern novels will show that the author has not reproduced the dialect of his character in detail. Rather, he has given the illusion of dialect. For one thing, unless the author were to use a phonetic alphabet, it would be as a rule impossible to give a faithful transcript of any very distinctive dialect. Such a transcript would be unintelligible to all readers not specially trained. What the author actually does is to give the flavor of dialect by careful selection.

John Galsworthy reproduces the speech of an old German cobbler in his short story "Quality":

I cannot forget that day on which I had occasion to say to him: "Mr. Gessler, that last pair of town walking-boots creaked, you know."

He looked at me for a time without replying, as if expecting me to withdraw or qualify the statement, then said:

"Id shouldn'd 'ave greaked."

"It did, I'm afraid."

"You goddem wed before dey found demselves?"

"I don't think so."

At that he lowered his eyes, as if hunting for memory of those boots, and I felt sorry I had mentioned this grave thing.

"Zend dem back!" he said; "I will look at dem."

A feeling of compassion for my creaking boots surged up in me, so well could I imagine the sorrowful long curiosity of regard which he would bend on them.

"Zome boods," he said slowly, "are bad from birdt. If I can do noding wid dem, I dake dem off your bill."

In the *Return of the Native,* Hardy frequently records the conversation of the natives of Egdon Heath. As the following incident shows, he is more interested in preserving the rhythms of Christian Cantle's talk than he is in stressing the vocabulary variations. The episode is highly important to the progress of the narrative and especially significant in its revelation of character. Observe that Christian is not a trained narrator. To him, the parson's suit of clothes is more important than the ignorant attack upon Eustacia Vye, although he is ready enough to agree with his shocked listeners that something should be done:

The silence was broken by the clash of the garden gate, a tap at the door, and its opening. Christian Cantle appeared in the room in his Sunday clothes.

It was the custom on Egdon to begin the preface to a story before absolutely entering the house, so as to be well in for the body of the narrative by the time visitor and visited stood face to face. Christian had been saying to them while the door was leaving its latch, "To think that I, who go from home but once in a while, and hardly then, should have been there this morning!"

" 'Tis news you have brought us, then, Christian?" said Mrs. Yeobright.

"Ay, sure, about a witch, and ye must overlook my time o' day; for, says I, 'I must go and tell 'em, though they won't have half done dinner.' I assure ye it made me shake like a driven leaf. Do ye think any harm will come o't?"

"Well—what?"

"This morning at church we was all standing up, and the pa'son said, 'Let us pray.' 'Well,' thinks I, 'one may as well kneel as stand;' so down I went; and, more than that, all the rest were as willing to oblige the man as I. We hadn't been hard at it for more than a minute when a most terrible screech sounded through the church, as if somebody had just gied up their heart's blood. All the folk jumped up, and then we found that Susan Nunsuch had pricked Miss Vye with a long stocking-needle, as she had theatened to do as soon as ever she could get the young lady to church, where she don't come very often. She've waited for this chance for weeks, so as to draw her blood and put an end to the bewitching of Susan's children that has been carried on so long. Sue followed her into church, sat next to her, and as soon as she could find a chance in went the stocking-needle into my lady's arm."

"Good heaven, how horrid!" said Mrs. Yeobright.

"Sue pricked her that deep that the maid fainted away; and as I was afeard there might be some tumult among us, I got behind the bass-viol and didn't see no more. But they carried her out into the air, 'tis said; but when they looked round for Sue she was gone. What a scream that girl gied, poor thing! There were the pa'son in his surplice holding up his hand and saying, 'Sit down, my good people, sit down!' But the deuce a bit would they sit down. O, and what d'ye think I found out, Mrs. Yeobright? The pa'son wears a suit of clothes under his surplice!—I could see his black sleeve when he held up his arm."

" 'Tis a cruel thing," said Yeobright.

"Yes," said his mother.

"The nation ought to look into it," said Christian.

HOW TO STUDY AND ANALYZE A NARRATIVE

When you have read Bret Harte's famous short story *The Outcasts of Poker Flat*, which commences on page 179, ask yourself these questions about the story and the author:

(1) What kind of people are portrayed in the story?
(2) Are they individualized?
(3) What do you learn about their social status?
(4) Does the story remind you of any others you have read?
(5) To which of your friends would you recommend it?
(6) Did you learn anything about the life or interests of the author?
(7) Have you read any other stories by him?
(8) What is his attitude towards life?
(9) Could he have told the story as effectively from another point of view?
(10) Is the author's interest primarily in action or in character?

In analyzing a narrative, with a view to learning how to write narrative prose, ask yourself such questions as the following about the plot, the characters, and the setting:

(1) What is the opening situation? the generating circumstance?
(2) What events make up the rising action?
(3) How is the passage of time shown?
(4) What is the climax?
(5) What is the denouement?
(6) Can you differentiate between major and minor characters?
(7) How does the author use his minor characters?
(8) How well do you know them?
(9) What is the setting?
(10) Does the setting influence the action?

THE OUTCASTS OF POKER FLAT

By Bret Harte

As Mr. John Oakhurst, gambler, stepped into the main street of Poker Flat on the morning of the 23rd of November, 1850, he was conscious of a change in its moral atmosphere since the preceding night. Two or three men, conversing earnestly together, ceased as he approached, and exchanged significant glances. There was a Sabbath lull in the air, which, in a settlement unused to Sabbath influences, looked ominous.

Mr. Oakhurst's calm, handsome face betrayed small concern in these indications. Whether he was conscious of any predisposing cause was another question. "I réckon they're after somebody," he reflected; "likely it's me." He returned to his pocket the handkerchief with which he had been whipping away the red dust of Poker Flat from his neat boots, and quietly discharged his mind of any further conjecture.

In point of fact, Poker Flat was "after somebody." It had lately suffered the loss of several thousand dollars, two valuable horses, and a prominent citizen. It was experiencing a spasm of virtuous reaction, quite as lawless and ungovernable as any of the acts that had provoked it. A secret committee had determined to rid the town of all improper persons. This was done permanently in regard of two men who were then hanging from the boughs of a sycamore in the gulch, and temporarily in the banishment of certain other objectionable characters. I regret to say that some of these were ladies. It is but due to the sex, however, to state that their impropriety was professional, and it was only in such easily established standards of evil that Poker Flat ventured to sit in judgment.

Mr. Oakhurst was right in supposing that he was included in this category. A few of the committee had urged hanging him as a possible example and a sure method of reimbursing themselves from his pockets of the sums he had won from them. "It's agin justice," said Jim Wheeler, "to let this yer young man from Roaring Camp—an entire stranger—carry away our money." But a crude sentiment of equity residing in the breasts of those who had been fortunate enough to win from Mr. Oakhurst overruled this narrower local prejudice.

Mr. Oakhurst received his sentence with philosophic calmness, none the less coolly that he was aware of the hesitation of his judges. He was too much of a gambler not to accept fate. With him life was at best an uncertain game, and he recognized the usual percentage in favor of the dealer.

A body of armed men accompanied the deported wickedness of Poker Flat to the outskirts of the settlement. Besides Mr. Oakhurst, who was known to be a coolly desperate man, and for whose intimidation the armed escort was intended, the expatriated party consisted of a young woman familiarly known as "The Duchess"; another who had won the title of "Mother Shipton"; and "Uncle Billy," a suspected sluice-robber and confirmed drunkard. The cavalcade provoked no comments from the spectators, nor was any word uttered by the escort. Only when the gulch which marked the uttermost limit of Poker Flat was reached, the leader spoke briefly and to the point. The exiles were forbidden to return at the peril of their lives.

As the escort disappeared, their pent-up feelings found vent in a few hysterical tears from the Duchess, some bad language from Mother Shipton, and a Parthian volley of expletives from Uncle Billy. The philosophic Oakhurst alone remained silent. He listened calmly to Mother Shipton's desire to cut somebody's heart out, to the repeated statements of the Duchess that she would die in the road, and to the alarming oaths that seemed to be bumped out of Uncle Billy as he rode forward. With the easy good humor characteristic of his class, he insisted upon exchanging his own riding-horse, "Five-Spot," for the sorry mule which the Duchess rode. But even this act did not draw the party into any closer sympathy. The young woman readjusted her somewhat dragged plumes with a feeble, faded coquetry; Mother Shipton eyed the possessor of "Five-Spot" with malevolence, and Uncle Billy included the whole party in one sweeping anathema.

The road to Sandy Bar—a camp that, not having as yet experienced the regenerating influences of Poker Flat, consequently seemed to offer some invitation to the emigrants—lay over a steep mountain range. It was distant a day's severe travel. In that advanced season the party soon passed out of the moist, temperate regions of the foothills into the dry, cold, bracing air of the Sierras. The trail was narrow and difficult. At noon the Duchess, rolling out of her saddle upon the ground, declared her intention of going no farther, and the party halted.

The spot was singularly wild and impressive. A wooded amphitheatre, surrounded on three sides by precipitous cliffs of naked granite, sloped gently toward the crest of another precipice that overlooked the valley. It was, undoubtedly, the most suitable spot for a camp, had camping been advisable. But Mr. Oakhurst knew that scarcely half the journey to Sandy Bar was accomplished, and the party were not equipped or provisioned for delay. This fact he pointed out to his companions curtly, with a philosophic commentary on the folly of "throwing up their hand before the game was played out." But they were furnished with liquor, which in this emergency stood them in place of food, fuel, rest, and prescience. In spite of his remonstrances, it was not long before they were more or less under its influence. Uncle Billy passed rapidly from a bellicose state into one of stupor, the Duchess became maudlin, and Mother Shipton snored. Mr. Oakhurst alone remained erect, leaning against a rock, calmly surveying them.

Mr. Oakhurst did not drink. It interfered with a profession which required coolness, impassiveness, and presence of mind, and, in his own language, he "couldn't afford it." As he gazed at his recumbent fellow exiles, the loneliness begotten of his pariah trade, his habits of life, his very vices, for the first time seriously oppressed him. He bestirred himself in dusting his black clothes, washing his hands and face, and other acts characteristic of his studiously neat habits, and for a moment forgot his annoyance. The thought of deserting his weaker and more pitiable companions never perhaps occurred to him. Yet he could not help feeling the want of that excitement which, singularly enough, was most conducive to that calm equanimity for which he was notorious. He looked at the gloomy walls that rose a thousand feet sheer above the circling pines around him, at the sky ominously clouded, at the valley below, already deepening into shadow; and, doing so, suddenly he heard his own name called.

A horseman slowly ascended the trail. In the fresh open face of the newcomer Mr. Oakhurst recognized Tom Simson, otherwise known as "The Innocent," of Sandy Bar. He had met him some months before over a "little game," and had, with perfect equanimity, won the entire fortune —amounting to some forty dollars—of that guileless youth. After the game was finished, Mr. Oakhurst drew the youthful speculator behind the door and thus addressed him: "Tommy, you're a good little man, but you can't gamble worth a cent. Don't try it over again." He then handed him his money back, pushed him gently from the room, and so made a devoted slave of Tom Simson.

There was a remembrance of this in his boyish and enthusiastic greeting of Mr. Oakhurst. He had started, he said, to go to Poker Flat to seek his fortune. "Alone?" No, not exactly alone; in fact (a giggle), he had run away with Piney Woods. Didn't Mr. Oakhurst remember Piney? She that used to wait on the table at the Temperance House? They had been engaged a long time, but old Jake Woods had objected, and so they had run away, and were going to Poker Flat to be married, and here they were. And they were tired out, and how lucky it was they had found a place to camp, and company. All this the Innocent delivered rapidly, while Piney, a stout, comely damsel of fifteen, emerged from behind the pine-tree, where she had been blushing unseen, and rode to the side of her lover.

Mr. Oakhurst seldom troubled himself with sentiment, still less with propriety; but he had a vague idea that the situation was not fortunate. He retained, however, his presence of mind sufficiently to kick Uncle Billy, who was about to say something, and Uncle Billy was sober enough to recognize in Mr. Oakhurst's kick a superior power that would not bear trifling. He then endeavored to dissuade Tom Simson from delaying further, but in vain. He even pointed out the fact that there was no provision, nor means of making a camp. But, unluckily, the Innocent met this objection by assuring the party that he was provided with an extra mule loaded with provisions, and by the discovery of a rude attempt at a log house near the trail. "Piney can stay with Mrs. Oakhurst," said the Innocent, pointing to the Duchess, "and I can shift for myself."

Nothing but Mr. Oakhurst's admonishing foot saved Uncle Billy from bursting into a roar of laughter. As it was, he felt compelled to retire up the cañon until he could recover his gravity. There he confided the joke to the tall pine-trees, with many slaps of his leg, contortions of his face, and the usual profanity. But when he returned to the party, he found them seated by a fire—for the air had grown strangely chill and the sky overcast—in apparently amicable conversation. Piney was actually talking in an impulsive girlish fashion to the Duchess who was listening with an interest and animation she had not shown for many days. The Innocent was holding forth, apparently with equal effect, to Mr. Oakhurst and Mother Shipton, who was actually relaxing into amiability. "Is this yer a d—d picnic?" said Uncle Billy, with inward scorn, as he surveyed the sylvan group, the glancing firelight, and the tethered animals in the foreground. Suddenly an idea mingled with the alcoholic fumes that disturbed his brain. It was apparently of a jocular nature, for he felt impelled to slap his leg again and cram his fist into his mouth.

As the shadows crept slowly up the mountain, a slight breeze rocked the tops of the pine-trees and moaned through their long and gloomy aisles. The ruined cabin, patched and covered with pine boughs, was set apart for the ladies. As the lovers parted, they unaffectedly exchanged a kiss, so honest and sincere that it might have been heard above the swaying pines. The frail Duchess and the malevolent Mother Shipton were probably too stunned to remark upon this last evidence of simplicity, and so turned without a word to the hut. The fire was replenished, the men lay down before the door, and in a few minutes were asleep.

Mr. Oakhurst was a light sleeper. Toward morning he awoke benumbed and cold. As he stirred the dying fire, the wind, which was now blowing strongly, brought to his cheek that which caused the blood to leave it, —snow!

He started to his feet with the intention of awakening the sleepers, for there was no time to lose. But turning to where Uncle Billy had been lying, he found him gone. A suspicion leaped to his brain, and a curse to his lips. He ran to the spot where the mules had been tethered—they were no longer there. The tracks were already rapidly disappearing in the snow.

The momentary excitement brought Mr. Oakhurst back to the fire with his usual calm. He did not waken the sleepers. The Innocent slumbered peacefully, with a smile on his good-humored, freckled face; the virgin Piney slept beside her frailer sisters as sweetly as though attended by celestial guardians; and Mr. Oakhurst, drawing his blanket over his shoulders, stroked his mustaches and waited for the dawn. It came slowly in a whirling mist of snowflakes that dazzled and confused the eye. What could be seen of the landscape appeared magically changed. He looked over the valley, and summed up the present and future in two words, "Snowed in!"

A careful inventory of the provisions, which, fortunately for the party, had been stored within the hut, and so escaped the felonious fingers of Uncle Billy, disclosed the fact that with care and prudence they might last ten days longer. "That is," said Mr. Oakhurst *sotto voce* to the Innocent, "if you're willing to board us. If you ain't—and perhaps you'd better not

—you can wait till Uncle Billy gets back with provisions." For some occult reason, Mr. Oakhurst could not bring himself to disclose Uncle Billy's rascality, and so offered the hypothesis that he had wandered from the camp and had accidentally stampeded the animals. He dropped a warning to the Duchess and Mother Shipton, who of course knew the facts of their associate's defection. "They'll find out the truth about us *all* when they find out anything," he added significantly, "and there's no good frightening them now."

Tom Simson not only put all his worldly store at the disposal of Mr. Oakhurst, but seemed to enjoy the prospect of their enforced seclusion. "We'll have a good camp for a week, and then the snow'll melt, and we'll all go back together." The cheerful gaiety of the young man and Mr. Oakhurst's calm infected the others. The Innocent, with the aid of pine boughs, extemporized a thatch for the roofless cabin, and the Duchess directed Piney in the rearrangement of the interior with a taste and tact that opened the blue eyes of that provincial maiden to their fullest extent. "I reckon now you're used to fine things at Poker Flat," said Piney. The Duchess turned away sharply to conceal something that reddened her cheeks through their professional tint, and Mother Shipton requested Piney not to "chatter." But when Mr. Oakhurst returned from a weary search for the trail, he heard the sound of happy laughter echoed from the rocks. He stopped in some alarm, and his thoughts naturally reverted to the whiskey, which he had prudently cachéd. "And yet it don't somehow sound like whiskey," said the gambler. It was not until he caught sight of the blazing fire through the still blinding storm, and the group around it, that he settled to the conviction that it was "square fun."

Whether Mr. Oakhurst had cachéd his cards with the whiskey as something debarred the free access of the community, I cannot say. It was certain that, in Mother Shipton's words, he "didn't say 'cards' once" during that evening. Haply the time was beguiled by an accordion, produced somewhat ostentatiously by Tom Simson from his pack. Notwithstanding some difficulties attending the manipulation of this instrument, Piney Woods managed to pluck several reluctant melodies from its keys, to an accompaniment by the Innocent on a pair of bone castanets. But the crowning festivity of the evening was reached in a rude camp-meeting hymn, which the lovers, joining hands, sang with great earnestness and vociferation. I fear that a certain defiant tone and Covenanter's swing to its chorus, rather than any devotional quality, caused it speedily to infect the others, who at last joined in the refrain:—

> "I'm proud to live in the service of the Lord,
> I'm bound to die in His army."

The pines rocked, the storm eddied and whirled above the miserable group, and the flames of their altar leaped heavenward, as if in token of the vow.

At midnight the storm abated, the rolling clouds parted, and the stars glittered keenly above the sleeping camp. Mr. Oakhurst, whose professional habits enabled him to live on the smallest possible amount of sleep, in dividing the watch with Tom Simson somehow managed to take upon himself the greater part of that duty. He excused himself to the Innocent by saying that he had "often been a week without sleep." "Doing what?" asked Tom. "Poker!" replied Oakhurst sententiously. "When a man gets a streak of luck,—nigger-luck,—he don't get tired. The luck gives in first. Luck," continued the gambler reflectively, "is a mighty queer thing. All you know about it for certain is that it's bound to change. And it's finding out when it's going to change that makes you. We've had a streak of bad luck since we left Poker Flat,—you come along, and slap you get into it, too. If you can hold your cards right along you're all right. For," added the gambler, with cheerful irrelevance—

> " 'I'm proud to live in the service of the Lord,
> And I'm bound to die in His army.' "

The third day came, and the sun, looking through the white-curtained valley, saw the outcasts divide their slowly decreasing store of provisions for the morning meal. It was one of the peculiarities of that mountain climate that its rays diffused a kindly warmth over the wintry landscape, as if in regretful commiseration of the past. But it revealed drift on drift of snow piled high around the hut,—a hopeless, uncharted, trackless sea of white lying below the rocky shores to which the castaways still clung. Through the marvelously clear air the smoke of the pastoral village of Poker Flat rose miles away. Mother Shipton saw it, and from a remote pinnacle of her rocky fastness hurled in that direction a final malediction. It was her last vituperative attempt, and perhaps for that reason was invested with a certain degree of sublimity. It did her good, she privately informed the Duchess. "Just you go out there and cuss, and see." She then set herself to the task of amusing "the child," as she and the Duchess were pleased to call Piney. Piney was no chicken, but it was a soothing and original theory of the pair thus to account for the fact that she didn't swear and wasn't improper.

When night crept up again through the gorges, the reedy notes of the accordion rose and fell in fitful spasms and long-drawn gasps by the flickering campfire. But music failed to fill entirely the aching void left by insufficient food, and a new diversion was proposed by Piney, story-telling. Neither Mr. Oakhurst nor his female companions caring to relate their personal experiences, this plan would have failed too, but for the Innocent. Some months before he had chanced upon a stray copy of Mr. Pope's ingenious translation of the Iliad. He now proposed to narrate the principal incidents of that poem—having thoroughly mastered the argument and fairly forgotten the words—in the current vernacular of Sandy Bar. And so for the rest of that night the Homeric demi-gods again walked the earth. Trojan bully and wily Greek wrestled in the winds, and the great pines in the cañon seemed to bow to the wrath of the son of Peleus. Mr. Oakhurst listened with quiet satisfaction. Most especially was he interested in the fate of "Ash-heels," as the Innocent persisted in denominating the "swift-footed Achilles."

So, with small food and much of Homer and the accordion, a week passed over the heads of the outcasts. The sun again forsook them, and again from leaden skies the snowflakes were sifted over the land. Day by day closer around them drew the snowy circle, until at last they looked from their prison over drifted walls of dazzling white, that towered twenty feet above their heads. It became more and more difficult to replenish their fires, even from the fallen trees beside them, now half hidden in the drifts. And yet no one complained. The lovers turned from the dreary prospect and looked into each other's eyes, and were happy. Mr. Oakhurst settled himself coolly to the losing game before him. The Duchess, more cheerful than she had been, assumed the care of Piney. Only Mother Shipton—once the strongest of the party—seemed to sicken and fade. At midnight on the tenth day she called Oakhurst to her side. "I'm going," she said, in a voice of querulous weakness, "but don't say anything about it. Don't waken the kids. Take the bundle from under my head, and open it." Mr. Oakhurst did so. It contained Mother Shipton's rations for the last week, untouched. "Give 'em to the child," she said, pointing to the sleeping Piney. "You've starved yourself," said the gambler. "That's what they call it," said the woman querulously, as she lay down again, and, turning her face to the wall, passed quietly away.

The accordion and the bones were put aside that day, and Homer was forgotten. When the body of Mother Shipton had been committed to the snow, Mr. Oakhurst took the Innocent aside, and showed him a pair of snow-shoes, which he had fashioned from the old pack-saddle. "There's one chance in a hundred to save her yet," he said, pointing to Piney; "but it's there," he added, pointing toward Poker Flat. "If you can reach there in two days she's safe." "And you?" asked Tom Simson. "I'll stay here," was the curt reply.

The lovers parted with a long embrace. "You are not going, too?" said the Duchess, as she saw Mr. Oakhurst apparently waiting to accompany him. "As far as the cañon," he replied. He turned suddenly and kissed the Duchess, leaving her pallid face aflame, and her trembling limbs rigid with amazement.

Night came, but not Mr. Oakhurst. It brought the storm again and the whirling snow. Then the Duchess feeding the fire, found that some one had quietly piled beside the hut enough fuel to last a few days longer. The tears rose to her eyes, but she hid them from Piney.

The women slept but little. In the morning, looking into each other's faces, they read their fate. Neither spoke, but Piney, accepting the position of the stronger, drew near and placed her arm around the Duchess's waist.

They kept this attitude for the rest of the day. That night the storm reached its greatest fury, and, rending asunder the protecting vines, invaded the very hut.

Toward morning they found themselves unable to feed the fire, which gradually died away. As the embers slowly blackened, the Duchess crept closer to Piney, and broke the silence of many hours: "Piney, can you pray?" "No, dear," said Piney simply. The Duchess, without knowing exactly why, felt relieved, and, putting her head upon Piney's shoulder, spoke no more. And so reclining, the younger and purer pillowing the head of her soiled sister upon her virgin breast, they fell asleep.

The wind lulled as if it feared to waken them. Feathery drifts of snow, shaken from the long pine boughs, flew like white winged birds, and settled about them as they slept. The moon through the rifted clouds looked down upon what had been the camp. But all human stain, all trace of earthly travail, was hidden beneath the spotless mantle mercifully flung from above.

They slept all that day and the next, nor did they waken when voices and footsteps broke the silence of the camp. And when pitying fingers brushed the snow from their wan faces, you could scarcely have told from the equal peace that dwelt upon them which was she that had sinned. Even the law of Poker Flat recognized this, and turned away, leaving them still locked in each other's arms.

But at the head of the gulch, on one of the largest pine-trees, they found the deuce of clubs pinned to the bark with a bowie-knife. It bore the following, written in pencil in a firm hand: —

✝

BENEATH THIS TREE
LIES THE BODY
OF
JOHN OAKHURST,
WHO STRUCK A STREAK OF BAD LUCK
ON THE 23D OF NOVEMBER 1850,
AND
HANDED IN HIS CHECKS
ON THE 7TH DECEMBER, 1850.

⊥

And pulseless and cold, with a Derringer by his side and a bullet in his heart, though still calm as in life, beneath the snow lay he who was at once the strongest and yet the weakest of the outcasts of Poker Flat.

CHAPTER VII

PUNCTUATION

PUNCTUATION AND GRAMMAR

PUNCTUATION depends upon grammar. Until we understand how one part of a sentence is related to another, we cannot punctuate efficiently. Commas and semicolons are not marks to be added to a completed sentence for artistic effect; they are as much a part of a well-rounded sentence as are correctly placed pronouns and adverbs. Punctuation takes the place, in written sentences and paragraphs, of gestures, pauses, rising inflections, and the like in spoken sentences. Most people make use of some system of "vocal punctuation" in their speech.

Some sentences would be clear enough without any marks of punctuation. But readers have come to expect that sentences which are structurally alike will be punctuated in the same way. Certain "rules of punctuation" have therefore come into being, and the sensible writer will adhere to them.

The greatest number of problems in punctuation have to do with the use of the comma and the semicolon. We shall therefore take up the comma and the semicolon first, and then consider the colon, period, question mark, exclamation point, dash, apostrophe, quotation marks, parentheses, and square brackets.

THE COMMA

The **comma** [,] indicates a very short pause. Writers may differ about a few of its uses, but most of them agree about the four main uses which we shall now consider.

PRINCIPAL USES OF THE COMMA

(I) The comma is used in a compound sentence to separate clauses which are joined by a coordinating conjunction.

In our discussion of the conjunction in Chapter II, we learned that *and, but, for, or, nor,* and sometimes *yet* are coordinating conjunctions used to connect elements of equal grammatical value. When one of these conjunctions joins two independent clauses it must usually be preceded by a comma. If the clauses are so short that there is no danger of misreading, the comma may be omitted; if the clauses are long and contain other commas, a semicolon may replace the comma before the coordinating conjunction. The following sentences illustrate this use of the comma:

Santa Fé is one of the oldest cities in the United States, *and* it is also one of the most interesting.

Some historians claim that St. Augustine, a city in Florida, is older, *but* all agree that northern New Mexico has been continuously inhabited for centuries.

Perhaps you have read about this old city, *or* perhaps you have even visited Santa Fé.

Every year thousands of visitors attend the annual Fiesta, *for* this ancient celebration is as well-known in its way as is the Mardi Gras festival in New Orleans.

It is not a carnival precisely, *nor* is it a country fair.

Rather it is a combination of the two, *and* the narrow streets of the old city are thronged for three days with native New Mexicans, Indians, and tourists from all parts of the country.

Notice in the last sentence that *for* in the expression *for three days* is a preposition, not a conjunction. The coordinating conjunction *and* joins the two clauses of this compound sentence. In the fourth sentence beginning "Every year," *for* is a coordinating conjunction.

The plaza is crowded but the merrymakers are friendly.
    (Short clauses: no comma)

Some are costumed as Indians, with feathered headdresses, moccasins, and silver jewelry; some masquerade as Spanish conquerors, with helmet and breastplate; and some appear disguised as frontiersmen, with coonskin caps and fringed leather jackets.
    (Longer clauses with interior punctuation: semicolons instead of commas)

(II) The comma is used to set off an introductory modifier.

The normal order of the English sentence (**subject, predicate, modifiers**) is often varied and instead of

> The Fiesta gets off to a rousing start with the ceremony of burning Zozobra, or Old Man Gloom, in effigy

we may have

> With the ceremony of burning Zozobra, or Old Man Gloom, in effigy, the Fiesta gets off to a rousing start.

As in the preceding rule, the comma may be omitted if the clause or phrase is so short that misreading is unlikely:

> As the flames rise the crowd gives a shout.

(III)   The comma is used to separate items in a series of three or more items.

Words, phrases, or clauses may be used in a series, as in these examples:

WORDS   The Indians sold pottery, baskets, blankets, and silver rings.

PHRASES   They spread their wares on the sidewalks, on doorsteps, and especially under trees in the plaza.

CLAUSES   The Indian men took part in the tribal dances, the women sold pottery and trinkets, and the children ran gleefully about through the crowd.

However, where the final coordinating conjunction connects two words or expressions more closely bound together than the other items in the series, no comma is used before this final conjunction:

> The Indians brought beads, blankets, and bows and arrows.

> At the picnic we had steak, corn, and bread and butter.

Where the series consists of only two items, the comma is not used:

> The Indians sold blankets and silver rings.

> The Indian was able to speak in Spanish and in English.

Commas are used to separate members of a series or of a pair of co-ordinate words not connected by a conjunction:

> The Indian tried to sell me beads, arrowheads, pottery, blankets; finally he brought out a silver necklace.

> He was able to speak in his Indian language, in Spanish, in English.

> He was a tall, thin man with black, stringy hair.
> (Pairs of coordinate adjectives)

> He leaned against an old elm tree.
> (In this sentence, *old* and *elm* are not coordinate modifiers. *Old* modifies the two words *elm tree*)

> NOTE: If the series is made up of long clauses containing commas or other interior punctuation, semicolons instead of commas may be used to separate the clauses from each other as in the last sentence under section I above.

(IV) The comma is used to set off non-restrictive modifiers.

(A) Relative clauses are either **restrictive** or **non-restrictive**. A restrictive clause restricts or limits the meaning of the word modified in such a way that the clause cannot be removed without changing the meaning of the sentence:

> The visitors *who refuse to wear costumes* seldom enjoy the Fiesta.

> Costumes *that are gaily colored* are suitable for both day and night, but costumes *that impede free movement* are undesirable.

The adjective clauses in the last two sentences are **restrictive** modifiers and should not be separated from their nouns by commas. If the clauses are removed, the sentences are radically changed. Observe that a single word may be substituted for each clause:

> *Uncostumed* visitors seldom enjoy the Fiesta.

> *Gay* costumes are suitable for both day and night, but *hampering* costumes are undesirable.

No comma is used to separate such single-word modifiers from their nouns. No comma is used with restrictive adjective clauses.

Some adverbial clauses are restrictive:

> We advise you not to eat Mexican food *unless you are accustomed to it.*

The dancing continues *until the sun comes up.*

Everyone is exhausted *when the three-day Fiesta ends.*

(B) **Non-restrictive** adjective clauses do not limit or restrict; they merely give additional information and have the value of appositives. Consequently, they may be removed without destroying the sentence, and they should be set off from the rest of the sentence by commas.

The Palace of the Governors, which occupies one side of the plaza, is worth visiting.

Lew Wallace, who in 1878 became governor of New Mexico, lived here for three years.

Ben Hur, which is his best-known book, was written in this building.

The scenery of New Mexico, *which resembles that of Palestine,* inspired Wallace to write his famous novel.

Some adverbial clauses are non-restrictive:

It is worthy of note that he had not visited the Holy Land when he wrote the book, *although he did visit it later.*

The rest of the building consists, *as you will discover,* of a museum.

Non-restrictive phrases or single words are set off by commas:

The cathedral, *built of brown stone,* was finally completed about 1880.

Willa Cather, *writing of Archbishop Lamy in a well-known book,* tells about his interest in the building of this church.

Standing before the cathedral, a statue commemorates the great archbishop.

NOTE: Restrictive phrases, like restrictive clauses, are not set off by commas:

The large building *adjoining the cathedral* is St. Vincent's Sanitarium.

The building *across the street* is the post office.

The postoffice having been built to resemble a Spanish mission, it harmonizes well with the older buildings nearby.

(See Absolute Phrases, pp. 65–66.)

Miscellaneous Uses of the Comma

(I) Parenthetical elements, such as transitional expressions or appositives, (when they are non-restrictive) are set off from the rest of the sentence by commas:

There are, to be sure, many other churches in Santa Fé.

One of them, in fact, is called the oldest church in the United States.

This church, the church of San Miguel, is very small.

(II) Dates, geographical expressions, parts of an address, titles and initials after proper names are, as a matter of convention, set off by commas:

Santa Fé was reconquered September 1, 1692.

Santa Fé, New Mexico, is today a city of some 35,000 inhabitants.

Her uncle's address is 500 Pecos Road, Santa Fé, New Mexico.

A lecture at the auditorium was given by James A. Purcell, Ph.D., who was introduced by Professor W. M. Whitney, curator.

The curator is listed in the directory as follows: Whitney, William Maxwell, M.A., Ph.D., Litt.D., curator of the Museum of Art.

(III) Short quotations, words of direct address, mild interjections, and the words *yes* and *no* are set off by commas:

"Dr. Purcell, do you mind if I ask a question?" said a man in the audience.

"Why, not at all," replied the speaker.

"Is it true, sir, that the ancestors of the present-day Indians were cliff-dwellers?"

"Yes, I believe that is true."

"Thank you, Dr. Purcell."

(IV) Commas are often used to emphasize a contrast between expressions which are coordinate:

The speaker dealt with the Pueblo Indians, not with the Apache Indians.

His speech was factual, yet interesting.

The audience was quiet, but interested.

(V) A comma is used to prevent misreading:

> Dr. Purcell is a recognized authority at home, and abroad his scholarly articles are widely read.

> As soon as the lecture ended, we went home, for our friends from New York were to arrive during the evening.

> The newspaper account next day said that Purcell's speech was an important one. That it was, was obvious to everyone who heard it.

Unnecessary Commas

Beginning writers, especially those who are uncertain about sentence structure, show a tendency to use the comma where it is not needed. In some sentences an extra comma does no particular damage; in others, an unnecessary comma may make the sentence difficult to read. As a general rule, do not use a comma between subject and verb, between verb and complement, between preposition and object, or between an adjective and the noun it modifies:

> The scenery of the Southwest has attracted many artists. (No comma after "Southwest")

> Many painters have bought or built homes in Santa Fé. (No comma after "built")

> Many of their homes are located on the Camino del Monte Sol. (No comma after "on")

> A number of well-known writers also live there most of the year. (No comma after "well-known")

(A) Do not use a comma before a title in italics or before an indirect quotation:

> I have recently been reading *Death Comes for the Archbishop*. (No comma after "reading")

> Martha was reading *Laughing Boy* by LaFarge. (No comma before or after *Laughing Boy*)

> One of my friends said recently that he did not care much for historical novels. (No comma after "recently")

(B) Do not use a comma before the first member of a series:

He reads short-stories, plays, and poetry. (No comma after "reads")

(C) Do not use a comma after the last member of a series:

He especially likes short, exciting, vivid tales. (No comma after "vivid")

(D) Do not use a comma to set off restrictive modifiers:

He spoke unkindly of the one man who had taken an interest in him. (No comma after "man")

(E) Do not use a comma after a descriptive expression which has the value of an adjective, when it precedes the name of a person:

The American playwright Eugene O'Neill wrote *Strange Interlude*. (No comma after "playwright")

However, when a descriptive expression follows the person's name, and is in apposition to the name, a comma should be used:

Eugene O'Neill, the American playwright, wrote *Strange Interlude*.

(See p. 191 for fuller discussion.)

THE SEMICOLON

The **semicolon** [;] indicates a longer pause than a comma.

PRINCIPAL USES OF THE SEMICOLON

The semicolon has three important uses:

(I) The semicolon is used to separate two independent clauses not joined by a coordinating conjunction:

The area of the United States in 1790 was 892,135 square miles; in 1960 it was 3,628,150 square miles.

The first important accession came in 1803; it is called the Louisiana Purchase.

When a conjunctive adverb or a transitional expression used like a conjunctive adverb occurs at the beginning of the second independent clause, use a semicolon before it:

194

The area acquired from Spain extended from Canada to the Gulf of Mexico; *in short,* the total area of the United States was now almost doubled.
(Transitional expression)

The Republic of Texas was acquired in 1845; *furthermore,* the successful conclusion of the Mexican War brought in an even vaster territory in 1848.
(Conjunctive adverb)

An important addition was Alaska, acquired in 1867; *equally important* were the Hawaiian and Philippine Islands and other outposts in the Pacific.
(Transitional expression)

The following list includes some of the most important of these transitional or explanatory expressions. (See also p. 53 for a list of conjunctive adverbs.)

after all	in addition
at length	in any event
at the same time	in brief
e.g. (= *exempli gratia*)	in fact
equally important	in the meantime
for example	on the contrary
for instance	on the other hand
for this purpose	to be sure
i.e. (= *id est*)	viz. (= *videlicet*)

(II) The semicolon is used to separate two independent clauses joined by a coordinating conjunction, if the clauses are long and if they contain commas:

In 1904, by an agreement with the Republic of Panama, the United States acquired control over a strip of land ten miles wide; and this acquisition of territory, though small, has proved to be of the utmost importance.

(III) The semicolon is used to separate clauses in a series if the clauses are long and if one or more of the clauses has interior punctuation:

The Canal Zone, as it is called, has an area of 549 square miles; for it the United States paid ten million dollars and agreed to make payments, annually, of $250,000; but the United States control does not extend to the cities of Panama and Colon.

Misuses of the Semicolon

(A) Do not use a semicolon between an independent clause and a dependent clause:

> The Canal Zone is a U.S. government reservation which is administered under the jurisdiction of the Secretary of the Army.
>> (No semicolon after "reservation")

(B) Do not use a semicolon before a participial modifier:

> Another great canal is the Suez Canal, extending a total distance of 100 miles.
>> (A comma, not a semicolon, after "Canal")

(C) Do not use a semicolon after the salutation in a letter:

> WRONG: Dear Sir;
> RIGHT: Dear Sir:
> RIGHT: Dear Sir,

(D) Do not use a semicolon before a direct quotation:

> WRONG: He said; "I see you got here all right."
> RIGHT: He said, "I see you got here all right."

THE COLON

The **colon** [:] is a mark of punctuation frequently used to show that something is to follow: a list, an important appositive, a series cf items, or a formal or lengthy quotation. The following sentences are illustrations:

> The article contains references to four kings: Louis XIV, Charles II, Philip I, and William II.

> When the speaker concluded, the audience remembered one word of his talk especially: cooperation.

> Marion has several reasons to be happy: she likes her apartment, she likes her children, and she likes her work.

> The question before us today is: How long are we to permit such graft and corruption to continue?

To emphasize the second of two clauses in a compound sentence, a colon may be used instead of a semicolon:

> Because of the leaky roof the room was more than uncomfortable: it was actually dangerous.

A colon is often used when the second clause is a restatement or amplification of the first, as in this sentence:

> The trouble with Mr. McCabe is that he is lazy and dishonest: lazy about everything not directly connected with his personal comforts, dishonest in minor matters.

Certain uses of the colon have become fixed by convention. They include the following:

1. When a quotation is introduced directly, that is, without a verb such as *said, remarked, answered,* and the like:

    > George hesitated for a moment or two: "Just what do you expect me to say?"

2. To separate the minute figures from the hour figures in expressions of time, chapters from books of the Bible, scenes from acts of a play, sub-titles from titles of books, and publisher from place of publication in a bibliography:

    > 3:30 a.m.
    > the 5:15 train
    > I Kings 8:1-6
    > *Macbeth* III:3
    > New York: Doubleday & Co., Inc.,1966.

3. After the salutation in a formal or business letter:

    > Gentlemen:
    >
    > Dear Dr. Phillips:

4. Often after such words as *namely:*

    > He had two especial favorites among French novelists, namely: Anatole France and Marcel Proust.

THE PERIOD

The **period,** or "full stop," [.] indicates the completion of a thought unit.

A declarative sentence is followed by a period:

> James telephoned us yesterday.
> He said that he had enlisted in the Navy.
> We were surprised, because we had always thought he preferred the Marines.

Unless an imperative sentence is also an exclamatory sentence, it is followed by a period:

> Be sure to see him before he leaves.
> Give him my best regards.

But a strongly imperative sentence requires an exclamation point:

> Do it now!

Fragments that do the work of complete sentences require the appropriate end punctuation:

> "You won't forget, will you?"
> "No."
> "Will you do it soon?"
> "Yes."
> "At what time?"
> "Ten."
> "Good!"

With certain exceptions, all abbreviations require the period. (See list on pp. 216–220.)

> My brother lives in Watertown, N.Y., a city north of Syracuse, N.Y.
> He is employed by the construction firm of Baker, Wilson, and Co.; his immediate superior is Capt. Joseph M. Baker.
> This firm has built a number of large buildings, e.g., the Bijou Theater, the Robinson Department Store, the new post office, etc.

Observe that these sentences are punctuated as if the abbreviated words were spelled out in full. Commas, semicolons, and the like may follow the period marking an abbreviation If a sentence ends with a period and an abbreviation requiring a period, one period only is used. But if an interrogative or exclamatory sentence ends with an abbreviation, the question mark or exclamation point follows the period:

> Do you mean Watertown, N.Y. or Watertown, Me.?
> You can't mean Watertown, Me.!

ELLIPSIS PERIODS

An omission is usually indicated by three spaced periods [. . .], called **ellipsis periods,** when the omission is in the middle of a sentence. When the ellipsis indicates the omission of words at the end of a declarative sentence, four periods are used, the fourth showing the end of the sentence. The following example illustrates both cases:

> "I enter'd upon the execution of this plan for self-examination, and continu'd it . . . for some time. I was surpris'd to find myself so much fuller of faults than I had imagined . . ."—FRANKLIN.

If the thought ending in an ellipsis is a question or an exclamation, the appropriate punctuation mark should follow three ellipsis periods.

> "Leave at once, or . . . !" shouted his father.
> "Do you think he . . . ? No. It's out of the question."

THE QUESTION MARK

The **question mark** [?] is used after direct questions but not after indirect questions:

> Do you mean that?
> You mean that?
> "Do you mean that?" asked my mother.
> In debating the question, What shall be done with the surplus in the treasury? the group spent two hours.
>> (Direct question inserted in a declarative sentence)
> In debating the question of what shall be done with the surplus in the treasury the group spent two hours.
>> (Indirect question)

A question mark in parentheses indicates the author's doubt or uncertainty about the material immediately preceding:

> We believe there were three editions altogether: 1702, 1705 (?), and 1710.

In a long interrogative sentence, question marks after each of the interrogative elements provide greater emphasis:

> If this bill is passed, what is the average man to do about his job? his family? his home? his retirement?

THE EXCLAMATION POINT

The **exclamation point** [!] is used after expressions of strong feeling or emotion, but should be used sparingly:

> Heavens! Is it possible!
> Stop where you are!
> Help! I'm trapped!

THE DASH

The **dash** [—] shows a sudden change of thought within a sentence. It is used singly or in pairs, but it should be used sparingly. The following sentences illustrate the principal uses of the dash:

Interruption:

> Our entire supply of food—meat, potatoes, bread, and coffee—disappeared during the night.
>
> I've been waiting for—ah, there she is, across the street!
>
> Considering everything—Johnson thought to himself—it would be a mistake to decline the offer.

Before a summing-up statement:

> The heat, the need for close application, the lack of proper ventilation —these forced him to complain to his boss.

Special uses:

After date of birth:

> (1890—   )

After a quotation:

> —Emerson

After an unfinished sentence:

> He said, "I hope you mean that; if not—."

To show uncertainty:

"He can't be—he can't be gone!" Bill muttered.

After an emphatic appositive:

He knew then what he must do—send her a telegram.

THE HYPHEN

The **hyphen** [-] is used to join the parts of certain compound words or expressions. Another use of the hyphen is to indicate the division of a word at the end of a line.

For a discussion of the use of the hyphen, with rules and examples, see pages 226–228. See also pages 224–225 for rules on the correct division of words into syllables, and for the points at which words may be divided at the end of lines.

The general term for the use of hyphens is *hyphenation.*

THE APOSTROPHE

The **apostrophe** ['] is used in these ways:

The apostrophe and *s* ['s] are used to form the possessive case of singular or plural nouns not ending in *s.*

This is a man's job.
These are men's jobs.
Children's games are not always simple.
My brother-in-law's great love is conversation.
She reads Addison and Steele's essays.

The apostrophe alone forms the possessive case of plural nouns ending in *s.*

He rang the Wilsons' doorbell.
The two dogs' tracks were plainly visible.
The ladies' help was much appreciated.

The apostrophe and *s* ['s] form the possessive case of singular nouns ending in *s* or an *s*-sound, but the apostrophe alone may be used to avoid an unpleasant repetition of the *s*-sound.

> Willis's hat is old.
> Willis' shirt is torn.
> For goodness' sake, have him get a new one.

The apostrophe and *s* ['s] are used to form the possessive case of indefinite pronouns.

> It is anybody's game so far.
> One's opinion is as good as another's.
> He took somebody else's place by mistake.

The apostrophe and *s* ['s] are used to form the plurals of letters, figures, and words spoken of as words.

> Mind your p's and q's.
> Your 11's look too much like your 77's.
> There are too many *and's* in this sentence.

The apostrophe is used in contractions to show that letters or figures have been omitted.

> Don't do it. (Do not do it.)
> He was born in '05. (1905)
> It's a great opportunity. (It is)
> I'll be there at ten o'clock. (I will)

For discussion of Contraction, see pages 220–222.

QUOTATION MARKS

Double quotation marks [" "] and **single quotation marks** [' '] have certain conventional uses:

The exact words of a speaker quoted directly must be enclosed in double quotation marks. The quoted material may be a sentence, more than a sentence, or less than a sentence. Quotation marks are not to be used before and after each sentence of a quotation of several consecutive sentences. If such a quotation runs to more than one paragraph, double quotation marks are to be used at the beginning of each paragraph and at the end of the last one. If the quotation is interrupted by words of explanation such as *he said* or *she replied,* the actual quoted words only are to be enclosed in quotation marks.

Single quotation marks are used at the beginning and end of a quotation within a quotation.

When a comma, period, semicolon, or colon is needed at the point where closing quotation marks appear, it is customary to follow the rule preferred by most printers, namely to place commas and periods *inside* the quotation marks, and to place semicolons and colons *outside* the quotation marks. This practice is recommended by printers because it is considered pleasing in appearance.

However, the rule as to whether to place a question mark or an exclamation point inside or outside a closing quotation mark is that the question mark or exclamation point goes inside the quotation mark if the passage quoted is a question or exclamation, and goes outside if the passage quoted is not itself a question or exclamation, but is only part of a larger unit which is a question or exclamation.

The placing of question marks and exclamation points in relation to closing quotation marks is therefore a matter of whether they belong *logically* to the quotation or not. Although we have recommended the printer's rule, it should be pointed out here that many writers prefer to follow *logical* punctuation also in the placing of commas, periods, semicolons, and colons, namely, placing each mark either inside or outside the quotation mark, depending on whether the punctuation is or is not part of the quotation.

Either the *printer's* method or the *logical* method is correct provided it is followed *systematically.* Be sure to be *consistent* in applying the method which you decide to use.

Observe how quotation marks are used in the following:

As they reached home, Elizabeth said, "What a lovely day it has been!"

"I'm glad you were able to be with us," said her cousin. "Perhaps we can take another trip next week."

"Perhaps we can arrange it, but—" said Elizabeth hesitantly.

"But what?" asked her cousin.

"I may have to work overtime all next week." Elizabeth seemed upset at the thought.

"Do you know what Bill said about you? He said, 'She is the most interesting girl I've ever met.' "

Quotation marks are used to call attention to technical words, to words used in some humorous or ironical way, and to slang words.

> The lecturer referred to "relativity" in the sense in which Einstein uses the term.

> He also spoke of the Freudian method of psychiatric therapy, which is also known as "psychoanalysis."

> This rainy day is certainly "perfect" for seeing a football game.

> As my young brother put it, he "really went to town."

(See also Use of Italics, pp. 228–232.)

PARENTHESES

Marks of parenthesis, or **parentheses,** [( )] are used before and after expressions that are loosely related to the rest of the sentence. Punctuation marks at the end of parenthetical material are placed inside the parentheses if they belong to the parenthetical material. However, punctuation which belongs to a larger unit than the parentheses is placed outside the parentheses:

> I am trying to learn their names (there are over fifty of them, as it happens, in the one office), and it isn't easy to do.

> Burton's last novel (it is all about frontier life) was reviewed in yesterday's paper.

Parentheses are used for purposes of accuracy to enclose numerals which follow the same amount expressed in words, or to enclose numbers and letters used to separate items in a series:

> I am sending with this a postal order for eighty-five dollars ($85.00).

> We shall study (1) the comma, (2) the semicolon, and (3) the period.

SQUARE BRACKETS

Square brackets [[ ]] indicate that the writer is adding an explanation or comment to quoted material:

> "Your account of the memorial service [for Major Clark] is typical of the carelessness of modern journalism. Cancel my subscription at once."

> This young man [Christopher Marlowe] enjoyed a great reputation in his day. His first play [*Tamburlaine*] set the fashion for tragedy and was widely imitated.

EXERCISES

A. Re-write these sentences, using commas wherever needed to set off non-restrictive modifiers:

(1) The Nobel Fund through which prizes are awarded each year was established by Alfred B. Nobel.

(2) Nobel who was the inventor of dynamite died on December 10, 1896.

(3) The fund which he established is now managed by a Board of Directors.

(4) It was designed to reward those persons who in the opinion of the board had contributed most during the previous year to the service of mankind.

(5) Prominent persons including a number of Americans are among those who have received the Nobel Prize.

(6) Although the Nobel Prize for Peace was not awarded in 1924 it was awarded the next year to Charles G. Dawes an American and to Sir Austen Chamberlain an Englishman.

(7) Previously in 1919 it had been awarded to Woodrow Wilson.

(8) Mme. Curie who twice received the prize is among the best-known winners.

(9) The discoverer of insulin Dr. Banting shared the prize in 1923 with Dr. Macleod.

(10) Sinclair Lewis who has written many novels of distinction was the first American to receive the Nobel Prize for Literature.

B. Re-write these sentences, supplying any missing commas:

(1) Another famous trust fund was established by Cecil John Rhodes a South African who died in 1902.

(2) Originally according to the provisions of the will two scholarships at Oxford were established for eligible young men in each of the states in this country.

(3) In addition scholarships were made available to the several states and provinces in Canada South Africa and Australia and to students in Newfoundland New Zealand Jamaica Bermuda and Malta.

(4) The fund as subsequently modified assigns thirty-two scholarships each year to the United States and the country for the purposes of election is divided into districts each consisting of several states.

(5) Four scholars are chosen from each district yearly but each scholar represents his own state.

(6) A candidate must meet certain requirements: he must be over seventeen and not over twenty-four years of age he must be of at least junior standing in college and he must show evidence of ability and interest in scholarship and athletics.

(7) Normally a Rhodes Scholar remains at Oxford for two years but he may apply for an additional third year.

(8) The Rhodes Scholars numbering usually about two hundred are as a rule fairly equally divided between the British Empire and the United States.

(9) The five scholarships which were awarded to Germany were annulled in 1916 later restored and still later withdrawn once again.

(10) After the outbreak of the Second World War the Rhodes Scholarships were suspended for the duration.

C. Supply semicolons and colons wherever needed in the following sentences:

(1) Great trust funds for philanthropic purposes have been established in this country there are some twenty-five such public trusts now in operation.

(2) Those established with an original endowment of more than $10,000,000 include the following the Ford Foundation, the Rockefeller Foundation, the Carnegie Corporation of New York, the Juilliard Foundation, and the Duke Endowment.

(3) American foundations make possible research in a variety of fields education, social welfare, medicine, public health, housing, economics, and many others.

(4) The Guggenheim Memorial fellowships are granted for research in many fields of knowledge they are awarded to capable and talented persons, regardless of race, color, or creed.

(5) One of the many funds set up by Andrew Carnegie is the Carnegie Hero Fund Commission it awards medals and sums of money to heroes and heroines or to their dependents.

D. The following sentences contain unnecessary commas. Remove them.

(1) The Seven Wonders of the World are, the Pyramids, the Hanging Gardens of Babylon, the Temple of Diana, the Statue of Jupiter

Olympus, the Mausoleum, the Pharos of Alexandria, and the Colossus of Rhodes.

(2) The best-known of these, is the Pyramids of Egypt.

(3) The great stone lion called the Sphinx, was hewn, we believe, from a single stone.

(4) The Colossus of Rhodes must not be confused with the Coliseum: the former was a statue of Apollo; the latter is that great amphitheatre, which still stands in Rome.

(5) Another famous monument of antiquity, is Stonehenge, a group of huge stones on Salisbury Plain, in England.

E. Re-write the following sentences, supplying all necessary marks of punctuation:

(1) The Monroe Doctrine one of the important documents of history was incorporated in President Monroes message to Congress on December 2 1823

(2) The result of much consultation with the members of the Cabinet the doctrine asserted that "the American continents . . . are henceforth not to be considered as subjects for future colonization by any European powers

(3) Jefferson echoing the Farewell Address of Washington declared Our first and fundamental maxim should be never to entangle ourselves in the broils of Europe

(4) The Monroe Doctrine has been discussed re-examined and debated both at home and abroad during the last century

(5) This discussion we have every reason to believe will continue

F. Supply marks of punctuation wherever needed in the following passage and compare your version with that given on page 340.

It was near sunset I repeat and we were crossing the bay of Gibraltar I stood on the prow of the vessel with my eyes intently fixed on the mountain fortress which though I had seen it several times before filled my mind with admiration and interest Viewed from this situation it certainly if it resembles any animate object in nature has something of the appearance of a terrible couchant lion whose stupendous head menaces Spain Had I been dreaming I should almost have concluded it to be the genius of Africa in the shape of its most puissant monster who had bounded over the sea from the clime of sand and sun bent on the destruction of the rival continent more especially as the hue of its stony sides its crest and chine is tawny even as that of the hide of the desert king A hostile lion has it almost invariably proved to Spain at least since it first began to play a part in history which was at the time when Tarik seized and fortified it It has for the most part been in the hands of foreigners first the swarthy and turbaned Moor possessed it and it is now tenanted by a fair haired race from a distant isle Though a part of Spain it seems to disavow the connection and at the end of a long narrow sandy isthmus almost level with the sea raising its blasted and perpendicular brow to denounce the crimes which deform the history of that fair and majestic land.

—GEORGE BORROW, *The Bible in Spain.*

G. The following sentences are designed to test your ability to use the dash, the apostrophe, quotation marks, parentheses, and the like. Supply all necessary marks of punctuation:

(1) Halt who goes there

(2) The new boarder hes from Louisiana speaks with a delightful accent

(3) Everything important life liberty the pursuit of happiness seemed about to be lost forever

(4) Freedom of speech freedom from want freedom from fear freedom of religion these they felt were great ideals

(5) The applicant identified himself as follows George Albert Wilson 2205 Mill St Smithtown California

(6) Its its impossible stammered the young man Do you really think hed

(7) Because of his abilities as a leader Sam was more than just a likely candidate he was the one man for the job

(8) I have collected many things in my time stamps coins arrowheads books and cigarbands.

(9) Ill say hes upset said my room-mate He was shouting Down with examinations

(10) Our clubs last meeting was devoted to a debate on the question Shall the constitution be revised

CHAPTER VIII

CAPITALIZATION, ABBREVIATION, AND MANUSCRIPT FORM

CLOSELY ALLIED to punctuation are a number of problems, often grouped together under the heading "Mechanics of Writing." They include the use of capital letters, the proper use of abbreviations, the problem of whether to use figures or words in the representation of numerals, the proper division of words into syllables, the hyphen and its several uses, and the question of using roman or italic type.

In the preparation of the final draft of a manuscript or other written material, such matters as legibility, spacing, indention, page numbers, and titles are important. All of these are discussed in this chapter under the heading "Manuscript Form."

CAPITALIZATION

Modern writers use capital letters more sparingly than did writers of earlier times. The best usage calls for capitals under the following circumstances:

I. Capitalize the pronoun *I*, the word *O* (but not *oh* unless it comes at the beginning of a sentence), *No.* (the abbreviation of *number*), and *B.C.* and *A.D.* Use either *A.M.* and *P.M.* or *a.m.* and *p.m.*

> He asked me to do what I could about it.
> Andy replied, "I can't seem to find . . . oh, here it is, after all!"
> Oh, how pleased she was about it!
> "O wild West Wind, thou breath of Autumn's being . . ."
> He was born in 40 B.C. and died in A.D. 12.
>   (Notice that A.D. precedes the numeral.)
> The meeting began at 3:15 P.M. (or 3:15 p.m.)

II. Capitalize the first word of a sentence, of a line of poetry, of a sentence directly quoted, of a formal question or answer:

> What a glorious day it is!
> How are you enjoying your visit?
> We are having a splendid time, thank you.
> Bill added: "We hope to stay an extra week."
> "Come in for a minute," I said, "if you can spare the time."
> Resolved: That this meeting favors the sales tax.
> The question is, Can we raise enough money?

> > "Day after day, day after day,
> > We stuck, nor breath nor motion;
> > As idle as a painted ship
> > Upon a painted ocean.
> >
> > "Water, water, everywhere,
> > And all the boards did shrink;
> > Water, water, everywhere,
> > Nor any drop to drink."

Observe that capitals are not used with fragments incorporated in a sentence, unless the fragment stands for a complete sentence.

COMPARE: When we asked him to join us, he said he "wasn't feeling up to it."

When we asked him to join us, he said, "Unfortunately, I'm not feeling up to it."

BUT: When we asked them to join us, he said No and she said Yes.

A parenthetical sentence within another sentence does not begin with a capital:

> When he telephoned me (he actually did telephone) he said he was coming down with a cold.

III. Capitalize proper names, whether written in full or abbreviated:

PERSONS: John Quincy Adams
John Q. Adams
J. Q. Adams
William Wordsworth
William the Conqueror

John Smith
Captain John Smith
Capt. John Smith

PLACES AND
THINGS:
Atlanta, Georgia   (*city, state*)
Chrysler Building   (*building*)
Central Park   (*park*)
France   (*country*)
Hawthorne Boulevard   (*street*)
Tioga County   (*county*)
Oxfordshire   (*shire*)
Hunter College   (*educational institution*)
Forty-second Street   (*street*)
Australia   (*country*)
Lake Superior   (*lake*)
Lafayette   (*ship*)
Boy Scouts of America   (*organization*)
Mohawk River   (*river*)
City of Homes and Churches   (*nickname*)
the Empire State   (*nickname*)
Doubleday & Co., Inc.   (*organization*)
University Heights   (*section of city*)
East Texas   (*section of state*)
Mars   (*planet*)
Old Glory   (*flag*)
the U.S. Air Force   (*organization*)
U.S. Steel   (*stock*)
the Federal Bureau of Investigation   (*organization*)

IV. Capitalize proper adjectives:

Belgian
Indian
American
Germanic
Semitic
Portuguese

V. Capitalize the first word and all important words in literary titles and division headings:

Man and Superman
The Return of the Native
Appendix II
Chapter VII
Hail, Columbia!

Yankee Doodle
"Kubla Khan"
Washington's *Second Inaugural Address*
the New York *World-Telegram*
Hamlet
the *Bell Telephone Hour* (television program)
the *National Geographic* (periodical)

VI. Capitalize the names of days of the week, months, important events or documents, special days, seasons (if they are personified), points of the compass (if they refer to specific localities), and ideas or qualities (if they are personified):

> Wednesday
> Ash Wednesday
> July
> Independence Day
> St. Patrick's Day
> the Battle of Gettysburg
> the Middle West
> the Middle Ages
> Magna Charta
> Declaration of Independence

VII. Capitalize the names of the Deity, churches, creeds, sacred scriptures, titles of honor, and academic degrees:

> God the Father
> the Bible
> the Koran
> the Old Testament
> Episcopal
> Quaker
> the Book of Job
> Catholic
> Justice Stone
> King George VI
> His Majesty
> His Excellency
> the Secretary of State
> the Pope
> Professor James Hanover, Ph.D.
> ex-President Eisenhower
> Doctor Roberts
> Dr. Roberts

VIII. Do not capitalize names that denote relationship unless they are used with a proper noun or in place of a proper noun:

We wrote to Uncle Henry about Mother's trouble.
It is comforting to have an uncle to help us out.
I spoke to Father about what Sarah's father said yesterday.
Alice is my younger sister.

IX. In letters, capitalize only the first and last words of the salutation and only the first word of the complimentary close:

Dear Sir:
My dear Madam:
Very truly yours,
Respectfully yours,

X. Do not capitalize for emphasis.

NOTE A: Proper nouns often become common nouns and lose the initial capital. In some expressions, however, the capital letter is retained. When in doubt, consult a good dictionary. Do not capitalize the following:

boycott	pasteurization
platonic	voltmeter
paris green	watt
china cup	mackintosh (*raincoat*)
manila rope	roman type

NOTE B: Current practice calls for the following usages:

ex-Governor Smith
James A. Harvey, Jr.
Robert Cunningham, Esq.
Alfred Thompson, M.A.
a high-school teacher
Middletown High School
the Missouri River
the river Missouri
the city of San Antonio
President Overton
Dr. L. S. Overton, president of Central College
A. L. Houghton, professor of chemistry
the Department of Chemistry
a senior at Hunter College
a member of the Freshman Class

213

ABBREVIATION

An abbreviation is a shortened form of a word and consists of certain key letters or of one or more beginning letters usually followed by a period. *New Jersey,* for example, is abbreviated *N.J.*

WHEN NOT TO ABBREVIATE

Where possible, avoid abbreviations in formal writing. Abbreviations often suggest informality, haste, or an attitude of indifference on the part of the writer, and they can be obscure or misleading.

Certain abbreviations, however, are almost obligatory in formal writing: *Mr., Mrs., Messrs., M., Mme., Mlle.,* and *St.* (for Saint). Observe that these abbreviations are used only before proper names:

> Mr. Frederick Smythe
> Messrs. Jackson and Hull
> St. Augustine (NEVER WRITE: He lived like a St.)

Because *Miss* (as a title) is not an abbreviation, no period is used after it:

> Miss Sarah Andrews
> the Misses Andrews

The following abbreviated titles are also permissible: *Sr., Jr., Esq., D.D., M.D., Ph.D.* and the like, when used after proper names:

> Richard Simpson, Jr.
> Archibald McVain, M.D.

Titles such as *Dr., Rev., Hon., Gen., Col., Lieut., Prof., Gov., Pres.,* and the like should be used only in informal writing and then only before full names:

> RIGHT: I wrote to Rev. George Philips about it.
> I wrote to the Reverend Dr. Philips.
> WRONG: I wrote to the Rev. about it.
> I wrote to Rev. Philips about it.
> I wrote Reverend Philips about it.

Such common abbreviations as *No., $, Co., A.M., P.M.* (or *a.m., p.m.*), *A.D.* and *B.C.* when used with other words, figures, or dates are sometimes appropriate but should be avoided whenever possible:

> She arrived home at 10:30 A.M. (or a.m.)
> (NOT: She arrived home during the A.M.)

Certain abbreviations of foreign words or expressions must be italicized; certain others in common use need not be italicized:

Use italics for:	*aet.*	*id.*
	et al.	*loc. cit.*
	et seq.	*op. cit.*
	ibid.	*vid.*
Do not italicize:	a.m.	etc.
	p.m.	i.e.
	cf.	viz.
	e.g.	vs.

It is considered inadvisable to abbreviate given names, names of days of the week, names of months, cities, states, and the like, except in lists. Even in addressing envelopes it is well to spell out names of states and countries:

Oregon	(NOT: Ore.)	Friday	(NOT: Fri.)
January	(NOT: Jan.)	George	(NOT: Geo.)
Missouri	(NOT: Mo.)	Canada	(NOT: Can.)

WHEN TO CAPITALIZE ABBREVIATIONS

Abbreviations are usually capitalized only if the full form of the word requires a capital. There are some exceptions, such as *No.* (for *number*) and *Q.E.D.* (for *quod erat demonstrandum*); also see some exceptions noted in the section immediately following.

ABBREVIATIONS THAT OMIT PERIODS

Some abbreviations, through their frequency of use or their clear advantage over long and cumbersome forms, have taken on some of the character of new words in their own right. There is a tendency today, especially in journalistic, scientific, technical, and political writing, to omit the periods in certain abbreviations. Good examples are: UN (United Nations); AFL-CIO (American Federation of Labor and Congress of Industrial Organizations); FBI (Federal Bureau of Investigation); FM (frequency modulation); DNA (deoxyribonucleic acid). When the periods are omitted, the abbreviation is capitalized whether or not the longer form is composed of proper names.

Periods are almost always omitted in an "acronym"—a new term coined to denote a pronounceable word that is made up of the initial letters of other words: ZIP code (Zone Improvement Plan code); UNESCO (United Nations Educational, Scientific, and Cultural Organization); SEATO (Southeast Asia Treaty Organization); LASER or laser (Light Amplification by Stimulated Electron Radiation). Similarly, "telescope words" such as COMSAT (Communications Satellite Corporation) and FORTRAN (Formula Translation—a data processing term) omit periods. Acronyms and telescope words are pronounced as words, and are sometimes written, like ordinary words, in lower-case letters.

For very long phrases or words, or in writing that repeatedly uses a term that happens to have a well-known abbreviation, acronym, or telescope word, it is preferable, even in formal writing, to use the shorter form. Unless the full meaning of this form is obvious to your audience, however, it is well to explain it at the first mention: "NASA (the National Aeronautics and Space Administration) was established in 1958."

ABBREVIATIONS COMMONLY USED

A.B.	*Artium Baccalaureus* (Lat., Bachelor of Arts)
abbr.	abbreviation; abbreviated
abl.	ablative
Abp., abp.	Archbishop
A.D.	*Anno Domini* (Lat., in the year of our Lord)
ad fin.	at the end
adj.	adjective
ad lib.	*ad libitum* (Lat., to the amount desired)
adv.	adverb
advt.	advertisement
A.L.A.	American Library Association
A.M.	*Artium Magister* (Lat., Master of Arts)
A.M. or a.m.	forenoon
anon.	anonymous
arch.	archaic
AS, A.S.	Anglo-Saxon
assn.	association
assoc.	associate; associated
A.V.	Authorized Version (of the Bible)
A.W.O.L.	absent without leave
B.A.	*Baccalaureus Artium* (Lat., Bachelor of Arts)
Bart.	Baronet

B.B.C. or BBC	British Broadcasting Corporation
B.C.	before Christ
Bib.	Biblical; Bible
Bibl., bibl.	Biblical; bibliographical
bibliog.	bibliography
biog.	biography; biographer; biographical
Brit.	Britannica; British; Britain
B.S.	Bachelor of Science
B.S.A.	Boy Scouts of America
c., circ.	*circa, circum* (Lat., about)
cap.	capitalize; capital
caps.	capital letters
cat.	catalogue
cc., c.c.	cubic centimeters; chapters; carbon copy
cf., cp.	compare
ch., chap.	chapter
cm.	centimeter
Co.	company; county
colloq.	colloquial
conj.	conjunction
contd. or cont.	continued
contr.	contraction; contrary
cop.	copyrighted
crit.	criticism; critical
cu. cm.	cubic centimeter
cwt.	hundredweight
d.	died
D.A.R. or DAR	Daughters of the American Revolution
D.D.	*Divinitatis Doctor* (Lat., Doctor of Divinity)
def.	definition; defined; definite
diag.	diagram
diam.	diameter
dial.	dialectal; dialect
dict.	diction; dictionary
D.N.B.	Dictionary of National Biography
do.	ditto (*Ital.*, the same)
D.V.	*Deo volente* (Lat., God willing)
DX	distance (radio term)
E.	east; English
ea.	each
ed.	edited; editor; edition
e.g.	*exempli gratia* (Lat., for example)
enc., encl.	enclosure
ency., encyc.	encyclopedia
Eng.	England; English
engr.	engineer; engraved; engraver; engraving
erron.	erroneous; erroneously

217

esp., espec.	especially
Esq., Esqr.	Esquire
est.	established
et al.	*et alii* (Lat., and others)
etc.	*et cetera* (Lat., and other things)
et seq.	*et sequens* (Lat., and the following)
etym., etymol.	etymology; etymological
f.	following (page)
fem.	feminine
ff.	following (pages)
fict.	fiction
fig.	figure; figurative
for.	foreign
Fr.	*Frater* (Lat., Brother); French; Father
ft.	foot; feet
G., Germ.	German
Gk., Gr.	Greek
hist.	history; historical
ibid.	*ibidem* (Lat., in the same place)
id.	*idem* (Lat., the same)
i.e.	*id est* (Lat., that is)
illust.	illustration; illustrated
imit.	imitative
incl.	inclusive; including
incog.	incognito
inf.	*infra* (Lat., below)
interj.	interjection
introd.	introduction
I.Q.	intelligence quotient
It., Ital.	Italian; Italy
ital.	italic (type)
Jr., jr.	junior
k.o.	knock out
kw.	kilowatt
L., Lat.	Latin
lb.	*libra* (Lat., pound)
L.C.	Library of Congress
l.c.	lower case (type)
LL.	Late Latin
ll.	lines
loc. cit.	*loco citato* (Lat., in the place cited)
log	logarithm
Ltd.	limited
M.A.	*Magister Artium* (Lat., Master of Arts)
mas., masc.	masculine
M.D.	*Medicinae Doctor* (Lat., Doctor of Medicine)

Messrs.	Messieurs
Mlles.	Mesdemoiselles
Mme., Mmes.	Madame; mesdames
MS., ms.	manuscript
MSS., mss.	manuscripts
n.	noun; number
N.B., n.b.	*nota bene* (Lat., note well)
n.d.	no date (of publication)
No., nos.	number; numbers
n.p.	no place (of publication)
N.S.	New Style (of dating, after 1752)
num.	numeral; number
ob.	*obiit* (Lat., he died)
obs.	obsolete
OE., O.E.	Old English
O.E.D.	Oxford English Dictionary
o.p.	out of print
op. cit.	*opere citato* (Lat., in the work cited)
Oxon.	*Oxonia* (Lat., Oxford; Oxfordshire)
p., pp.	page; pages
pam., pamph.	pamphlet
par.	paragraph; parallel
perh.	perhaps
pinx.	*pinxit* (Lat., he painted it)
pl., plur.	plural
P.M., p.m.	afternoon
poet.	poetical; poetic; poetry
poss.	possessive
pop.	popularly; population
pref.	preface; prefix
prep.	preposition; preparatory
prin.	principal; principally
Prof., prof.	professor
pron.	pronoun; pronunciation; pronounced
pro tem.	*pro tempore* (Lat., for the time being)
prov.	provincial
pseud.	pseudonym
P.T.O.	please turn over (a leaf)
pub., publ.	published; publisher; public
punct.	punctuation
Pvt.	Private
Q.E.D.	*quod erat demonstrandum* (Lat., which was to be demonstrated)
qto.	quarto
quot.	quotation
q.v.	*quod vide* (Lat., which see)

ref.	reference
rev.	revised; revise; review
rhet.	rhetorical; rhetoric
R.I.P.	*requiescat in pace* (Lat., may he rest in peace)
Rom.	Roman; romance
R.O.T.C.	Reserve Officers' Training Corps
R.S.V.P.	*Répondez, s'il vous plaît* (Fr., please reply)
R.S.V. or RSV	Revised Standard Version (of the Bible)
scil.	*scilicet* (Lat., to wit)
Scot.	Scottish
sec., secs.	second; seconds; section; sections
seq., seqq.	*sequentia* (Lat., the following)
sing.	singular
S.J.	Society of Jesus
Sp.	Spanish
sp.	spelling
Sr.	senior
S.R.O.	standing room only
SS.	*Sancti* (Lat., saints)
S.S., S/S	steamship
subj.	subject; subjunctive; subjective
suf.	suffix
sup.	*supra* (Lat., above)
supp., suppl.	supplement
s.v.	*sub verbo* (Lat., under the word)
syn.	synonym
tech.	technical
tr.	transpose; translate; translated
ult.	*ultimo* (*mense*): Lat., in the last (month)
v.	verb; verse; voice; volume; (law cases) versus
var.	variant; variable
vb.	verb
v.i.	intransitive verb
viz.	*videlicet* (Lat., namely)
vocab.	vocabulary
vol., vols.	volume; volumes
vox pop.	*vox populi* (Lat., voice of the people)
vs.	versus (however, present usage prefers v.)
v.t.	transitive verb
vv.	verses

CONTRACTION

Contractions are shortened forms of a word or phrase. In spoken English, unstressed syllables are frequently dropped, and *would not* becomes *wouldn't, I am* becomes *I'm,* and *they will* becomes *they'll.*

When such contractions are written, the apostrophe (see p. 202) shows the omission of a letter or letters. No period is used at the end of a contraction (as contrasted with an abbreviation which is followed by a period).

Contractions, suggesting as they do the easy give-and-take of familiar conversation, are frowned upon in formal writing. They are often necessary, of course, in reproducing conversation, whether in a short story or a play. Often, too, contractions are used with effect in informal compositions such as the familiar essay or the personal letter.

The following list includes the more common contractions (in addition to those mentioned above), together with the expressions which they represent:

I'll	I will; I shall
I'd	I would; I had
I've	I have
They shan't	They shall not
They won't	They will not
He doesn't	He does not
They don't	They do not
She's	She is
It's	It is
They're	They are
You're	You are
We're	We are

Special care must be taken to avoid three common errors in the use of contractions:

1. Be sure to make the verb agree with the subject in person and number.

> He *doesn't* care. (**Not,** He don't care.)
>
> *Aren't* there two ways of doing it? (**Not,** Isn't there two ways of doing it?)

2. Be sure to place the apostrophe where it belongs.

> He *hasn't* come back yet. (**Not,** He has'nt.)
>
> *I've* been waiting. (**Not,** Iv'e been waiting.)
>
> He *won't* be long. (**Not,** He wo'nt be long.)

3. Be sure to distinguish carefully between *it's* (it is) and *its* (the possessive case of *it*) :

> The bird got *its* wings wet.
>
> The team won *its* first game.
>
> *It's* obvious that *it's* going to be a hard campaign for the Administration and *its* supporters.

NUMERALS

In books in which numbers appear very extensively, as in works on mathematics and the sciences, numerals are used in preference to spelling out numbers. In writing that is strictly literary, where few numbers are used, it is preferable to spell them out; but even in formal literary work, numbers are used in lists and in footnotes.

Certain special rules concerning numerals should be noted:

I. If the spelling out of numbers in literary work becomes cumbersome, it is permissible to use figures for all numbers that cannot be expressed in one or two written words. The following list carries out this practice:

> twenty-eight
> ninety-nine
> eighteen
> eighteen hundred
> 199
> 1,801
> the year 1801
> Fifth Avenue

If many numbers are used in a sentence or paragraph, it is appropriate to use figures, except at the beginning of a sentence:

> The hotel guests totaled 210 persons, of whom 101 were local people, 53 were from New England, 22 were from Texas, 21 were from Pennsylvania, and 13 were from California.
>
> Thirteen were from California.
>
> The Californian visitors totaled 13.
>
> (NOT: 13 were from California.)

Observe that fractions and compound numbers (twenty-one to ninety-nine) are to be spelled out when they occur in a normal English sentence. Observe also that they require the hyphen:

> Forty-two dollars and twenty-five cents covered his expenses.
> (*Or:* His expenses came to $42.25.)
> Butter is fifty-eight cents a pound.
> The work is nine-tenths finished.

II. Use figures in the following:

Dates:

> RIGHT: October 16, 1905; October 16; the 16th of October.
> MORE FORMAL: the sixteenth of October
> IMPROPER: October 16th, 1905

Hours:

> RIGHT: 5 P.M.; 5 p.m.; 11:30 A.M.
> MORE FORMAL: five in the afternoon; eleven-thirty in the forenoon
> IMPROPER: five p.m.

Page or section numbers, room numbers, street numbers, telephone numbers, and the like:

> RIGHT: pages 6–10; room 110; 200 Main Street; RAymond 9–1577; 10,465 books; license number 8,640; Chapter III, Section 2.

II. Use Roman numerals to indicate large divisions; use Arabic nerals for smaller divisions:

ARABIC	ROMAN	ARABIC	ROMAN
1	I	15	XV
2	II	20	XX
3	III	30	XXX
4	IV	40	XL
5	V	50	L
6	VI	60	LX
7	VII	90	XC
8	VIII	100	C
9	IX	500	D
10	X	1000	M

IV. Use Roman numerals in titles:

> George V
> Pope Pius XII
> Louis XIV

V. Use small Roman numerals for page numbers in a preface or introduction:

> p. xxvii
> pp. ii-xii
> pp. iv. ff.

SYLLABLES

A syllable is a unit of speech or utterance and forms either a complete word or one of the divisions of a word. Examples of monosyllables (words of one syllable) are *boy, sun, air, but, plague.* Examples of polysyllables (words of more than one syllable) are such words as *boyish, sunshine, butter, ague,* and the word *polysyllable* itself. Good dictionaries indicate the division of words into syllables, and the writer should familiarize himself with the devices used for this purpose in his own dictionary. In *Webster's Collegiate,* the end of a syllable is shown by a centered period, except when accent marks or hyphens occur. The word *flowering,* for example, appears as *flow'er·ing.*

In writing, it is frequently necessary to divide a word at the end of a line. Such division is indicated by the use of a hyphen after the first part of the word, the remainder of the word appearing at the beginning of the next line. The principal rule for division of this sort is: **Divide words only between syllables.** The following practical suggestions are designed to help the beginning writer:

A. Do not divide a syllable or a word of one syllable.

> *floor*   (not *flo-or*)
> *ridge*   (not *ri-dge*)

The whole word should be carried over to the beginning of the next line.

B. Do not divide a hyphenated word except at the hyphen.

> *self-explanatory*   (not *self-ex-planatory*)
>
> *a never-to-be-forgotten experience* (not *a never-to-be-for-gotten experience*)
>
> *a light-minded person* (not *a light-mind-ed person*)

C. If the word consists of a root and a prefix or suffix, divide between prefix and root or between root and suffix. Avoid setting off only one or two letters from the rest of the word.

> *avert*   (not *a-vert*)
> *away*   (not *a-way*)
> *studio*   (not *studi-o*)
> *hippo-potamus*   (not *hip-popotamus*)
> *prepared-ness*   (not *prepar-edness*)

D. Do not separate two letters representing a single sound.

> *proph-et*   (not *prop-het*)
> *mathe-matics*   (not *mat-hematics*)
> *cro-quet*   (not *croq-uet*)

E. Do not separate a final *ed* from the rest of the word unless it is itself a syllable.

> *joined*   (not *join-ed*)
> *walked*   (not *walk-ed*)
>
> BUT: *point-ed*
> *lift-ed*
> *repeat-ed*

F. Do not divide names of persons.

> *Roosevelt*   (not *Roose-velt*)
> *William*   (not *Will-iam*)
> *Hemingway*   (not *Heming-way*)

G. Wherever possible, divide so that the first part of the word will suggest the complete word.

> *distress-ing*   (not *dis-tressing*)
> *patriot-ism*   (not *patri-otism*)
> *dogmati-cal*   (not *dog-matical*)
> *social-istic*   (not *so-cialistic*)

USE OF THE HYPHEN

The hyphen [-] has two chief uses: to join the parts of certain compound words or expressions; and to indicate the division of a word at the end of a line. (See The Hyphen, p. 201, and Syllables, p. 224.)

Current practice in the handling of compound words is extremely varied. Although the hyphen is necessarily used in certain instances, the tendency of modern writers is to avoid the hyphen wherever possible and to write compound words as two words or as one word without the hyphen, as in the following examples:

life insurance	bookstore
oak table	notebook
dining room	workshop
back door	workman

Here are definite recommendations for the use of hyphens:

I. Use a hyphen to join two or more words used as a single adjective preceding the noun:

> a never-to-be-forgotten occasion
> a ten-foot pole
> a well-stocked cupboard
> a second-class ticket
> a high-school student

Omit the hyphen if the words follow the noun, if the first word ends in *ly*, or if the compound is a proper name:

> The cupboard was well stocked.
> She is a student in high school.
> It was an eagerly awaited moment.
> The South Carolina accent is delightful.

II. Use a hyphen in compound numbers and in fractions used as modifiers:

> thirty-six dollars
> three-tenths wood and seven-tenths metal
> ninety-nine per cent
> seven twenty-fourths
> twenty-one twenty-fourths

Observe that no hyphens are used when the first of two words in a numerical expression is really an adjective modifying the second word, as in the following:

> One third of the work has been completed.
>
> Nine tenths of the time he is right.

III. Use the hyphen with any stressed prefix, especially before a proper name, with the prefixes *ex-* and *vice-*, and with the adjective *-elect* used as a suffix:

the president-elect	pre-World War I
the ex-president	non-native
ex-President Eisenhower	all-important
ex-husband	G-man
fellow-member	U-boat
anti-Communist	by-product
pro-Roosevelt	the Vice-President

IV. Use a hyphen if the second member of a compound word is an adverb or if the first member is equivalent to a phrase:

> an also-ran
>
> the sorting-out of this problem
>
> run-around
>
> self-satisfaction
>
> a self-made man
>
> the summing-up
>
> the filling-out of a questionnaire

V. Use a hyphen to prevent misreading. Words in which the prefix is to be emphasized can be contrasted with words spelled identically or very similarly by using a hyphen between the prefix and the root of the word:

> co-respondent (CP. correspondent)
>
> re-collect   (CP. recollect)

Separate words which should be closely connected in thought in a given sentence may be united by a hyphen:

> a light-blue hat (CP. a light blue hat = a blue hat light in weight)
>
> a party for three-, four-, and five-year-old children (the hyphens prevent ambiguity)

In order to prevent mispronunciation of words with a prefix ending in a vowel followed by a root commencing with the same vowel, it is permissible to separate the prefix by a hyphen or to place a dieresis over the second vowel, but neither of these devices is necessary:

cooperate   *or* co-operate   *or* coöperate
coordinate   *or* co-ordinate   *or* coördinate
preeminent   *or* pre-eminent   *or* preëminent

Though in general there is now a tendency away from using the hyphen, usage is divided about many words. The following may be written with or without the hyphen, but the writer should be consistent in his use of one or the other form:

nationwide	nation-wide
tomorrow	to-morrow
trademark	trade-mark
goodby	good-by
weekend	week-end

Write the following as single words without the hyphen:

textbook	bookcase
sailboat	beefsteak
airplane	forehead
taxpayer	iceberg

Well-known pronouns, adverbs, and prepositions are written as single words:

anybody	itself
nowhere	within
myself	into

USE OF ITALICS

Italic type is sometimes used instead of ordinary, or roman type. In longhand or typewritten papers, it is conventional to underline words to be set in italics.

LONGHAND:

The American Language is by H. L. Mencken.

TYPEWRITTEN:

The American Language is by H. L. Mencken.

In formal writing, italics are used in certain special ways, and the beginning writer will do well to follow in his manuscript the rules discussed here. He will avoid overworking italics as a mechanical device for emphasis. He will, of course, in preparing copy for the printer, follow any special instructions relating to italics and other kinds of type.

I. Underline quoted titles of separate publications: books, periodicals, newspapers, bulletins, pamphlets, musical compositions, radio and television programs, moving pictures, and plays. One sometimes sees quotation marks used to indicate titles, but current practice reserves quotation marks for sub-titles, titles of chapters or divisions in a longer work, and for titles of individual poems in a collection of poems. In general, separate publications require italics.

A new magazine called *Challenge* has appeared.

Lost Horizon was a bestseller.

Book I of *The Return of the Native* is called "The Three Women."

He discovered a useful pamphlet entitled *Practical Gardening*.

Brutus is a well-developed character in *Julius Caesar*.

His parents always enjoy the *Meet the Press*.

My friend Everett writes for the New York *Times*.

Harper's, Life, and *Vogue* are always found on their coffee table.

He suggested that I read "Lycidas" in the *Poetical Works of John Milton*.

It was a splendid performance of *Tristan und Isolde*.

The American Language is a scholarly work by H. L. Mencken.

NOTE A: The articles *a, an,* and *the* at the beginning of a title are placed in italics if they form part of the title. Often, they are not italicized:

She subscribes to the *Nation* and to the *Readers' Digest*.

As a child, she was fond of *The Tale of Two Cities*.

One of the best films I have seen is *The Informer*.

He referred to a character in Scott's *The Antiquary*. (OR: in Scott's *Antiquary*.)

NOTE B: Do not italicize the name of the city in newspaper titles:

RIGHT: I read the New York *World Journal Tribune*.
He wrote a letter to the Los Angeles *Times*.
The advertisement appeared in the Denver *Post*.

NOTE C: Short forms of names of books of the Bible may be italicized:

The text of the sermon was taken from *Matthew* xi: 17.

II. Underline names of works of art, ships, boats, docks, railway coaches, and aircraft:

Civic Virtue, a group of statuary, used to stand near the City Hall.

My uncle often crossed the Atlantic on the *Aquitania*.

He was at the airport when the President stepped down from his official airplane, the *Columbine*.

As a Christmas present, I received a reproduction in color of the *Mona Lisa*.

III. Underline foreign words and their abbreviations used in English sentences. English has always "borrowed" freely from other languages. Sometimes the borrowed words become completely anglicized, sometimes they become only partially naturalized, and sometimes they remain alien in appearance and sound. Italicize words not completely adopted; use ordinary type for others. If in doubt, consult a good dictionary.

The following list contains a number of examples of naturalized words and abbreviations that may be printed in ordinary type:

agenda	chic	gratis
aide-de-camp	communiqué	hors d'oeuvres
à la carte	connoisseur	kindergarten
à la mode	corps	liaison
alias	crescendo	lingerie
alibi	debonair	matinee
Alma Mater	debut	mayonnaise
amateur	detour	menu
a priori	dramatis personae	naïve
apropos	encore	negligee
au revoir	ennui	nil
blitzkrieg	en route	nom de plume
bona fide	ersatz	per cent
buffet	et cetera	protégé
café	ex officio	questionnaire
camouflage	fiancé	ragout
chaperon	fiancée	rendezvous
chassis	finis	repertoire
chauffeur	garage	salon

status quo	verbatim	e.g.
stein	versus	etc.
subpoena	via	i.e.
tableau	vice versa	v.
table d'hôte	cf.	viz.
tête-à-tête	cp.	

Italics are required for the following, and, of course, for all other foreign words and expressions not yet adopted into English:

ancien régime	*in medias res*	*q.v.*
circa	*in situ*	*s.v.*
coiffeur	*in toto*	*seriatim*
coup d'état	*laissez faire*	*sic*
de novo	*loc. cit.*	*sotto voce*
en rapport	*modus operandi*	*supra*
et al.	*nouveau riche*	*terminus ad quem*
ex parte	*op. cit.*	*vide*
gemütlichkeit	*par excellence*	*Weltanschauung*
ibid.	*pari passu*	*Weltschmerz*
infra	*passim*	

NOTE A: Scientific names of genera and species are to be italicized:

> *Anthropoides virgo*
> *Colaptes auratus*
> *Pediculus capitis*

NOTE B: Foreign names and titles are not italicized:

> RIGHT: Monsieur DuPont lived in Paris on the Rue de Rivoli. They rode down Unter den Linden.

IV. Italicize letters, figures, words, phrases, and clauses spoken of as such:

Your *1*'s and *7*'s look alike.

Mind your *p*'s and *q*'s.

You overwork the word *and* and the phrase *by the way*.

Every once in a while is a curious expression.

In the sentence *We were very late*, *very* is used as an intensive.

Except in textbooks and the like, the writer will do well to avoid placing long sentences in italics.

V. Underline for emphasis, but only if emphasis can be secured in no other way:

> ACCEPTABLE: The witness again asserted that he *was* in his home at nine o'clock.

> JUVENILE: He is the *handsomest* man I have *ever* seen in *all* my life.

NOTE A: In referring to court cases, italicize the names:

> *The State of New York* vs. *Jones*
> *Schwartz* vs. *Granby*

NOTE B: In resolutions, italicize the word *Resolved* and put the word WHEREAS in capitals.

NOTE C: In typewritten documents italics are used for emphasis:

> *See also* the account on page 10
> *Note 3:*
> *Wrong:*
> *Right:*
> Page 12, 1. 3, *for* well, *read* we'll.

MANUSCRIPT FORM

There are certain standards of good appearance which should be borne in mind in putting any written material into final form:

For a handwritten manuscript, use white paper of a standard size (8½ by 11 inches), write on one side only, and write legibly in black or blue-black ink. Failure to space words properly, failure to distinguish commas from periods, failure to distinguish between *a*'s and *o*'s and between *e*'s and *i*'s, failure to distinguish small letters from capitals, failure to dot *i*'s and *j*'s and to cross *t*'s—these are the things that make for illegibility.

For a typewritten manuscript, use double space between lines of the text and single space between lines of a lengthy quotation. Leave one space after a comma or semicolon; leave two after a period, colon, question mark, or exclamation point. Distinguish between the hyphen and the dash, and leave one space before the dash and one after it. Use the lower-case *l* for the numeral "one."

Leave margins of an inch and a half at the top and at the left, and margins of an inch at the right and at the bottom of the page.

Indent uniformly to indicate paragraphs. If the manuscript is hand-written, indent one inch; if typewritten, indent five spaces. Quoted lines of poetry must be presented as they appear in the original. Note following example:

> I was late. As I hurried to my seat in the rear of the room, I heard the voice of my teacher droning out some lines from Lord Byron:
>
>> " 'Eternal Spirit of the chainless Mind!
>> Brightest in dungeons, Liberty! thou art,
>> For there thy habitation is the heart—
>> The heart which love of thee alone can bind . . .' "
>
> He glared at me while he read.

Center the title about an inch and a half from the top of the page, capitalize important words, and remember that although a question mark or an exclamation point may be used, no period follows a title. Do not put your own title in italics or in quotation marks unless there is a special reason for doing so, and do not repeat the title on subsequent pages. Number the pages by using arabic numerals in the upper right-hand corner of each page except the first. If your manuscript is to be published, put your name and address in the upper left-hand corner of the first page.

EXERCISES

A. Use capital letters wherever needed in the following sentences:

(1) On saturday night joe masters and his rhythm boys entertained the yorkville social club.

(2) My cousin robert has a decided french accent.

(3) He referred to his section of the southwest as god's country.

(4) The street was named sherman street in honor of general sherman.

(5) I remember that there was a chinese boy in my class in burton high school.

(6) Father and mother both approve of the United Nations.

(7) Bill said, "oh, there goes dr. jones now!"

(8) We wrote to captain anderson of the 95th coast artillery.

(9) He has a book about the stone age.

(10) They stayed with their uncle from thanksgiving until christmas.

B. Change unnecessary capitals to small letters and use capitals wherever needed:

(1) In High School we studied Physics, English, Latin, History, and Civics.

(2) I suffer during the Winter and go South if I can.

(3) Please go to the Drugstore, sally, and get Mother some ice-cream.

(4) The crew included Mexicans, indians, negroes, and Portuguese.

(5) He reads the bible regularly and especially likes the letters of the apostle Paul.

(6) Sometimes Gypsies are called Bohemians.

(7) The area around times square is known as the great white way.

(8) Theirs is a Platonic friendship.

(9) The missouri river flows into the mississippi.

(10) Mrs. McDermott, a High-school Teacher, threatened to call in the board of health.

C. Correct any misuses of abbreviations and numbers:

(1) 85 pedestrians were killed on Linden Blvd. last mo.

(2) The mts. form a splendid background for the U. of Colo.

(3) Chas. Miller, Prof. of Chem., will be 50 next Jan. the 8th.

(4) Enclosed please find one ($1.00) dollar.

(5) My address is sixteen Fremont st., Middletown, O.

(6) His library contains one thousand three hundred and forty-two vols.

(7) When he is in Chi. he goes sailing on Lake Mich.

(8) The 5th of November is called Guy Fawkes Day in Engl.

(9) Over 10,000 people saw the game between N.D. and Nebraska.

(10) This box is 2 inches longer and 3 inches wider than the other one.

(11) Telephone me at Central six three thousand at five p.m.

(12) They called on the Rev. to arrange the wedding details.

(13) The word in question occurs in chapter five, p. 110, line 3.

(14) Xmas parties mean work for the docs.

(15) Early last mo. he left for N. Zealand.

D. None of the compound words in the following sentences is hyphenated. With the aid of a dictionary, decide which should be written as one word, which hyphenated, and which as two words:

(1) In the anteroom of the lifeinsurance company's mainoffice the workingman sat patiently for thirtyfive minutes.

(2) He wore a lightgray suit and a fourinhand tie.

(3) The fillingout of the application for an interview with the vice-president took up onethird of his time.

(4) He had never been much of a letterwriter, and it was with a feeling of selfsatisfaction that he answered the last of the twentyone questions.

(5) He handed the allimportant document to the goodlooking secretary and watched her as she went into the inneroffice.

E. Underscore all words that should be in italic type:

(1) He preferred the France to the Queen Elizabeth for trans-Atlantic crossings.

(2) Did you enjoy Together by Norman Douglas?

(3) The w in the word Harwich is not pronounced.

(4) They attended a performance of Rigoletto at the Metropolitan Opera House.

(5) The Spirit of St. Louis was one of the world's most famous airplanes.

(6) Like most epics, Milton's Paradise Lost begins in medias res.

(7) The story deals with his experiences en route to his Alma Mater.

(8) Johnson's Rasselas is a tale of Abyssinia.

(9) Child Care, a sixty-page pamphlet, has a chapter called Clothing.

(10) The words damask and calico are derived from city-names: Damascus and Calicut.

CHAPTER IX

DICTION

THE WORD *diction* as used in this book means "choice of words to express ideas" (*Webster's Collegiate Dictionary*). If we are tremendously interested in saying something, we find that we are constantly searching for the proper word—for the word that will convey the exact shade of meaning which we have in mind.

IMPORTANCE OF VOCABULARY

The student of writing must take an interest in words. He must collect words as ardently as others collect stamps or coins. He must pay close attention to the speech of educated persons and he must increase his knowledge of words by careful study of the diction of reputable writers. He should remember, of course, that a large vocabulary is valuable only insofar as it makes for effective speech and writing; but he will also remember that a man whose diction is constantly becoming more varied and more exact is, beyond question, a man whose mind is improving.

An indispensable book in a writer's library is his dictionary. We shall therefore first of all devote some time to the problem of using the dictionary intelligently.

USE OF THE DICTIONARY

Every writer should have access to a reputable, unabridged dictionary and should, if possible, own one of the abridged, one-volume dictionaries. Students are encouraged to acquire the "dictionary habit," for an inexpensive dictionary such as *Webster's Collegiate Dictionary* if properly used will be of immense value to anyone interested in learning to write.

Certain general suggestions may be given here for the effective use of the dictionary. The reader will, of course, interpret these suggestions in terms of the particular dictionary he owns and uses.

It is perhaps safe to say that most people consult a dictionary either to find the exact meaning of a word or to find out how it is spelled. But even an abridged dictionary will supply much additional information about most words. Let us examine a typical entry, for example, the word *tarantella,* in *Webster's Collegiate.* (See p. 239.)

The entry is a short one, but a good deal of information is compressed into it. Let us read the entry in expanded form:

The word *tarantella* (we find) is, first of all, a word of four syllables (tar/an·tel/la), accented lightly on the first and more heavily on the third syllable. Its pronunciation is given as (tăr'ăn·těl'à), and the key to the pronunciation appears conveniently at the bottom of the page. We next learn from the abbreviation *n.* that the word is a noun. The etymology of *tarantella* comes next, and it is enclosed in square brackets. The word is one borrowed from the Italian language and is derived (by the process of antonomasia*) from the city-name *Taranto* by way of a diminutive form, as shown by the *-ella* ending. There are two meanings of the word: first, "a lively, passionate Neapolitan folk dance in 6/8 time or a social dance evolved from it"; and second, the "music for such a dance."

From this short entry we have learned the following things about the word:

1. Spelling
2. Syllabication
3. Accent
4. Correct pronunciation
5. Part of speech
6. Etymology or history
7. Two meanings

It is often useful, when consulting a dictionary entry, to examine nearby words. The next word listed is *tarantism,* the etymology of which reveals that this medical name for a "nervous affection" is

---

*Antonomasia means the process of deriving common nouns from proper nouns.

Tann'häu.ser (tän'hoi-zĕr; tän'), n. [G.] A German knight and minnesinger, identified with a legendary hero in Wagner's opera *Tannhäuser* who entered the enchanted cavern, and his final release form the therefrom, his return, and his final release form the plot of the opera.

tan'nic (tăn'ĭk), *adj.* Of, like, or derived from tan.

tan'nin (-ĭn), n. [F. *tanin*.] Also **tannic acid.** *Chem.* A A strongly astringent substance obtained in scales from galnuts, sumac, etc. It is used in tanning, dyeing, etc. b Any of a group of substances having similar uses.

tan'ning (tăn'ĭng), *pres. part.* of TAN. Specif. n. Art or process by which a skin is tanned.

tan'sy (tăn'zĭ), n. [OF. *tanoise*, *tanesie*, fr. ML., fr. Gr. *athanasia* immortality.] Any of a genus (*Tanacetum*) of carduaceous plants, esp. one species (*T. vulgare*) having an aromatic odor, a very bitter taste, and tonic properties.

tan'ta.late (tăn'tȧ-lāt), n. A salt of tantalic acid.

tan.tal'ic (tăn-tăl'ĭk), *adj. Chem.* Of, pertaining to, or derived from tantalum; specif., designating any of several acids derived from tantalum pentoxide and known chiefly in their salts, the tantalates.

tan'ta.lite (tăn'tȧ-līt), n. A heavy iron-black mineral of submetallic luster, essentially iron tantalate, $Fe(TaO_3)_2$. H, 6. Sp. gr., up to 7.3.

tan'ta.lize (-līz), *v. t. & i.* [From TANTALUS.] To tease by keeping something desirable in view but out of reach.— **tan'ta.li.za'tion**, n.— **tan'ta.liz'er**, n.— **tan'ta.liz'ing.ly**, *adv.*

tan'ta.lum (-lŭm), n. [NL.; ref. to the difficulties met in isolating it. See TANTALUS.] *Chem.* A hard, ductile, gray-white, acid-resisting metallic element of the vanadium family, found (combined) in tantalite, columbite, and other rare minerals. Symbol, *Ta*; at. no., 73; at. wt., 180.88.

Tan'ta.lus (-lŭs), n. [L., fr. Gr. *Tantalos*.] *Gr. Myth.* A wealthy king, son of Zeus and father of Pelops and Niobe. For an atrocious sin he was punished in the lower world by being placed in water up to his chin with fruit-laden branches over his head. The water or fruit receded whenever he sought to drink or eat.

tan'ta.mount' (tăn'tȧ-mount'), *adj.* [From *tantamount*, n. & v., fr. AF. *tant amunter* to amount to as much. See AMOUNT.] Equivalent in value, signification, or effect.—**Syn.** See IDENTICAL.

tan'ta.ra (tăn'tȧ-rȧ; tăn-tä'rȧ; -tā'rȧ), n. [Imitative.] The blare of a trumpet or horn.

tan.tiv'y (tăn-tĭv'ĭ), *adv. Archaic.* Swiftly, headlong.— *adj.* Swift, speedy.— n.; *pl.* -TIVES (-ĭz), 1. An impetuous rush. 2. *Hunting.* A call to signal full chase.

tan'to (tän'tō), *adv.* [It.] So much; specif., *Music*, not too much; as, *direttio*

---

tape'line' (tāp'līn'), n. Also **tape measure.** A tape marked with linear dimensions and used for measuring.

ta'per (tā'pĕr), n. [AS. *taper*, *tapor*, *tapur*, fr. L. *papyrus* papyllus, in ML. also taper, wick.] 1. Oriz., a small wax candle; now esp., a long wax red wick; hence, a small light. 2. A tapering form or figure, as a spire; hence, gradual diminution of thickness or width in an elongated object; as, the *taper* of a spire.— *adj.* Regularly narrowed toward a point; conically pyramidical.— *v. i. & t.* To become or make gradually smaller toward one end; hence, to diminish gradually.—**ta'per.ing.ly**, *adv.*

ta.pes.try (tā'pĕs-trĭ), n.; *pl.* -TRIES (-trĭz). [F. *tapisserie*, fr. *tapis* a carpet, carpeting, fr., OF., fr. Gr. *tapēion*, dim. of *tapēs* a carpet, rug.] A heavy, hand-woven, reversible textile, commonly figured and used as a wall hanging, carpet, or furniture covering; also, a machine-made imitation of it.— *v. t.; -TRIED* (-trĭd), -TRY.ING. To furnish or adorn with or as if with tapestry.

ta.pe'tum (tȧ-pē'tŭm), n. [LL. fr. L. *tapete* a carpet, a tapestry.] 1. *Bot.* A layer of nutritive tissue commonly investing the archespore in a developing sporangium. 2. *Anat. & Zool.* Any of certain membranous layers or areas, esp. of the choroid and retina of the eye.

tape'worm' (tāp'wûrm'), n. Any of numerous cestode worms (*Taenia* and allied genera) parasitic when adult in the intestine of man and various animals.

tap'house' (tăp'hous'), n. A tavern; a taproom.

tap'i.o'ca (tăp'ĭ-ō'kȧ), n. [Pg., Sp., F., fr. Tupi & Guarani *tipyóca*, *tipióca*, fr. by juice + *pi'a* heart, bowels + *ocõ* to be removed.] A granular preparation of cassava starch.

ta'pir (tā'pĕr), n.; see PLURAL, *Note*, 3. [Sp., fr. Tupi *tapyra*, *tapira*, any large mammal.] Any of several large ungulates (family Tapiridae), all but one of which, the Malayan) inhabit South or Central America. They are chiefly nocturnal, shy, and gentle, and are the nearest living allies of horses and rhinoceroses.

Malayan Tapir (*Tapirus indicus*). ($\frac{1}{40}$)

tap'is (tăp'ē; tȧ'pḗs; tȧp'; also F. tȧ'pḗ'), n. [F.] See TAPESTRY.] Tapestry; a floor or tablecover.— now chiefly in *on*, or *upon*, *the tapis* (*pron. in this use* perh. *more often as* F. tȧ'pḗ'), [Transl. of F. *sur le tapis.*] On the floor; hence, under consideration.

tap'per (tăp'ĕr), n. [From 1st TAP.] One that taps; specif., a telegraph key, esp. one (in full *Morse tapper*) that makes one contact and breaks another by one movement.

238

Tan'trum (tăn'trŭm), *n. Colloq.* A fit of ill temper.

Tao'ism (dou'ĭz'm; tou'-), *n.* [Chin. (Pek.) *tao'* road, way.] A religion and philosophy of China, traditionally founded by Lao-tse, 6th century B.C., and teaching conformity to the cosmic order and simplicity of social and political organization. — **Tao'ist** (-ĭst), *n. & adj.* — **Tao-is'tic** (-ĭs'tĭk), *adj.*

tap (tăp), *v.t. & i.;* TAPPED (tăpt) TAP'PING. [ME. *tappen*, fr. OF. *taper*, of imitative origin.] **1.** To strike with a slight blow; rap lightly. **2.** To give a light blow or blows with (cane, feet, etc.). **3.** To make, as a hole, by tapping. **4.** To repair (a shoe) by putting a tap on. — *n.* **1.** A light blow; a rap; also, its sound. **2.** *pl.* A signal, by drum, bugle, or trumpet, to extinguish all lights in soldiers' or sailors' quarters, to go to bed and preserve silence. **3.** A partial sole put on over the worn sole of a boot or shoe.

tap, *n.* [AS. *tæppa.*] **1.** *Chiefly Brit.* A cock, faucet, or small valve, esp. for turning on water. **2.** A hole or pipe through which liquor is drawn. **3.** A plug or spile to stop a hole, as in a cask; as a spigot. **4.** Liquor drawn through a tap; hence: **a** A certain kind or quality of liquor. **b** *Colloq.* A taproom; bar. **5.** A tool for forming an internal screw thread. **6** In an electric circuit, a point where a connection may be made. — **on tap, a** Ready to be drawn; as, ale *on tap.* **b** Broached or furnished with a tap. On hand. — *v.t.* **1.** To let out by piercing, or by drawing (anything) from the containing vessel. **2.** Hence, to draw, as a liquor, from the source. **3.** To pierce (a cask, a tree, tumor, etc.) so as to let out, or draw off a fluid. **4.** To connect (a street, a water main) with a local supply. **5.** To form a female screw in by means of a tap. — *v.t.* To be, or act as, a tapster.

ta'pa (tä'pä), *n.* [Native name in Marquesas Isls.] The bark of a kind of mulberry tree, from which a cloth (**tapa cloth**) is made.

tap dance. Any step dance, tapped out audibly with the feet, toes, or heels. — **tap'-dance',** *v. i.*

tape (tāp), *n.* [AS. *tæppe.*] **1.** A narrow woven ribbon of cotton or linen. **2.** Hence, any narrow strip or band, as of paper, steel, or the like. **3.** Short for RED TAPE, TAPE-LINE. **4.** *Sports.* A string stretched breast-high above the finishing line to aid the judges in determining the winner of a race. — *v. t.* **1.** To furnish with tape; fasten, tie, bind, or the like, with tape. **2.** To measure with a tape-line; *Scot.* to measure sparingly. — **tap'er** (tāp'ẽr), *n.*

by some other piece, as a cam, or intended to tap something else, to cause a certain motion.

tap'ping (tăp'ĭng), *n.* **1.** Act, process, or means by which something is tapped. **2.** *pl.* That which is taken from a tap or from something tapped.

tap'pit-hen' (tăp'ĭt-hĕn'), *n. Scot.* **a** A crested hen. **b** A large drinking vessel with a knob on its lid.

tap'room' (tăp'rōōm'), *n.* A barroom. — **tap'room',** *adj.*

tap'root' (-rōōt'), *n.* A primary root which grows vertically downward, giving off small lateral roots.

tap'ster (tăp'stẽr), *n.* [AS. *tæppestre* a female tapster.] Orig., a barmaid; later, anyone employed to tap, or draw, liquors. — **tap'stress** (-strĕs; -strĭs), *n.*

Ta-pu'ya (tä-pōō'yä), *n. sing. & pl.* [Prg. *Tapuyo, Tapuya,* fr. Tupi *tapuya* savage, enemy.] An Indian of the important linguistic family of South American Indians, formerly of central Brazil.

Ta-pu'yan (-yän), *adj.* Pertaining to or designating an Ta-pu'yan stock. — **Ta-pu'ya,** *adj.*

tar (tär), *n.* [AS. *teru, teoru.*] **1.** A thick, dark-brown or black, viscous liquid obtained by distillation of wood, coal, peat, etc. **2.** [Abbr. fr. TARPAULIN.] A sailor; seaman. — *v. t.;* TARRED (tärd); TAR'RING. To smear with or as with tar. — *adj.* Of, from, or like tar.

ta'ran-tas', ta'ran-tas' (tä'rän-täs'), *n.* [Russ. *tarantas.*] A low four-wheeled carriage used in Russia.

tar'an-tel'la (tär'än-tĕl'ä), *n.* [It., dim. fr. *Taranto.*] A lively, passionate Neapolitan folk dance in 6/8 time or a social dance evolved from it. **b** Music for such a dance.

tar'ant-ism (tär'ăn-tĭz'm), *n.* Also **tar'ent-ism** (târ'ĕn-). [NL. *tarantismus,* fr. It. *tarantismo,* fr. *Taranto.* See TARANTULA.] *Med.* A nervous affection characterized by melancholy, stupor, and an uncontrollable desire to dance.

ta-ran'tu-la (tä-răn'tū-lä), *n.; pl.* -LAS (-läz) -LAE (-lē). [ML. *tarantula,* It. *tarantola,* fr. L. *Tarentum,* now *Taranto,* in the south of Italy.] Any of several large venomous spiders; esp., a European species (*Lycosa tarentula*) whose bite was supposed to cause tarantism.

European Tarantula (*L. tarentula*). (⅓)

āle, châotic, câre, ădd, àccount, ärm, àsk, sofá; ēve, hẽre (27), évent, ĕnd, sĭlĕnt, makẽr; ice, ĭll, charĭty; ōld, ŏbey, ôrb, ŏdd, sŏft, cŏnnect; food, fŏot; out, oil; cūbe, ûnite, ûrn, ŭp, circŭs, menü;

By permission. From Webster's Collegiate Dictionary, Fifth Edition
Copyright, 1936, 1941
by G. & C. Merriam Co.

also derived from the city-name *Taranto*. Because one of the symptoms of *tarantism* is "an uncontrollable desire to dance," it is easy to see the connection between the two words. We are further advised to consult the word *tarantula,* which, we discover, means a venomous spider and which is also derived from the same city-name. But in this longer etymology we learn in addition that the older, Latin name for Taranto, in the south of Italy, was *Tarentum*. If we wish further information about the city of Taranto, we may consult the *Pronouncing Gazetteer* in the latter part of the dictionary. There (on page 1220) we learn that Taranto is a seaport of some 106,000 inhabitants. The word *tarantism* is sometimes spelled *tarentism,* but since the two words are not merely separated by a comma (a sign that they are of equal standing) we assume that *tarantism* is the preferred spelling. The abbreviation *Med.* indicates that *tarantism* is a term used in the medical profession. The word *tarantula,* we find, has two plural forms: *tarantulas* and *tarantulae*. The first of these is the preferred form.

Thus we have found that the dictionary yields even further information:

8. Information about places
9. Preferred spelling
10. Technical terminology
11. Variations in the plural form

The word *tantalize* also appears on this page of *Webster's Collegiate*. The abbreviations *v. t. & i.* show that *tantalize* is a verb and that it may be either transitive or intransitive. For the etymology we are referred to the entry *Tantalus* on the same page, and we learn that the verb is derived from a Greek proper name by way of the Latin (*L., fr. Gr. Tantalos*). The brief explanation of the story of *Tantalus* from Greek mythology gives a richer meaning to the modern verb *tantalize* and to the technical term *tantalum,* used in chemistry. The proper name *Tantalus* appears, we observe, in the regular vocabulary of the dictionary; many other names, most of them fairly modern, are collected in a separate *Pronouncing Biographical Dictionary* immediately following the *Gazetteer*. On the basis of the verb *tantalize* two nouns (*tantalization* and *tantalizer*) and an adverb (*tantalizingly*) have been formed. For suggestions about possible synonyms, we are referred to the entry *harass,* where we find a discussion of the closely allied verbs *harass, annoy, vex, fret, worry, plague, torment, molest, tease,* and *tantalize,* with nice shades of meaning pointed out. Antonyms are also given: *soothe, solace, comfort, relieve.*

Our study of the dictionary has thus revealed that the following information is also obtainable:

12. Kind of verb
13. Biographical information
14. Oblique or derivative forms
15. Synonyms (words having nearly the same meaning)
16. Antonyms (words opposite in meaning)

The word *tanto* is preceded by a symbol ‖ to indicate that it is not yet completely naturalized and is consequently to be set in italic type. The word *tantrum* is labelled *Colloq.* (colloquial), an indication that it is not acceptable in formal writing. The adverbial use of *tantivy,* we discover, is to be avoided today, for it is labelled *Arch.* (archaic or out of date). In the somewhat lengthy account of the word *tap,* we observe particularly the idiomatic expression *on tap* (printed in bold-face type) for which there are three different meanings. We observe, too, that the noun *tap dance* is written as two words and that the verb *to tap-dance* is hyphenated. *Taphouse* and *taproom* are, however, to be written as single words. The verb *to tap* has, we find, two possible forms for the past participle: *tapped* and *tapt.*

Thus we may add the following to our list:

17. Use of italics for foreign words
18. Colloquialisms and archaic words
19. Idiomatic usage
20. Compound words
21. Principal parts of verbs

PROBLEMS OF USAGE

The remainder of this chapter is devoted to certain problems of usage: present, national, idiomatic, reputable, and exact usage. The chapter concludes with a Glossary listing a number of common violations of acceptable English.

Present-Day Usage

Use words that are intelligible today: this means avoiding old-fashioned words and words, once current, but now not in general use. Such words are labelled *Archaic* or *Obsolete* in the dictionary and should not be employed except to create a special effect. A historical novel written today, for example, may well contain words and expressions peculiar to, say, the seventeenth century.

Some words have become completely obsolete; others have lost earlier meanings; still others have changed completely in meaning during the course of time. Examples of archaic words are:

forsooth	olden
whilom	aroint
erstwhile	wot
prithee	y-clept
spake	perchance
thou	mayhap
anent	dight
Gadzooks	peradventure
ods bodkins	enow
quoth	eftsoons
wight	gramercy
yesteryear	

If words of this sort are used today, they are used either through ignorance or for humorous effect. Some archaic terms, it is true, survive in set expressions:

> much ado
> stand him in good stead
> the twain
> wherein
> whereupon

The Authorized Version of the Bible has given currency to many archaic phrases involving *thee, thou,* and *ye,* but these are readily recognizable and afford no particular problem.

Words completely out of use likewise cause the writer little trouble. If he knows them at all, he will realize that they must be avoided. The word *wanthrift* once meant "extravagance," *bene* meant "prayer," *word-hoard* was used for "vocabulary." *Dole* once meant "grief," and although the word *doleful* survives, *dole,* today, rather suggests the distribution of food or money to the needy.

Standard Usage

Use words that are understood in all sections of the country: this means avoiding not only what are called **provincialisms** but also unnaturalized foreign words and expressions, British usages, and technical terms.

USE OF PROVINCIALISMS

Provincialisms are words and expressions peculiar to one part of the country. If the writer has heard *tote* used all his life to mean "carry," he may not realize that *tote* is a provincialism. But because not everyone will immediately understand that *tote* means "to carry," the careful writer will not use it except to give a local flavor to his writing. The following short list will serve to warn the beginning writer about the dangers of provincialisms:

chuck	(to throw)
allow	(to think)
draw	(gulley)
boughten	(bought)
anywheres	(anywhere)
piece	(distance)
disremember	(forget)
calculate	(think)
chunk	(fragment)
bunk into	(bump into)
dasen't	(dare not)

Thanks to the radio, moving pictures, newspapers, and magazines, localisms of this sort tend to become familiar to persons living in even the remotest sections of the country. Yet the careful writer will nevertheless avoid them in his writing unless he wishes to reproduce the speech of a particular locality.

USE OF ANGLICISMS

What has just been said applies also to **Anglicisms,** or words and expressions peculiar to British English. Films, television, and the like have familiarized the British with such American terms as *elevator, truck,* and *gasoline,* and, similarly, British films have made Americans familiar with such Anglicisms as *lift, lorry,* and *petrol.* Fashionable tradesmen in the United States often prefer *shop* (or even *shoppe*) to *store,* and *luggage* to *baggage;* there are always persons who will affect not only such terms as *cinema* and *hire-purchase system* (= installment buying) but also a strange accent supposed to be British. But the writer will do well to follow American usage whenever possible. And he should remember that there are more resemblances than differences between the two forms of English. The following will indicate a few additional variations:

AMERICAN	BRITISH
radio	wireless
crackers	biscuits
automobile	motor car
ice cream	cream ice
laborer	navvy
faucet	tap
second floor	first floor

USE OF FOREIGN WORDS

Foreign words—those not yet a part of the English language—should be used with great care. In general, they should be avoided if an English equivalent is in current use. If such foreign words and expressions are used, they must be put in italic type. See pages 230 and 231 for examples of "borrowed" words and abbreviations.

USE OF TECHNICAL TERMS

By **technical terms** are meant words and expressions peculiar to a particular trade, profession, or occupation. If we are writing for an average audience, we ought to use technical terms only as a last resort. Sometimes a term originates in a profession or science and finds its way into popular speech. But it is nevertheless true that most scientific and technical language is baffling to the average reader and should therefore be avoided.

Idiomatic Usage

Use words and expressions that are in accord with English idiom: this means avoiding all violations of idiomatic usage.

An **idiom** is an expression peculiar to a language and one that is acceptable even though it may seem to violate the laws of grammar. Idioms can seldom be translated literally into another language. *It* *vient d'arriver* does not mean "he comes from arriving" but rather "he has just arrived." Such English idioms as "to be taken in" by something or "the sooner the better" cannot be turned directly into a foreign language without loss of meaning.

No complete list of English idioms has ever been compiled. A few common violations of idiom (principally those involving prepositions) are listed here for convenience or reference. Further information will be found in the Glossary (p. 253).

UNIDIOMATIC	IDIOMATIC
accord to	accord with
acquitted from	acquitted of
adverse against	adverse to
aim at proving	aim to prove
all the farther	as far as
angry at (a person)	angry with (a person)
as regards to	as regards
blame it on him	blame him for it
can't help but feel	can't help feeling
comply to	comply with
different than	different from
doubt if	doubt whether
free of	free from
graduated (college)	graduated from (college)
have got to	must
in accordance to	in accordance with
independent from	independent of
in search for	in search of
kind of a	kind of
lest it becomes	lest it become
oblivious to	oblivious of
out loud	aloud
plan on staying	plan to stay
providing	provided
superior than	superior to
to home	at home
try and	try to
unmindful about	unmindful of

Reputable Usage

Use words that are in reputable use. Avoid the following in formal writing: vulgarisms, improprieties, colloquialisms, and slang.

245

AVOIDANCE OF VULGARISMS

Some words and expressions, used by some uneducated people, are known as vulgarisms. The careful writer will guard against using such expressions as those listed below:

hadn't ought	disremember
used to could	to enthuse
drownded	still and all
he ain't	hisself
irregardless	that there
nohow	this here
to burgle	them people

AVOIDANCE OF IMPROPRIETIES

Improprieties include errors in grammar and errors resulting from the confusion of one word with another. Do not use verbs as nouns, nouns as verbs, adjectives as adverbs, and the like, until such transference has become sanctioned by good use. A few examples are listed here; the Glossary (p. 253) will provide others:

Nouns used as verbs:
to suspicion
to loan
to doctor

Verbs used as nouns:
an invite
a combine

Adjectives used as adverbs:
I *sure* will
real attractive

Improprieties sometimes result from failure to distinguish between words similar in sound. (See Glossary, p. 253.)

accept	except
advice	advise
affect	effect
all ready	already
all together	altogether
berth	birth
born	borne
breath	breathe
capital	capitol
coarse	course

complement	compliment
choose	chose
council	counsel
dairy	diary
desert	dessert
decent	descent
dining	dinning
dying	dyeing
elude	allude
fair	fare
farther	further
formally	formerly
forth	fourth
healthful	healthy
hear	here
ingenious	ingenuous
its	it's
know	no
later	latter
lead	led
loose	lose
ought	aught
past	passed
peace	piece
plain	plane
precede	proceed
principal	principle
prophecy	prophesy
quiet	quite
respectfully	respectively
right	write
sight	cite; site
stationary	stationery
staid	stayed
straight	strait
than	then
their	there; they're
therefore	therefor
threw	through
to	too; two
weather	whether
whose	who's

Colloquialisms are conversational or informal expressions and are, of course, appropriate to informal writing. In general, however, they should be avoided in serious, formal, or literary writing, except to reproduce actual speech. Contractions and abbreviations are to be considered colloquialisms. The Glossary (p. 253) contains a number of typical colloquialisms, and a few others are listed below:

> take it easy
> every which way
> a lot of
> so long (good-by)
> auto
> pal
> funny (queer or odd)
> laid off
> to go in for
> to get away with (something)
> to make no bones about
> thusly
> gumption
> cute
> show up
> in back of
> spunk
> skedaddle
> nifty

USE OF SLANG

Slang is out of place in formal writing. Because most slang terms are short-lived, because these terms are too often vague substitutes for more exact diction, and because many of them are still tainted by unsavory origins, careful writers, for the most part, avoid weakening their writing with slang. Young people are fond of slang. They coin new words and expressions almost daily. To this extent it is true that slang is a living language; but some stability is required in language as in other social institutions. Last year's (or sometimes last week's) slang for drinking, for girls, for sports is every bit as antiquated as the slang which makes many of O. Henry's stories incomprehensible today.

Slang expressions are sometimes defended on the ground that they are more colorful and consequently more precise than normal English expressions. This does not appear to be a valid defense. Very little discrimination is shown when a book, a football game, a player, and the weather are all called *lousy* or *swell*. The noun *chiseller* has found its way into respectable use, but other terms such as *scram, gat,* and *to take the rap* still reek of the underworld.

The following are examples of words and expressions labelled as slang:

> far out (= peculiar)
> goofy
> dough (= money)
> crummy
> behind the eight ball
> sky-pilot
> joint (= establishment)
> nuthouse
> vamoose
> chick (= girl)
> cop (= policeman)
> kid (= child)
> beat it (= go away)
> stinks (= is bad)
> to doll up
> grand (= thousand dollars)
> shebang
> hoofer (= dancer)

Exact Usage

Use words that are exact. Avoid vague words, trite or hackneyed expressions, and harsh or unpleasant combinations of sounds.

USE OF CONCRETE, VIGOROUS EXPRESSIONS

Prefer the specific or concrete word to the general or abstract word. Gain emphasis by using words that make a direct appeal to the mind.

GENERAL: There were *flowers* in her garden.

SPECIFIC: There were *dahlias and tulips* in her garden.

VAGUE: He *ate* the sandwich.

MORE EMPHATIC: He *bit hungrily into* (*wolfed, nibbled at, bolted*) the sandwich.

VAGUE: The work is *nice*.

BETTER: The work is *pleasant* (*stimulating, interesting, agreeable*).

VAGUE: His conversation is *poor*.

BETTER: His conversation is *dull* (*lifeless, spiritless, stale, dead, vapid, mawkish*).

VAGUE: They *walked* down the street.

SPECIFIC: They *trudged* (*rambled, swaggered, ambled, jogged, strolled, plodded, tramped*) down the street.

VAGUE: She is a *happy* child.

SPECIFIC: She is a *sunny* (*joyous, cheery, buoyant, joyful, light-hearted, gay, merry*) child.

AVOIDANCE OF TRITE OR HACKNEYED EXPRESSIONS

Prefer vigorous, fresh expressions to trite or hackneyed expressions. Phrases are said to be trite or hackneyed if they are worn smooth from overwork. Just as coins lose their original engraving if rubbed together long enough, so words and expressions, originally fresh and stimulating, often become stale and spiritless. It is not always easy to avoid them; they slip readily from the pen. But the writer must guard against weakening his sentences by careless use of these overworked expressions. The following will serve as an introduction to the subject. The writer will have no difficulty in adding to this list.

abreast of the times	brave as a lion
aching void	breathless silence
acid test	briny deep
after all is said and done	budding genius
all in all	busy as a bee
a long-felt want	by leaps and bounds
agree to disagree	captain of industry
all work and no play	caught like rats in a trap
along this line	checkered career
arms of Morpheus	cheered to the echo
as luck would have it	clear as crystal
at a loss for words	clinging vine
at one fell swoop	conspicuous by its absence
beat a hasty retreat	course of true love
beggars description	deadly earnest
better half	devouring element
better late than never	doomed to disappointment
bitter end	downy couch
blushing bride	drastic action
bolt from the blue	dull thud

each and every
easier said than done
fair sex
favor with a selection
few and far between
filthy lucre
goes without saying
great open spaces
green with envy
grim reaper
heart's content
holy bonds of matrimony
in all its glory
in the last analysis
irony of fate
it stands to reason
last but not least
looking for all the world like
mantle of snow
meets the eye
method in his madness
monarch of all I survey
Mother Nature
motley crowd
nipped in the bud
none the worse for wear

no sooner said than done
partake of refreshments
powers that be
proud possessor
psychological moment
red as a rose
reigns supreme
riot of color
sadder but wiser
self-made man
sleep of the just
slow but sure
strong, silent man
sumptuous repast
sweat of his brows
tired but happy
to the bitter end
too funny for words
venture a suggestion
with bated breath
words fail to express
work like a Trojan
worse for wear
wreathed in smiles
wrought havoc

EUPHONY

Rhyme, regular meter, alliteration, and other metrical devices should be limited to poetry. If they are used in prose, they must be handled with extreme care. Avoid needless repetition and harsh combinations of sounds.

The morning warning did not deter her.
They weakened astonishingly willingly when we told old man Oakes.
The tall wall served to prevent her from entering.
Put it back on the rack or in this sack.
She bakes cakes for four men and three children.
It is curious how furious she became when called by that name.
Often open doors are a fine sign.

If the above sentences are read aloud, it will not be difficult to discover their lack of **euphony** (or "pleasing sound") and to suggest ways of improving them.

251

Appropriate Usage

Use words that are appropriate. Most words have both **denotation** (or literal meaning) and **connotation** (or suggested meaning), and the careful writer will, so far as he can, choose words that are suitable not only to the subject but also to the audience for which he is writing. The dictionary does much to help him select the proper word. It lists synonyms and often gives examples of acceptable usage. But the dictionary cannot give the connotation of words because that connotation varies from person to person, depending upon the association which the word has for the individual. The words *dog, heat, neighbor,* and *work* suggest different things to different people. Some people like dogs; others do not. The word *home* strictly means one's dwelling place; but *home* suggests a multitude of varied associations depending upon the person who reads or hears the word. To one man, *home* suggests the native land as opposed to a foreign country; to another, it suggests a log cabin; to another the family circle.

SPEECH LEVELS

The most casual student of English soon becomes aware of the fact that there are several different speech levels. Some words are unmistakably literary or bookish; some are neutral; still others are colloquial or informal. Every trade and profession has its own technical jargon. There are words that are used only for humorous effect. There are words that one hesitates to use at all. Between informal speech and profanity we find the noisy language of slang.

We may say that a word is the "wrong" word if it fails to meet three requirements. To be considered the "right" word, it must be appropriate to the subject, to the occasion, and to the audience. Under certain circumstances, we may describe a person as *contumacious;* under other circumstances, the "right" word may be *pig-headed.* The word *stubborn* belongs somewhere between these two extremes and is suitable for most contexts. *Slain* does not differ in actual meaning from *bumped off;* the two words are, however, on different speech levels, and we choose one or the other depending upon circumstances.

GLOSSARY OF FAULTY EXPRESSIONS

**accept,
  except**
These verbs should not be confused.

The committee decided to *accept* the gift of ten thousand dollars.

We *except* (i.e., "exclude") those persons under twelve years of age.

ad.
Informal abbreviation for *advertisement*. (See "advt.", p. 216.)

**affect,
  effect**
As verbs, *affect* means "to influence" and effect means "to cause." The noun *effect* means "result."

His speech is sure to *affect* the vote.
It will have a great *effect*.
As governor, he will *effect* certain changes in local practices.

aggravate
This verb means "to make heavier or more severe."

The draught from the open door will *aggravate* the patient's condition.

Do not use *aggravate* to mean "annoy" or "irritate," as in "The child aggravates me."

**agree to,
  agree with**
My brother agreed *to* his employer's proposal. ("gave assent to")
I agreed *with* her that the hour was a poor one ("was in accord with")

ain't
Incorrect for "am not," "are not," and the like. Do not use it.

**all right,
  alright**
Observe that the dictionaries do not recognize *alright* as an acceptable word. *All right* (two words) form a colloquial phrase equivalent to "Correct" or "Very well."

all the farther
The correct idiom is *as far as:*

This is *as far as* I am willing to go. (**Not:** This is *all the farther* I am willing to go.)

Similarly for **all the quicker** and **all the faster.**

allusion, **illusion**	These nouns must not be confused. An *allusion* is an indirect reference; an *illusion* is "an unreal or misleading image." (*Webster's Collegiate.*)
	His poem is full of *allusions* to his boyhood friends.
	Illusion, delusion, and *hallucination* are closely allied words.
allusive, **elusive**	*Allusive* is the adjective form of *allusion; elusive,* derived from the word *elude,* means "evasive or baffling."
	The poet's style is *allusive.*
	The *elusive* criminal outwits the police.
alone, **only**	Do not confuse these words:
	I made the trip to camp *alone* ("unaccompanied").
	Of the group of us, *only* I had the right change for the telephone ("I and no other").
already, **all ready**	The adverb *already* means "prior to some specified time."
	We were surprised to find the boy *already* there when we arrived.
	All ready (two words) form a phrase meaning "completely prepared."
	They were *all ready,* apparently, for the work to begin.
alternative	Careful writers and speakers preserve the literal meaning: "a choice between two things or courses."
	He was tempted by the second alternative.
	Informally, *alternative* is often used when more than two possibilities are concerned.
altogether, **all together**	*Altogether* is an adverb meaning "wholly" or "thoroughly" and must not be confused with the phrase *all together* (two words) meaning "simultaneously" or "all at once."

The customers were *altogether* dissatisfied.

They were *all together* in the waiting-room by nine o'clock.

among, between   *Among* refers to more than two; *between* refers to two:

Between you and me, I think this is one of the finest novels produced this year.

Let us divide the toys *among* the eight children.

Informally, *between* may refer to more than two:

We divided it *between* Jim, Henry, and Frank.

and etc.   Omit the *and*. *Etc.* is an abbreviation for *et cetera* ("and the rest").

anent   *Anent* is a pompous word for *concerning*.

I spoke to him *concerning* (not *anent*) his unusual views.

angry about, with, at   We are angry *about* occasions or situations; we are angry *with* people; we are angry *at* things or animals:

Father was angry *about* the increased taxes.

He was angry *with* Mr. Williams for supporting the new mayor.

He showed his dissatisfaction by becoming angry *at* the car for stalling.

any   This word is sometimes misused in the sense of *at all* or of *any other:*

She says she has not slept *at all* (not *any*) for three nights.

New York is larger than *any other* (not *any*) city in this country.

I like New York better than any European city. (*Any* is correctly used for two classes are involved.)

any place   See *place*.

255

apt,
liable,
likely

Liable and *apt* are sometimes improperly used for *likely*. Something is "apt" if it is "suited for, appropriate to" something else, or a person is "apt" if he has a tendency to do something or is ready to learn. *Liable* means "answerable for" and often suggests an undesirable possibility. *Likely* means "probably."

They are not *apt* students.
He is *liable* to arrest.
It will very *likely* rain tomorrow.

around

Do not confuse *around* with *about*:
Philip went *about* (not *around*) with older men.

as

Do not use *as* when *that* or *whether* is required:
They didn't know *whether* (not *as*) they could be there.

Do not use *as* instead of *for* or *because*:
We were uneasy, *for* (not *as*) it was our first visit.
Because (not *As*) we were uneasy, we said nothing to the man.

In negative comparisons use the correlatives *so . . . as* rather than *as . . . as*:
He is not *so* young *as* he was.

For prepositional misuse see *like*.

at about

Do not substitute *at about* for *about*:
The party will begin *about* (not *at about*) four.

awful,
awfully

These words are overworked:
His disappointment was *intense* (not *awful*).
We had an *exceedingly* (not *awfully*) enjoyable round of golf.

balance

Do not confuse *balance* and expressions such as "the rest" or "the others."

256

Twenty students were present; *the others* (not *the balance*) were ill.

The *rest* (not *balance*) of the day we shall spend in the garden.

being as,
being that
These are improper expressions intended to mean *since* or *because:*

Because (not *Being as*) he was only fifteen, he could not enlist.

beside,
besides
Do not confuse these words. *Beside* is a preposition:

I stood *beside* a tall man ("by the side of").

Besides, an adverb or preposition, means "in addition to, moreover, or except."

Besides understanding French, he speaks and writes Italian and Spanish.

blame it on
Use *blame* or *blame* (someone) *for.*

CORRECT: We *blamed him for* the failure of our plan.

INCORRECT: We *blamed* the failure *on* him.

INCORRECT: *Blame* for the failure was laid *on* him.

brainy
This is slang for *intelligent.*

My father is an *expert* (not *brainy*) accountant.

bunch
Do not use *bunch* as a loose synonym for *set, clique, group of people,* or *crowd.*

business
Incorrect synonym for *right:*

He thought they had no *right* (not *business*) to interfere.

bust,
busted
Incorrect equivalents of *burst.*

but,
but what,
but that
But often has negative force:

They had no doubt *that* (not *but that*) he could make it.

257

calculate	A colloquialism in the sense "to think" or "to expect" to "to plan": I *think* (not *calculate*) that it should be ready by Friday.
can, **may**	*Can* implies ability to do something; *may* implies permission granted or possibility: He may do it if all goes well; I know that he can do it.
cannot help but	This expression should be followed by the participle: I cannot help *feeling* (not *but feel*) sorry for them. *Can but feel* is somewhat formal: I can but feel unhappy about it.
center about, **center around**	Prefer the expressions *center on* or *center upon.*
certainly	Do not overwork *certainly* as an intensive: He looked most unhappy. (Not "He certainly looked unhappy.")
claim	*Claim* means "demand as one's own or as a right." Do not use it as a loose synonym for *say, assert,* or *maintain:* He *maintains* (not *claims*) that he was at home all evening.
combine	*Combine* is a verb, not a noun. Most dictionaries label as colloquial the noun *combine* meaning "combination of persons or organizations."
common, **mutual**	*Mutual* means "reciprocal." *Common* means "belonging to many or to all."
company	*Company* is an informal or colloquial expression for *visitors* or *guests.*
compare to, **compare with**	*Compare to* suggests that two things may be comparable; *compare with* suggests a detailed

comparison in which resemblances or lack of resemblances are pointed out.

The author *compares* life *to* a journey.
Compare Albert's story of what happened *with* Esther's.

complected

Do not use *complected* to mean *complexioned*:
A *dark-complexioned* (not *dark-complected*) woman left the house.

considerable

This adjective must not be used as an adverb:
She was *considerably* (not *considerable*) upset at the news.

Do not use *considerable* to mean "much":
Much (not *considerable*) time was spent making plans.

contrary

Contrary means "opposite."
I was of the *contrary* opinion.

Do not use it to mean "obstinate" or "perverse."
Tommy is a *vexatious* (not *contrary*) boy.

could of

This is incorrect for *could have*. Similar expressions, also to be avoided, are *would of, might of, had of*:
He *could have* (not *could of*) been here on time if he *had* (not *had of*) started earlier.

couple

Do not use *couple* for more than two, or for some indefinite number:
Some (not *A couple*) of my friends are in the army.
CORRECT: We know a married *couple* in Scarsdale.

**data,
phenomena,
strata**

These words are plurals of *datum, phenomenon*, and *stratum*:
RIGHT: His *data* for the paper are correct.
RIGHT: The *strata* in this cliff are being investigated by geologists.

date

This is a colloquialism used to mean *appointment, casual meeting,* or *engagement.*
I have *an appointment* (not *a date*) with the dentist at ten.

deal

This noun is a slang word for business or political transaction or bargain. *New deal* is a figurative use borrowed from card-playing. Such well-known expressions as "a good deal" or "a great deal" are sometimes acceptable:
RIGHT: Mary talks a great *deal.*
INADVISABLE: She is a good *deal* like her mother.

die with

If we are stating the cause of death, we must use *die of, die by, die from,* or *die through:*
James *died of* (not *died with*) pneumonia.

differ with,
differ from

To express unlikeness, use *differ from;* to express disagreement, use *differ with:*
American English *differs from* the British English.
We *differ with* them on several points.

different than

The correct idiom is *different from:*
Middletown was *different from* (not *different than*) other small villages in a number of ways.

doesn't,
don't

The contracted form of *does not* is *doesn't:*
He *doesn't* (not *don't*) like golf.

doubt

Uncertainty is expressed by *doubt whether . . . or:*
I *doubt whether* she will be on time *or* not.

Strong negative probability is expressed by *doubt that:*
I *doubt* very much *that* she will come.

dove

The past participle of the verb *dive* is *dived:*
My young brother *dived* (not *dove*) from the highest diving-board.

due to,
   owing to,
   caused by
	These expressions must follow some form of the verb *to be*. For a preposition which has the meaning of these expressions, use either *because of* or *on account of*.
	
	Because of (not *Due to*) conditions beyond our control, we must interrupt the broadcast.

each other, **one another**	*Each other* implies two persons; *one another* implies more than two: My brother and sister get along with *each other* fairly well. My two brothers and my cousin are always quarreling with *one another*.
emigrate, **immigrate**	These words, and the corresponding nouns *emigrant* and *immigrant* must be carefully distinguished. *To emigrate* means "to go out from"; *to immigrate* means "to go into."
etc.	This is an abbreviation of the Latin *et cetera*. Do not use a needless *and,* as in the faulty expression *and etc.* (See also p. 255.)
equally as good	Improper for *equally good:* The speeches were *equally good* (not *equally as good*).
except	Do not use *except* as a conjunction to mean "unless." I won't go *unless* (not *except*) you will, too.
expect	Do not use *expect* as a synonym for *suspect* or *suppose:* I *suppose* (not *expect*) he will have a good story to tell us. *Expect* means "to look forward to" or "to hope." I *expect* to see you tomorrow at the store.

extra

Do not use *extra* as a synonym for *unusually* or *extremely:*

She is looking *extremely* (not *extra*) well today.

fellow

Do not misuse this word. Except in special usages, say *one, man, person, boy,* or *sweetheart:*

Sadie has a new *sweetheart* (not *fellow*).

I told Mr. Walters about a *man* (not *fellow*) I met last summer.

fewer, less

Fewer refers especially to number; *less* is used with words expressing degree or quantity:

There have been *fewer* (not *less*) street accidents this year.

We have *less* coal now than we had last year at this time.

fix

Fix is not to be used instead of the nouns *predicament* and *condition:*

He found himself in a dangerous *predicament* (not *fix*).

The verb *to fix* means "to fasten or attach securely." Do not use it instead of *repair, mend,* or *arrange:*

Joe will *repair* (not *fix*) the clock.

I'll *arrange* (not *fix*) things for you.

former, latter

Use *former* and *latter* in reference to two persons or things; as a general rule, use *first* and *last* for more than two.

The *latter* half of his talk was amusing.

The *first* to arrive was William. George came in five minutes later, and Bill was the *last* to get there.

funny

Funny means "comical." Do not use it as a loose synonym for *queer, odd, strange, remarkable,* or *unusual:*

Hearing about automobile accidents always has an *odd* (not *funny*) effect on me.

**good,
well**
Do not use the adjective *good* when the adverb *well* is required:

Sam speaks French very *well* (not *good*).

Well can also be an adjective:

Mother is *well*, thank you.

**got,
gotten**
The principal parts of *get* are *get, got, got*. *Gotten* is no longer acceptable as a past participle, although the expression *ill-gotten* is still heard.

Have they *got* (not *gotten*) around to doing it yet?

American usage regards "have got" as colloquial:

Have you any news for me? (NOT: *Have* you *got* any news for me?)

guess
The verb *guess* means "to conjecture." Do not use it to mean "think" or "suppose."

I *think* (not *guess*) it will run all right now.

had of
See *could of*.

**hanged,
hung**
Hanged means "put to death by hanging."

The murderer was *hanged* (not *hung*) last week.

Hung is the proper past participle in other situations:

He had *hung* his hat on the third hook upon entering.

have got to
Do not use *have got to* to mean "must."

I *must* (not *have got to*) hurry if I am to catch the train.

**healthful,
healthy**
Distinguish between these words:

The boy is *healthy*.
Walking is a *healthful* pastime.

| human, humans | *Human* is an adjective. Do not use it as a noun: |
| | He said that *human beings* (not *humans*) are often unreasonable. |

if, whether	Careful writers and speakers use *whether* rather than *if* after verbs of doubting, seeing, knowing, and the like:
	CORRECT: She was not sure *whether* her mother would approve or not.
	ALSO CORRECT: She was not sure *whether* her mother would approve.

| immediately | Do not use *immediately* as a conjunction. Use *as soon as:* |
| | I'll let you know *as soon as* (not *immediately*) I hear from him. |

in, into	Some constructions require one rather than the other of these words:
	He backed the car *into* (not *in*) the garage.
	He then walked *into* (not *in*) the house.
	He usually gets *in* late.
	He leaves his overcoat *in* the vestibule.

| in back of | Prefer *back of, behind,* or *at the back of:* |
| | The tennis court is *behind* (not *in back of*) the house. |

| individual, party | Do not use these words as loose synonyms for *man, person, woman,* and the like: |
| | He is a strange *person* (not *individual*). |

Party suggests a group:

They held the train for a *man* (not *party*) of fifty.

Party also has a legal meaning, as in "party of the first part."

Use *individual* to point a contrast to a group:

I like the students as *individuals,* but I dislike them as a group.

inferior than	The correct expression is *inferior to:* His training has been *inferior to* (not *than*) his brother's.
ingenious, ingenuous	*Ingenious* means "clever, talented, skillful." *Ingenuous* means "frank, open, naïve." Most inventors are *ingenious* (not *ingenuous*) persons.
inside of	In expressions of time, use *within* instead of *inside of:* Can you meet me *within* (not *inside of*) an hour?
is when, is where	*When* and *where* introduce adverbial clauses. Do not use them to introduce predicate nominatives: A gazetteer is a list of geographical items. (Not: A gazetteer *is where* you find geographical items.) Rhyme is the correspondence of two final sounds. (Not: Rhyme *is when* two sounds correspond.)
its, it's	*Its* is the possessive of *it. It's* is a contraction of *it is:* When he saw my tie, he said, *"It's* an unusual one, but I like *its* color."
just	Avoid using *just* as an intensive: I think your idea is a splendid one. (Not: I think your idea is *just* splendid.)
kind, sort	*Kind* and *sort* are singular nouns: Betty prefers *this* (not *these*) kind of silk stockings. Her father objects to *this sort* of idea. (Not: Her father objects to *these sort* of ideas.)
kind of a, sort of a	As adjective phrases, *kind of* and *sort of* are followed by nouns: This is the *sort of* (not *sort of a*) day I like. What *kind of* (not *kind of a*) person do you think I am? Use *rather, somewhat,* and the like in adverbial functions: I was *somewhat* (not *kind of*) disappointed.

**last,
latest**

     Last is used in several ways; *latest* is used to mean "most recent" in order of time:

The *latest* ("most recent") news we have had about him was in last month's letter from Arizona.

He was *last* seen getting off the train.

The *last* letter he ever wrote was dated in April.

**lay,
lie**

     Lay is transitive and means "to put down." *Lie* is intransitive and means "to recline." The principal parts of *lay* are *lay, laid, laid.* The principal parts of *lie* are *lie, lay, lain.*

I shall *lay* the blanket on the floor and then I shall *lie* on it.

I have *lain* on it many times before.

The first time I *laid* it on the floor was the day we moved in.

I *lay* on it for two hours that time.

**lead,
led**

     Led is the past tense and past participle of the verb *to lead:*

We must *lead* the child by the hand.

I *led* him by the hand last week.

I have *led* (not *lead*) him by the hand many times.

**leave,
let**

     These words are often confused:

Let (not *Leave*) her have her own way.

We shall *leave* her to her own devices.

Before you *leave*, let me give you a road-map.

led

     See *lead*.

**like,
as,
as if**

     Like is a preposition:

Jimmy looks *like* (not *as*) me.

     As and *as if* are conjunctions:

It looks *as if* (not *like*) we are going to have trouble.

I wish I could play golf *like* my father.

I wish I could play the game *as* my father plays it.

loan	Do not use *loan* as a verb:
	Lend (not *Loan*) me your fountain pen for a moment, will you?
	The bank will *lend* (not *loan*) you the money.
	Why don't you apply for a *loan?*
locate	Do not use *locate* to mean "settle in a place" or "find."
	They intend to *settle* (not *locate*) in Ohio.
	I can't seem to *find* (not *locate*) my galoshes.
lose, loose	These words are often incorrectly used for each other:
	I'm afraid they will *lose* (not *loose*) their way.
	Loose (not *Lose*) the dog.
	Turn the dog *loose* (not *lose*).
lot, lots of	These are colloquialisms for *many* or *much:*
	Much (not *A lot*) of his trouble arises from his home life.
	She told us that *many* (not *lots of*) people objected to the newspaper report.
mad	*Mad* means "insane." Avoid using it to mean "angry."
	The poor man was clearly *mad* when he committed the murder.
	She has been *angry with* (not *mad at*) me for days.
mean	*Mean* as an adjective suggests poor circumstances or something common, vulgar, or ignoble. Do not use it in formal writing to mean "irritable, selfish, or malicious."
	That was an *unkind* (not *mean*) thing to do.
might of	See *could of.*
mighty	A colloquialism for *very* or *exceedingly.* Properly, *mighty* means "of great size or bulk or power."
	The smith a *mighty* man was he.
	This is a *very fine* (not *mighty fine*) book.

most, **almost**	Do not confuse these words: Which of you boys has the *most* money? My mother is *almost* (not *most*) always willing to chat with him. She sees him *almost* (not *most*) every week.
nice	Properly, *nice* means "discriminating, fastidious, subtle, or precise." Avoid using it to mean "pleasant, agreeable, or delightful." There is a *nice* distinction between the two words. He has a *nice* taste in wines. The dinner was an *enjoyable* (not *nice*) one. Yesterday was a *pleasant* (not *nice*) day.
no place	See *place*.
out	*Out* is often added unnecessarily: Do you think he will *lose* (not *lose out*)?
out loud	The correct expression is *aloud:* The teacher read the letter *aloud* (not *out loud*).
outside of	Do not use this expression to mean "except for." *Except for* (not *Outside of*) the clothes on my back, I have lost everything.
over	Do not use *over* to mean "more than." I haven't read it for *more than* (not *over*) ten years.
over with	Use *over.* The play was *over* (not *over with*) at ten-thirty.
per cent, **percentage**	Use *per cent* only after numerals. *Percentage* may be used to mean "proportion." Sixty *per cent* of the money went for expenses. The auditors thought this a larger *percentage* than necessary.
piece	Do not use *piece* to mean "a short distance."

place	Do not use *place* to mean "where":
	Anywhere (not *any place*)
	Nowhere (not *no place*)
	Somewhere (not *some place*)
plenty	Do not use the noun *plenty* as an adverb:
	The seat is *quite wide enough* (not *plenty wide enough*) for three persons.
poorly	Prefer *not well* or *in poor health*.
postal	*Postal* is an adjective, as in *postal card*.
	Post card is an acceptable form.
	How many words can you put on a *post card* (not *postal*)?
prefer	The correct form is *prefer to,* not *prefer than:*
	We prefer fishing *to* (not *than*) hunting.
principal, principle	These words are often confused. *Principal* is correctly used as a noun or adjective to mean "chief" or "chief teacher or official."
	Mrs. Williams is the *principal* of the girls' school.
	Principle is a noun meaning "a fundamental truth or primary law."
	It is the *principle* (not *principal*) of the thing.
prospect	Avoid the slang use of *prospect* to mean "prospective buyer" or "one likely to do something."
	He has a list of *likely contributors* (not *prospects*).
proven	The past participle of *prove* is *proved*. Prefer *proved* to *proven* in all constructions.
	He is a man of *proved* (not *proven*) ability.
	She has *proved* (not *proven*) a great help to him.
put in, over, across	*Put in* to mean "devote, make, or spend" is colloquial. *Put over* and *put across* are slang.
	Do you think he will *spend* (not *put in*) more than three hours on the job?

quite

Properly, this adverb means "completely" or "entirely."
I have *quite* finished.

Colloquially, it is used to mean "rather" or "very" or "to a great extent."
His home is *quite near* (*very near*) to his office.

Quite a few, quite a while are colloquialisms.

raise,
rear

Prefer *rear* to *raise* if the meaning intended is "to educate or take care of children."

raise,
rise

Raise is transitive; *rise* is intransitive.
Raise your right hand.
When your name is called, please *rise*.

rarely ever

See *seldom ever*.

real

Do not use *real* as an intensive, for emphasis:
We had a *very* (not *real*) enjoyable trip.

reason is because

The correct form is "the reason is that."

reckon

Reckon is dialectal for *suppose, think, guess:*
I *think* (not *reckon*) I'll be able to do it.

refer back,
repeat again

The words *back* and *again* are unnecessary:
I want you to *refer* (not *refer back*) to page two.
Will you please *repeat* that? (Not: Will you please *repeat* that *again?*)

regard,
respect

The acceptable idioms are *in regard to, with regard to, as regards,* and *with respect to.*

reminisce

A verb of doubtful standing used to mean "indulge in reminiscences."

right

The expressions *right away, right off, right smart,* and *right along* are colloquialisms.

run	Informal or colloquial for the verbs *manage, control, conduct,* or *amount to:* He *managed* (not *ran*) the business for his father.

same,
    said,
  such
	Business or legal jargon for *it, this, that, one,* and the like:
	He found the watch and returned *it* (not *same*) to the owner.

same as	This is a colloquialism used to mean "just as" or "in the same way as." He feels *just as* (not *the same as*) I do about the new tax.
seldom ever, **seldom or ever**	The correct expressions are *seldom, seldom if ever, seldom or never, hardly ever.* They *seldom* (not *seldom ever*) go to the theater. Frank *seldom if ever* (not *seldom ever*) reads a book.
set, **sit**	*Set* is a transitive verb; *sit* is intransitive. The principal parts of *set* are *set, set, set.* The principal parts of *sit* are *sit, sat, sat.* I asked my sister *to set* the table. Then I invited our guests *to sit* down. Father *sat* in his usual chair at the head of the table. During his absence, I *had sat* there several times. Whenever I *set* the table, I always get things wrong.
show	Colloquial for *play, operatic performance, public performance, moving picture:* He hasn't been to a *play* (not *show*) for three months. A *spectacle* or *pageant* may be called a *show. Show* is also used colloquially for *opportunity* or *chance.*
show up	Colloquial for *expose, appear, arrive:* The investigating committee will *expose* (not *show up*) the corruption in the city government. Do you think the doctor will *arrive* (not *show up*) in time?

271

size up	Colloquial or slang for *appraise* or *estimate:* Michael quickly *estimated* (not *sized up*) his chances for success.
so	Do not use *so* as an intensive: They are *very* (not *so*) excited today. Do not use *so* for *so that* or *and so:* The game was over at five, *and so* (not *so*) we left at once. We went home immediately *so that* (not *so*) we could hear the news broadcast at six.
some	Do not use *some* to mean "somewhat." The car is running *somewhat* (not *some*) better. *Some* as an intensive is slang: This is *some* game!
some place	See *place.*
species	*Species* means "a kind" or "a class." It is both singular and plural: The collection contains one rare *species* (not *specie*) of hawks and three *species* of eagles. *Specie* means "coined money."
stop	Colloquial of British for *stay* or *visit:* He is *staying* (not *stopping*) with relatives.
such	Do not use *such* as an intensive: She has *excellent* (not *such*) taste in clothes. Distinguish between *such . . . that* and *such . . . as:* Friday was *such* a fine day *that* I visited the zoo. *Such* talent *as* he shows ought to be developed.
superior than	The correct idiom is *superior to.*

sure	Colloquial and informal equivalent of *certainly, surely, indeed,* and the like:
	It *certainly* (not *sure*) is a hard problem.
	Sure is slang for *yes:*
	Can you manage it? *Sure.*
suspicion	Use *suspect.*
	They *suspected* (not *suspicioned*) that he was lying.
take	Colloquialisms involving *take* include:
	to take in for *to deceive* or *to attend*
	to take sick for *to become ill*
	to take off for *to ridicule* or *to parody*
	to take on for *to act violently*
	to take stock in for *to rely on*
	to take on too much work for *to attempt too much*
take and	See *try and.*
tend, attend	*Tend* is followed by a direct object; *attend* is followed by *to:*
	Please *attend to* the matter at once.
	Bessie always *tends* (not *tends to*) the children.
terrible, terribly	Do not use these words as mere intensives.
	We are *extremely* (not *terribly*) late.
through	Prefer the word *finished:*
	Have you *finished* with the paper?
	(Not: Are you *through* with the paper?)
transpire	*Transpire* means "to become known" or "to come to light" or "to exhale." Do not use it to mean "happen" or "occur."
	What he did after that has not *transpired.*
	The accident *happened* (not *transpired*) at five minutes to four.

**try and,
sure and**

These are colloquialisms for *try to* and *sure to:*

Be *sure to* (not *sure and*) be there by six.
I'll *try to* (not *try and*) get there promptly.

**uninterested,
disinterested**

Do not confuse these words. *Disinterested* means "unbiased" or "impartial." *Uninterested* means "indifferent" or "taking no interest in."
The judge was *disinterested.*
The spectators were not *uninterested* in the outcome.

unique

Unique means "the one of its kind."
His hobby is, I think, *unique.*

Do not use *unique* carelessly to mean "odd" or "unusual." (See p. 43.)

up

This adverb is frequently added in colloquial speech. Avoid the following in formal writing: *divide up, finish up, fold up, settle up, end up, rest up. Up* is correct in such expressions as *wake up, hang up, dig up.*

up until

Prefer *until:*
I was doing well *until* (not *up until*) last year.

wait on

Do not use *wait on* to mean "wait for" or "await."
What are you *waiting for?* (Not: What are you *waiting on?*)

want

The verb *want* cannot take a clause:
They *wanted* him to go to camp. (Not: They *wanted that* he should go to camp.)

Do not use *want in* to mean "want to get in."
Do not use *want to* for *should:*
You *should* (not *want to*) be careful crossing streets.

274

way, **ways**	Do not use *way* to mean *condition*. The patient is in a bad *condition* (not *way*). Do not use *way* for *away*: I saw her *away* (not *way*) down the street. Do not use *ways* for *distance*: I noticed her when she was a great *distance* (not *ways*) off.
while	Do not use *while* as a conjunction unless the intended meaning is "during the time that." I'll get the fire going *while* you peel the potatoes. (See p. 50.)
wire	*Wire* is colloquial for *telegram* or *telegraph*.
without	Do not use *without* to mean *unless*: I can't finish *unless* (not *without*) you help me.

worst way,
   worst kind,
   worst sort
	These are colloquialisms for *very much* or *very difficult*:
	This is a *very difficult* (not *the worst kind of a*) book.

would have	In conditional clauses, use *had*: If he *had* (not *would have*) stayed at home, it would not have happened at all.
would of	The correct form is *would have*: They *would have* (not *would of*) been able to come had it not been for the storm. See *could of*.
you all, **we all**	These are Southern colloquialisms for *you* (plural) and *we*.

275

EXERCISES

A. Re-write the following sentences, correcting any lapses from acceptable usage:

(1) The music critics were so interested in the concert and in one new specie of composition especially.

(2) The football game transpired at four o'clock.

(3) I saw the old man when he was way down the road and he seemed in a bad way.

(4) The workers agreed with the companies terms.

(5) Our grocer charges all together too much for eggs, butter, and etc.

(6) Being as he was not well, he stayed home.

(7) The cashier has less dollar bills today than usual.

(8) Having thrown them in the water, they can't help but swim.

(9) A queer individual stood in back of the desk talking to another queer party.

(10) The child lead the girl a kind of a merry chase in the park yesterday.

(11) Outside of Herbert, they are most always eager to play bridge.

(12) His principle hobby these days is to rear rabbits.

(13) She suggested that we set down and size up our chances of raising the money.

(14) "It is an allusion," said the instructor, "to think that this is all the farther you can go."

(15) Her mother wasn't sure as Mildred should go around with older girls.

(16) They certainly seem to be a bunch you can't help but like.

(17) The data for the construction of the bridge has been put in the safe.

(18) Due to some misunderstanding or other, the dark-complected man was extra late.

(19) A "comma splice" is when two sentences are joined by a comma.

(20) Hold the tennis racquet like Joe does.

(21) We seldom or ever have anyplace to go evenings.

(22) The reason he oversleeps is because he spends hours each night reminiscing.

(23) Try and return the book by Friday, will you?

(24) His parents wanted that he should go to college and so did he up until last year.

(25) The ticket collector suspicioned that we intended to try and slip by him.

(26) If my brother would have sent me a wire, I would of met his train.

(27) The poem sounds nice when you read it out loud.

(28) I know lots of people who will loan me an umbrella even if you won't.

(29) Mr. Watson laid on the couch all week.

(30) I like this game you've invented; I think its most ingenuous.

(31) The clerk said he would have some of these kind inside of a week.

(32) Immediately I finish work, we'll go to the zoo and spend the balance of the day there.

(33) Humans, he is convinced, have got to learn tolerance.

(34) Reading about the plagues in the Middle Ages always has a funny affect on me.

(35) Harvey and Paul get along with one another alright now.

(36) This chocolate cake sure tastes well.

(37) The two schemes are equally as good.

(38) He was at a loss to explain the cause of this phenomena.

(39) The Norrises go to considerable expense each year entertaining company.

(40) He told her she had no business interrupting him.

(41) If things go wrong, they are liable to blame it on him.

(42) His uncle is angry at the new traffic regulations.

(43) The rain will have a good affect on our garden.

(44) They fully expected he would die with heart disease.

(45) I know several New Yorkers who hope to immigrate to Brazil.

(46) Johnny is in a bad fix, but I think I can fix things for him.

(47) Golf is a healthy pastime, but my father thinks it inferior than tennis.

(48) She looked like she was sort of unhappy.

(49) I wrote to Mr. Mitchell with regards to the ad. in yesterday's paper.

(50) Up until last week I was disinterested in his offers of employment; but, now that I want a job the worst way, I guess I'll have an awful job finding one, owing to general conditions.

B. Normalize the diction of the following sentences. Avoid archaisms, improprieties, colloquialisms, provincialisms, and slang in the re-written sentences:

(1) Whilst waiting for the other guests to arrive, mine host and yours truly talked anent the new project.

(2) He dasen't go anywheres nowadays.

(3) Irregardless of what them people say, I'm going to go home now.

(4) He can't play the piano so good as he used to could.

(5) This here hat don't fit nohow.

(6) He loaned me the car hisself.

(7) It was real kind of them to send me an invite; I think I'll accept.

(8) Formally, there was a stationary store on this corner.

(9) As we drove passed the town hall, we noticed that it was latter then we had thought.

(10) Descent people do not use course language.

(11) He ain't the kind to enthuse about music.

(12) Let's scram outa this goofy burg.

(13) She writes in her dairy real faithful every night.

(14) I wasn't sure weather I should take it as a complement or an insult.

(15) It takes a lot of gumption to drive these kind of cars.

(16) Do you plan on staying to home every night?

(17) If he would have graduated high school, he would have been able to get a better kind of a job than the one he has now.

(18) He was convinced that 'twas no use for him to continue.

(19) The fortune-teller said he would either be drownded or hung.

(20) "There aught to be a law," he said.

C. Choose the word or phrase (synonym) which most closely corresponds in meaning to the italicized word in the numbered phrases:

(1) A *strident* voice — harsh-sounding   loud   plaintive   enthusiastic   angry

(2) *Tepid* water — medicated   lukewarm   soda   stagnant   hot

(3) A *satiated* condition — pleased   satisfactory   glutted   unhappy   satirical

(4) A *munificent* offer — bountiful   civic   niggardly   trifling   detailed

(5) *Extant* copies — early   new   illustrated   old   not destroyed

(6) To be *quixotic* — alert   enchanted   uncomfortable   unpractical   immune

(7) *Ribald* speech — humorous   scurrilous   halting   bold   fragmentary

(8) An *eclectic* writer — scientific   careful   witty   long-winded   selective

(9) *Synchronous* actions — simultaneous   immoral   dangerous   simple   uneven

(10) Devoted to *philately* — trifling   logic   stamp-collecting   social service   arguing

(11) Having a *sobriquet* — serious mind   new hat   nickname   sad face   foreign accent

(12) A *tenacious* memory — retentive   poor   hesitant   exceptional   unexpected

(13) A *clandestine* visit — hurried   desirable   early   surreptitious   uncalled-for

(14) A *sultry* afternoon — warm   rainy   sweltering   cloudy   sunny

(15) Unusual *temerity* — timidity   self-control   torpor   rashness   cowardice

(16) *Urbane* remarks — insulting   slangy   charming   boring   courteous

(17) A *furtive* glance — stealthy   foreign   nervous   impolite   humble

(18) An *intrepid* person — bold   melancholy   angry   frightened   rude

(19) An impressive *cortege* — casket   procession   bouquet collection   ceremony

(20) A *predilection* for roses — partiality   demand   dislike disgust   interest

(21) Under *surveillance* — control   close watch   guidance instruction   orders

(22) *Resonant* tones — sonorous   shrill   loud soft   grating

(23) *Sporadic* instances — dangerous   regular   connected inexplicable   scattered

(24) A *capricious* person — changeable   captivating   dizzy critical   headstrong

(25) To be a *sycophant* — clown   critic   glutton snob   parasite

(26) Addicted to *lucubration* — laborious study   laziness over-eating   talking   silence

(27) Fond of *repartee* — witty retorts   conversation insults   games   sneering

(28) A large *mausoleum* — tomb   library   statue museum   arcade

(29) A *parsimonious* person — saintly   poor   stingy hypocritical   funny

(30) The *requisite* facts — new   necessary   odd plain   desirable

(31) To *indemnify* someone — compensate   anger   vouch for introduce   endanger

(32) A *sententious* remark — long-winded   pithy   sensible irritating   clever

(33) *Secular* matters — earthly   heavenly   civic religious   improper

(34) Engage in *persiflage* — jesting   subtlety   practical jokes story-telling   punning

(35) Saying with *impunity* — eagerness   caution   impertinence freedom-from-punishment   boldness

(36) A *sapient* man — wise   stupid   energetic careless   monastic

(37) A *sedentary* life — dangerous   suitable   settled strange   boisterous

280

(38) An *officious* attitude   meddlesome helpful legal unkind surly

(39) A *callow* youth   promising studious rash fretful unsophisticated

(40) A *taciturn* man   silent sorrowful gifted loquacious talented

(41) An *eccentric* person   charming odd vicious sportive kindly

(42) His *minatory* expression   menacing instructive cordial simple hesitant

(43) An *obese* woman   lazy friendly voracious tall fat

(44) To be a *suppliant*   petitioner substitute informer messenger partner

(45) A *fractious* person   uncultured peevish busy carefree solemn

(46) One who *philanders*   flirts reasons gives alms idles studies

(47) *Spurious* relics   ancient not-genuine valuable priceless famous

(48) An *implacable* rival   important weak fearful dangerous inexorable

(49) My *confrere*   cousin teacher opponent partner fellow-worker

(50) A *jocund* group   merry miscellaneous large unruly silent

(51) *Impugn* his veracity   question praise comment on exaggerate belittle

(52) Her *petulant* attitude   peevish gentle unusual soothing sad

(53) *Querulous* tones   quizzical complaining quaint angry subdued

(54) *Countermanded* orders   special revoked endorsed preliminary countersigned

(55) *Mendacious* statements   domestic lying whining pleading threatening

(56) A *vigilant* person   lax alert small-town strong vigorous

281

CHAPTER X

STYLE

Before giving a definition of **style** we shall quote a passage which illustrates style at its best:

To put the matter more plainly and broadly: a civilized man reads books not to find in them the illustration of a ready-made theory of living which has his antecedent approval, nor that shallow emotional stimulus to his public morality which is known as "uplift"; nor, finally, the optimism that comes from seeing things as they are not. He goes to literature for life, for more life and keener life, for life as it crystallizes into higher articulateness and deeper significance. His own experience is limited and he desires to enlarge it; it is turbid and he seeks to clarify it. The enlargement and clarification of men's experience, that is,—so far as all formulation is not futile—the function of literature.

Literature, so used, will not make men "better," that is, more assiduous in the uncritical practice of a standardized morality, nor more given to the emotions deemed appropriate on public and private occasions. But it will make them wiser and, above all, deeper. For it will immeasurably heighten their consciousness of their own selves and of the other selves that fill the world. It opens the prison of the mind in which so many spirits lie in the bonds and thongs of ancient angers and in the delusions of hatred and of dread.

Its form, its varied beauty, contributes to the same end because it springs from the same source. For substance and form are in all vital work born together. Rhythmic and verbal symbols—however worthy of study for their own sake—are to this fundamental view but the voice of that creative personality who speaks of his experience to us in tones which the impact of that experience upon him has itself brought forth. Art is one. The music of a poem is of the very stuff of its meaning; the structure of a play the very rhythm of life here symbolized and set down. There is in art, as in any form of life, no outer or inner, neither kernel nor husk but an infinite complexity moulded into indissoluble oneness.

—Ludwig Lewisohn, *Literature and Life*

This is good modern prose. It is sincere, direct, forceful, and original. Such apparently effortless writing is actually the result of long practice and much study. It is not to be achieved except through effort and then only by one who brings to his writing not a mind merely but also a soul—not merely skillful craftsmanship and constructive ability but also originality and sincerity.

DEFINITIONS OF STYLE

Attempts to define prose style have been numerous. Probably the most famous remark about style is that of the French naturalist Buffon, who said that "style is man himself." Others have spoken of "literary excellence," of the distinctive manner in which the author reveals himself, of that quality in prose which satisfies the reader's craving for beauty, of the "mode of expressing thought in language, especially such use of language as exhibits the spirit and personality of an artist" (*Webster's Collegiate Dictionary*). As Edmund Gosse points out in the *Encyclopaedia Britannica,* 11th edition, the famous remark of Buffon *"le style est l'homme même"* means not "style is *the* man" but rather "style is man himself." Style distinguishes the language of man from "the monotonous roar of the lion or the limited gamut of the bird." Buffon as a naturalist was concerned with *Homo sapiens* as opposed to the other members of the animal kingdom. Although his observation has suffered the fate of all famous remarks—misquotation and misapplication—even the common interpretation makes sense: style *is* the man, for "the personal aspect of style is indispensable."

Most definitions of the word *style* are in agreement about one thing: ornament itself, we are told, is not style. What Woodrow Wilson once said of the young man who sets out consciously to cultivate "character" or a "new personality," we may say also of the young writer who sets out to develop a style by limiting himself to the surface features of unusual prose: figures of speech, affected and high-flown language, and cheap novelties of expression. He will cultivate nothing except what will make him intolerable to his fellowman. Style is based upon thought. Writing and thinking are inseparable. "Before there can be style," said Gosse, "there must be thought, clearness of knowledge, precise experience, sanity of reasoning power." The secret of style is the secret of all creative art: the ability to select details, to arrange them, and to present them artistically. Ornament there will be, but ornament that grows naturally out of structure.

Throughout this book, structure has been emphasized, for it is all-important. Firm structure is necessary for coherence and clarity. Structure need not (in fact, should not) be obtrusive, but the writer of good prose is a conscious artist who foresees the end in the beginning and who impresses upon the confused and chaotic materials of life a deliberate design. As Walter Pater expressed it: "The chief stimulus of good style is to possess a full, rich, complex matter to grapple with." For out of this grappling with complexity come order and clarity and a sense of movement towards a predetermined goal. Structure, in other words, is not static. The design develops and grows, and this union of order and movement is at the very heart of all good style.

THE GROWTH OF MODERN PROSE STYLE

It has often been pointed out that the best of modern prose is the final development of centuries of care and attention to the problems of writing. To read the history of English literature is to read of the gradual emergence of prose as an acceptable vehicle for transmitting thought. Let us note briefly some of the familiar passages from earliest times until the present.

EARLY ENGLISH

In the days of Alfred the Great, prose was, for the most part, utilitarian, especially by contrast to poetry, which was considered the only worthy medium for expressing thought and emotion. In our first passage, Alfred records the description of Scandinavia given him by a visitor at his court:

Ohthere said that the country of the Northmen was very long and narrow. All that his man can use for either grazing or ploughing lies by the sea, and even that is very rocky in some places; and to the east, along the inhabited lands, lie wild moors. In these waste lands dwell the Finns. And the inhabited land is broadest to the eastward, growing ever narrower the farther north. To the east it may be sixty miles broad, or even a little broader, and midway thirty or broader, and to the north, where it was narrowest, he said it might be three miles broad up to the moor. Moreover the moor is so broad in some places that it would take a man two weeks to cross it . . .

The fourteenth and fifteenth centuries witnessed the re-emergence of English as a reputable language after the Norman-French period. Wyclif translated the Bible into an English which slavishly followed the Latin Vulgate. Chaucer's prose is usually neglected even by lovers of his poetry, although it is often excellent. The prose *Tale of Melibeus,* for example, is noteworthy as an early experiment in the full-length prose narrative. It begins:

A young man called Melibeus, mighty and rich, begat upon his wife, that called was Prudence, a daughter which that called was Sophie. Upon a day befell that he for his disport is went into the fields him to play. His wife and eke his daughter hath he left inwith his house, of which the doors were fast y-shette. Three of his old foes it have espied, and set ladders to the walls of his house, and by the windows been entered, and beaten his wife, and wounded his daughter with five mortal wounds in five sundry places; that is to say, in her feet, in her hands, in her ears, in her nose, and in her mouth; and left her for dead, and went away. When Melibeus returned was into his house, and saw all this mischief, he, like a mad man, rending his clothes, 'gan to weep and cry . . .

The best prose of the fifteenth century is that of Sir Thomas Malory who gave us the first attempt at a unified history of King Arthur and his knights: *Morte d'Arthur.* Much of his book is based upon earlier verse, and Malory is extraordinarily successful in transmuting this often flabby and incoherent verse into a rhythmical prose characterized by simplicity and genuineness. Malory, we say, has the genius of style. Despite the frequent monotony of his subject matter, his prose gives the effect of variety. Often it rises to impressive heights as in the following well-known passage:

Then came word to Sir Mordred that King Arthur had araised the siege for Sir Launcelot, and he was coming homeward with a great host, to be avenged upon Sir Mordred; wherefor Sir Mordred made write to all the barony of this land, and much people drew to him. For then was the common voice among them that with Arthur was none other life but war and strife, and with Sir Mordred was great joy and bliss. Thus was Sir Arthur depraved and evil said of. And many there were that King Arthur had made up of nought, and given them lands, might not then say him a good word. Lo ye, all Englishmen, see ye not what a mischief here was! for he that was the most king and knight of the world, and most loved the fellowship of noble knights, and by him they were all upholden, now might not these Englishmen hold them content with him. Lo thus was the old custom and usage of this land; and also men say that we of this land have not yet lost nor forgotten that custom and usage. Alas, this is a great default of us Englishmen, for there may no thing please us no term. . . .

ELIZABETHAN

The influence of Malory's book upon prose during the time of Elizabeth can scarcely be exaggerated, although it was often indirect and subtle.

A notable pioneer in prose structure was John Lyly whose fantastic style is represented fairly in the following extract from his *Euphues, the Anatomy of Wit:*

He that today is not willing will tomorrow be more wilful. But, alas, it is no less common than lamentable to behold the tottering estate of lovers, who think by delays to prevent dangers, with oil to quench fire, with smoke to clear the eyesight. They flatter themselves with a feinting farewell, deferring ever until tomorrow, when as their morrow doth always increase their sorrow. Let neither their amiable countenances, neither their painted protestations, neither their deceitful promises, allure thee to delays. Think this with thyself, that the sweet songs of Calypso were subtle snares to entice Ulysses; that the crab then catcheth the oyster when the sun shineth; that hyena, when she speaketh like a man, deviseth most mischief; that women when they be most pleasant pretend most treachery.

Quaint and curious and even affected as this prose seems to us today, it represents nevertheless one of the earliest attempts to make prose an artistic medium. Lyly applied to prose some techniques usually associated only with poetry: balanced structure, antithesis, and alliteration. With all its exaggeration, Euphuism, as it came to be called, had much to teach later students of English prose style.

More important perhaps was the influence of the successive translations of the Bible, culminating in the Authorized, or King James, Version of 1611. The prose of the Authorized Version is an ornate and rhythmical prose:

Behold, a King shall reign in righteousness, and princes shall rule in judgment. And a man shall be as a hiding place from the wind, and a covert from the tempest; as rivers of water in a dry place, as the shadow of a great rock in a weary land. And the eyes of them that see shall not be dim, and the ears of them that hear shall hearken. The heart also of the rash shall understand knowledge, and the tongue of the stammerers shall be ready to speak plainly. The vile person shall be no more called liberal, nor the churl said to be bountiful. For the vile person will speak villainy, and his heart will work iniquity, to practise hypocrisy, and to utter error against the Lord, to make empty the soul of the hungry; and he will cause the drink of the thirsty to fail. The instruments also of the churl are evil: he deviseth wicked devices to destroy the poor with lying words, even when the needy speaketh right. But the liberal deviseth liberal things; and by liberal things shall he stand.

THE PURITAN AGE

And this rhythmical style influenced, and received further contributions from such men as John Donne, Francis Bacon, Sir Thomas Browne, and John Milton, as the following extracts will show:

Divers men may walk by the Sea side, and the same beams of the Sunne giving light to them all, one gathereth by the benefit of that light pebles, or speckled shells, for curious vanitie, and another gathers precious Pearle, or medicinall Ambar, by the same light. So the common light of reason illumins us all; but one imployes this light upon the searching of impertinent vanities, another by a better use of the same light, finds out the Mysteries of Religion: and when he hath found them, loves them, not for the lights sake, but for the naturall and true worth of the thing it self. Some men by the benefit of this light of Reason, have found out things profitable and usefull to the whole world; As in particular, *Printing,* by which the learning of the whole world is communicable to one another, and our minds and our inventions, our wits and compositions may trade and have commerce together, and we may participate of one anothers understandings, as well as of our Clothes, and Wines, and Oyles, and other Merchandize: So by the benefit of this light of reason, they have found out *Artillery,* by which warres come to quicker ends than heretofore, and the great expence of bloud is avoyded: for the numbers of men slain now, since the invention of Artillery, are much lesse than before, when the sword was the executioner . . .—DONNE: Sermon XXXVI (1621)

The first creature of God, in the works of the days, was the light of the sense; the last was the light of reason; and his sabbath work, ever since, is the illumination of his Spirit. First he breathed light upon the face of the matter or chaos; then he breathed light into the face of man; and still he breatheth and inspireth light into the face of his chosen . . .
—BACON: *Of Truth*

In vain do individuals hope for immortality, or any patent from oblivion, in preservations below the moon; men have been deceived even in their flatteries above the sun, and studied conceits to perpetuate their names in heaven. The various cosmography of that part hath already varied the names of contrived constellations; Nimrod is lost in Orion, and

287

Osyris in the Dog-star. While we look for incorruption in the heavens, we find they are but like the earth;—durable in their main bodies, alterable in their parts; whereof, beside comets and new stars, perspectives begin to tell tales, and the spots that wander about the sun, with Phaeton's favor, would make clear conviction . . .—Browne: *Urn Burial* (1658)

The end, then, of learning is, to repair the ruins of our first parents by regaining to know God aright, and out of that knowledge to love him, to imitate him, to be like him, as we may the nearest, by possessing our souls of true virtue, which, being united to the heavenly grace of faith, makes up the highest perfection. But because our understanding cannot in this body found itself but on sensible things, nor arrive so clearly to the knowledge of God and things invisible as by orderly conning over the visible and inferior creature, the same method is necessarily to be followed in all discreet teaching.—Milton, *Of Education*

The Augustan Age

In the Augustan Age which began with Dryden, we note the triumph of what has been called, by contrast to the ornateness of the early seventeenth century, the "plain" style. Augustan prose strove to be well-bred. At its best it was characterized by the ease and fluency and absence of discord that we look for in the best conversation. Dryden gave much thought to English prose, as he tells us himself, and with Dryden we may say that prose has come into its own at last. Speaking of his advancing age, Dryden says:

I think myself as vigorous as ever in the faculties of my soul, excepting only my memory, which is not impaired to any great degree; and if I lose not more of it, I have no great reason to complain. What judgment I had, increases rather than diminishes; and thoughts, such as they are, come crowding in so fast upon me that my only difficulty is to choose or to reject, to run them into verse, or to give them the other harmony of prose: I have so long studied and practiced both, that they are grown into a habit, and become familiar to me. . .

—Dryden, *Preface to the Fables*

Dr. Samuel Johnson, in a famous passage, recommended the prose of Addison as a model for all young aspirants to style. Johnson himself, we may believe, learned much from the *Spectator* papers. As a sample of Addison at his best, we may take the following passage:

Our ships are laden with the harvest of every climate; our tables are stored with spices, and oils, and wines: our rooms are filled with pyramids of china, and adorned with the workmanship of Japan: our morning's-draught comes to us from the remotest corners of the earth: we repair our bodies by the drugs of America, and repose ourselves under Indian canopies. My friend Sir Andrew calls the vineyards of France our gardens; the spice-islands our hot-beds; the Persians our silk-weavers, and the Chinese our potters. Nature indeed furnishes us with the bare necessities of life, but traffick gives us greater variety of what is useful, and at the same time supplies us with everything that is convenient and ornamental. Nor is it the least part of this our happiness, that whilst we enjoy the remotest products of the north and south, we are free from those extremities of weather which give them birth; that our eyes are refreshed with the green fields of Britain, at the same time that our palates are feasted with fruits that rise between the tropicks.   —ADDISON, *Spectator*

This is not the heightened style of Sir Thomas Browne nor is it intended to be. By contrast to the passage from the *Urn Burial* it is indeed the "plain" style. Swift, Addison's contemporary, put this familiar style to excellent use in his *Gulliver's Travels* and other satirical works. For no small part of Swift's power as a satirist comes from his ability to persuade his readers that he is telling the simple unadorned truth when he is at his most extravagant. Speaking of the customs of Lilliput, Swift says:

I shall say but little at present of their learning, which for many ages hath flourished in all its branches among them: but their manner of writing is very peculiar, being neither from the left to the right, like the Europeans; nor from the right to the left, like the Arabians; nor from up to down, like the Chinese; nor from down to up, like the Cascagians; but aslant from one corner of the paper to the other, like ladies in England.—SWIFT, *Gulliver's Travels*

What is called Johnsonese is the early manner of the great doctor. Compare this passage from *Rasselas,* an early work, with the selection from one of his later writings. Observe that while both passages have rhythm, the first is far less "modern" in tone than is the second:

Such is the common process of marriage. A youth and maiden, meeting by chance or brought together by artifice, exchange glances, reciprocate civilities, go home, and dream of one another. Having little to divert attention or diversify thought, they find themselves uneasy when they are apart, and therefore conclude that they shall be happy together. They marry, and discover what nothing but voluntary blindness before had concealed; they wear out life in altercations, and charge Nature with cruelty.

From those early marriages proceeds likewise the rivalry of parents and children: the son is eager to enjoy the world before the father is willing to forsake it, and there is hardly room at once for two generations. The daughter begins to bloom before the mother can be content to fade, and neither can forbear to wish for the absence of the other.

—SAMUEL JOHNSON, *Rasselas*

Gray's odes are marked by glittering accumulations of ungraceful ornaments; they strike, rather than please; the images are magnified by affectation; the language is laboured into harshness. The mind of the writer seems to work with unnatural violence. *Double, double, toil and trouble.* He has a kind of strutting dignity, and is tall by walking on tiptoe. His art and his struggle are too visible, and there is too little appearance of ease and nature.

To say that he has no beauties, would be unjust: a man like him, of great learning and great industry, could not but produce something valuable. When he pleases least, it can only be said that a good design was ill directed . . .

In the character of his Elegy I rejoice to concur with the common reader; for by the common sense of readers uncorrupted with literary prejudices, after all the refinements of subtilty and the dogmatism of learning, must be finally decided all claim to poetical honours . . .

—SAMUEL JOHNSON, *Life of Gray*

THE MODERN PERIOD

With Macaulay and Hazlitt, with Ruskin and Matthew Arnold and Hardy, all of whom are represented by quotation elsewhere in this volume, we reach the prose of today.

THE QUALITIES OF GOOD PROSE

The passages quoted in this chapter remind us that English prose has had a long and various history. From humble beginnings, it has slowly raised itself to its present-day commanding position. Once used almost exclusively for non-literary purposes, prose today, thanks to the triumph of the novel, has become almost more important than verse. We observe even in this rapid survey that different ideals have characterized different periods. We quite naturally tend to assume that our modern prose represents the culmination of a long series of experiments—that no further improvements will be made or will need to be made. Perhaps this is true; but let us not forget that our predecessors probably felt much the same about the prose written in their day.

Thanks to the devotion of a relatively small group in each generation, the question of style has been kept alive. There have always been a few—the "passionate few" as Bennett calls them—who have insisted that prose be kept clear and forceful and beautiful. The vast majority of users of the language cannot be depended upon to do this. As with a literary reputation, so with a prose style: it is maintained by the few rather than by the majority. What Arnold Bennett says of literature applies also to style:

> What causes the passionate few (he asks) to make such a fuss about literature? There can be only one reply. They enjoy literature as some men enjoy beer. The recurrence of this pleasure naturally keeps their interest in literature very much alive. They are forever making new researches, forever practising on themselves. They learn to understand themselves. They learn to know what they want. Their taste becomes surer and surer as their experience lengthens. They do not enjoy today what will seem tedious to them tomorrow. When they find a book tedious, no amount of popular clatter will persuade them that it is pleasurable; and when they find it pleasurable, no chill silence of the street crowds will affect their conviction that the book is good and permanent. They have faith in themselves.—BENNETT, *Literary Taste*

How may we, as apprentice writers, acquire style? We may, first of all, as is implicit in what has gone before, study and imitate the best models. We need not follow Johnson's advice completely and give our days and nights to the volumes of Addison, but we may do as Stevenson tells us he did: pattern our style upon that of some recognized master. By deliberately copying the styles (that is, by TRYING to copy the styles) of various moderns we may in time achieve a style of our own.

But far more meaningful to us than imitation are discipline and self-criticism. In previous chapters we have learned that there are technical devices for improving our written language. To write good prose we must be sincere and original, it is true; but we must also bring to our writing a tremendous capacity for the hard work of revision. We must pursue perfection by beginning with the sentence itself and we must not rest until we have made our sentence unified, coherent, and emphatic. As we have learned, this means that we must avoid confusion, obscurity, and incorrectness. We must also study the problem of grouping sentences into paragraphs and paragraphs into longer units. We must, that is, concern ourselves with structure. Beginnings and endings must receive attention. Shall we begin bluntly and abruptly? Or shall we adopt a more leisurely approach? Let us not be afraid to end when we have reached the end. The conclusion of an essay, like the end of a sentence or paragraph, is an emphatic position. Every type of composition presents its own special problems, and we must study our particular pattern diligently if we are to conclude successfully.

Of equal importance is our choice of words. The chapter on Diction is based on the belief that it is possible to cultivate a discriminating taste in words and phrases. Unity, coherence, and emphasis our essay must have, but beyond these minimum requirements are the qualities of realness and aliveness and all that makes for *interest*. No book of instruction can teach realness and aliveness except incidentally. There are no "rules" for style. But the writer who is constantly on the alert where words are concerned will ultimately improve his taste. By preferring the exact word to the vague word and the concrete word to the abstract word, he will before too long begin to write prose that is pleasant to the ear, vigorous and lively, easy and natural. He will bear in mind Swift's definition of style: "proper words in proper places" and will not only apply himself to the arrangement of words but will also search unweariedly for the "proper" words.

In the select company of contemporary stylists Christopher Morley occupies a position of eminence. As an example of a vigorous modern prose let us conclude by reading what Mr. Morley has to say about style:

STYLE

By CHRISTOPHER MORLEY

Thomas Hardy and I first met at a club in Piccadilly where he had asked me to lunch. It is a club where they afterward adjourn to the smoking room and talk for a breathless hour or two about style. Hardy's small contribution made no mark, but I thought, "How interesting it is that the only man among you who does not know all about style and a good deal more, is the only man among you who has got style."—SIR JAMES BARRIE, *at a dinner of the Society of Authors, as reported in the New York* Times, *Nov. 29, 1928.*

As Barrie's anecdote implies, those most likely to talk about it are least likely to have it. Style in writing corresponds to intonation in speaking. It may be harsh; shrill; nasal; affected; a soft Southern timbre, or a cockney vivacity. It is as personal as clothes or complexion. It can be controlled and educated, but beneath control it must partly remain instinctive, unconscious, and organic. As in clothes so in literature it is most admirable when least obtruded. Its very plainness implies high cost; the cost of thinking and study.

The word means the pen itself. Thence, the individual's way of using the pen. There are many different ways. When language, spacing, cadence, punctuation, are skilfully adapted to the intended purpose, the result may give extreme pleasure.

In school and college we hear a great deal about literary "style," and rarely think of it again. The word has come to have a disagreeable, self conscious, or snobbish taint. That is a pity, for it suggests important realities. Remember that the word means an instrument: one of those omnibus tools that can be put to a thousand uses.

There is, in the absolute, no such thing as good style or bad style. The question is, does it accomplish the intention. The intentions, involving human moods and characters, are innumerably diverse. Ford Madox Ford once said that good writing exhibits a constant succession of small surprises. This was a shrewd comment, but also there may be a constant succession of fulfilled expectations. But these trickeries are dangerous. What specially stultifies or stiffens a writer's method is constantly writing for the same audience. Boredom, regularity, laziness, fatigue, instantly show themselves. Style becomes stunt; a mannerism; an "act."

Where I sit now there is an open window near the table. If the wind is northwest it flutters the papers and is a nuisance. If I close the window, the room becomes stuffy. But for concentration sometimes the window must be shut. It would have a good sentimental sound if I were to say that we must keep the window open—the window into Reality—while we are writing, even if it blows our papers around. It's a temptation to say just that, which would have a hearty masculine ring; but it wouldn't be so. Genuine writing—as distinct from blather—cannot always be done in a strong draught of reality. Writing is an art; an illusion. "A prepared selected illusion of reality," or words to such effect, was the phrase Walter de la Mare once used in a lecture at the Town Hall. Style is the enzyme in the literary system; the digestive chemical that makes chunks of tough reality soluble. Lowell said it well, in his verses on Dr. Holmes—

> *Master alike in speech and song*
> *Of Fame's great antiseptic—style.*[1]

Some kinds of writing that you perhaps thought very offhand were prepared and selected with sharp care. Some of Ring Lardner's stories, for instance. Or, as examples of "prepared selected illusion" consider the advertisements of New York department stores; or circulars proposing to vend First Mortgage Bonds. These are masterpieces of condensed selec-

[1]Viz.—antiseptic against the corruption of time.

tion. Equal art, with purer motive, are the Notices to Mariners which Joseph Conrad praised as the finest writing he knew. I once asked a ship-master to copy out for me the *Admiralty Sailing Directions for Sable Island,* a good example of statement on which life or death may depend:

> . . . When seen from the north, from a distance of 8 to 10 miles, the Island presents the appearance of a long ridge of sandhills some of which are very white. From the south, the range of white sand appears more continuous, and very low towards West point. On a nearer approach many of the sandhills are seen to have been partly removed by the waves, so as to have formed steep cliffs next to the sea. In other parts they are covered by grass, and defended by a broad beach, which, however, cannot be reached without passing over ridges of sand covered with only a few feet of water. These ridges, which are parallel to the shore at distances not exceeding 4 cables, form heavy breakers, and are dangerous to pass in boats when there is any sea running . . .

This is the Robinson Crusoe style; there is none better—for its purpose.

Sensitiveness in these matters cannot be taught; we can only grope and guess. The distinctions are subtle. In London some years ago, when beer was served under strict licensing restrictions, I was amused by one regulation. If you went to a pub for an after-theatre supper you couldn't have beer unless you ordered a "meal." I suggested sardines on toast. That was not a meal. I tried jam omelet. That also was not considered serious enough. But a Welsh rabbit, said the waiter, was a meal within the meaning of the Act, and made beer legal. Evidently there had to be something the gastric juice must elaborate. (I chose the unusual verb *elaborate* there, because I assume the reader of these notes to be in a mood to relish accurate words. I should have preferred *work on;* but that closes the sentence on a weak tone. I had written *really elaborate,* and dropped the adverb because it clumsily duplicates the EAL sound. So pleasantly intricate are the considerings of sound and sense.)

The distinction between style and stunt is as delicate, as absurd, and yet as full of meaning, as that supper-table dilemma.

There are no rules. Let us remember that language is a living element and we can't learn all about it in textbooks. It is employed with many different purposes. Every time we instinctively vary our accent or choice of words to suit the recipient (whether reader or listener) we show our awareness of style as a reality. A telephone conversation, a dictated letter, a newspaper story, a book review, all differ utterly in tone and tact. When in search of meanings it is often helpful to take the suggestions of familiar common phrase. To "do the thing in style" is to do it in a way that is suitable to the mood of the occasion.

The minims of a really subtle style are a delicious secret between the author and the fit reader. That is reading that becomes ecstasy. Every student of Shakespeare has gloated over tricks of assonance and colliteration of which he imagines himself sole discoverer. The bombast opening of "Richard III," *Now is the winter of our discontent,* etc., have I not often thought that the play on the consonants D and S, varied first with B, then with M, then with MB, was put there for my joy alone? Or "Hamlet," Act I, Scene 4—*The King doth wake tonight:* with pursing lips one follows the KW changing to WS, the WS to SR and DR and TR. Trivial but happy examples! For any writer of real virtu plays a myriad tricks that he expects none but his own kin to notice—concealed satirics and burlesques, implied significances, buried allusions, broken or suspended rhythms, omissions of the obvious. In some kinds of writing the measure of art is how much can he convey without quite saying it. The sum total of what he did not need to write is the mutual triumph of writer and reader. This is the esthetic form of Squaring the Circle. I read once that the reading room of the Public Library is a famous place for trafficking forbidden drugs: buyer and seller, taking adjoining seats, can pass the stuff unnoticed under cover of pretended study. The dangerous drug of complete understanding also passes, in thrilling privacy, between book and reader. Our best joy in it is, it can rarely be made general or vulgarized by publicity. Something essential in ourselves floods out to meet it, helps to create it. Shakespeare, I say to myself, would never have written such delicious vulgarities unless he knew that someone as coarse as myself would come along who could understand them.

All this has not necessarily much to do with what we call "good" writing. Style is idiosyncrasy; it may be very annoying. Conrad, certainly a very great writer, often erred widely from the meridian of strict English. But his style, his quiddity, was unmistakable. Style is bad when it gives the wrong impression. There was a big advertisement in the newspapers the other day about a certain tobacco. "Old man Wellman," it said, "knew how to make pipe tobacco. —— is packed in a sensible, soft foil pouch and it keeps the tobacco just like it left the factory." Old man Wellman, we say to ourselves, didn't know how to write English; but his error doesn't in the least invalidate the ad. In fact, the more people notice the error, the more —— tobacco is fixed in their minds. But when a department store advertises "Our engineers have improved this lighter to such an extent that it will now light 500 cigarettes, instead of only 3 or 4," the stenographer's slip becomes painful. What was meant was "3 or 4 hundred."

The arts of writing were first acquired by imitation, as Stevenson insisted in a famous passage. Many of us in my generation began by aping Stevenson himself; in my own case I followed that by some educative paraphrase of Belloc, Don Marquis, and Simeon Strunsky. Each will find by chance or intuition the model that best pleases him. H. M. Tomlinson has admitted that he bred himself on Thoreau. C. E. Montague—whose

"A Writer's Notes on His Trade" is one of the few textbooks worth reading in this matter—was packed and primed with Shakespeare. Wherever his prose bursts open it shows the glint of Shakespeare underneath. It doesn't matter so much from whom you borrow if you pay it back, eventually, with earnings of your own.

I hope I have said enough to suggest some private thinking. Underneath the printed page, unconcealable from the skilled observer, is the quality, the personal coefficient, that reveals the performer himself. We come back inevitably to the old saying "Le style, c'est l'homme." It is the blood pressure of the mind.

LIBRARY REFERENCE AND RESEARCH

MUCH of the material of writing comes from books. The beginning writer, therefore, will do well to become familiar with the library. He will learn how to find information quickly and efficiently by becoming acquainted with the special procedures of his own local library in addition to those of any special libraries he may visit.

What follows is a simple statement of library usage plus an acceptable method to be used in gathering material for a paper based largely on secondary sources.

OBTAINING BOOKS

In a typical library, most books are stored in the "stacks." To obtain them, one must fill out the proper "call slip" and present it at the desk. Some books kept in the stacks may be taken away from the library for a specified length of time. Others must be used in the library itself, and still others—rare or especially valuable—may be used only with the permission of the library authorities. Many books will be found on the open shelves, and no slips need be filled out for them. They include dictionaries, encyclopedias, and other reference books. They must not be taken outside the reading room.

THE CARD CATALOGUE

A good library contains a card catalogue or master index to all books and periodicals owned by the library, whether shelved within the library building itself or elsewhere. Obviously, the first step is to become acquainted with this catalogue.

The card catalogue consists of cards, three by five inches in size, placed in sliding drawers and arranged alphabetically. Six types of cards are used: author cards, title cards, subject cards, reference cards, analytical cards, and editor cards. Most large libraries use the printed cards supplied by the Library of Congress, although some libraries may use typewritten cards or even cards in longhand. Let us examine a typical author card:

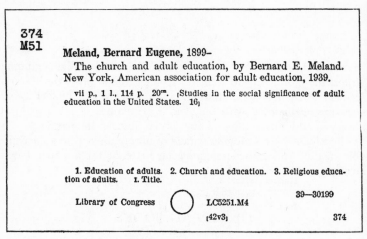

374
M51

Meland, Bernard Eugene, 1899–
    The church and adult education, by Bernard E. Meland. New York, American association for adult education, 1939.

    vii p., 1 l., 114 p. 20ᶜᵐ. ₍Studies in the social significance of adult education in the United States. 16₎

       1. Education of adults. 2. Church and education. 3. Religious education of adults. ɪ. Title.

    Library of Congress   ◯   LC5251.M4   39—30199

                      ₍42v3₎   374

Fig. 1—Author Card

The information on this Library of Congress card may be divided for our purposes into five parts. Part I contains a blank upper margin in which the library's call number (374–M51) or other information may be typed. The author's full name is given in bold face type (last name first) followed by the dates of his birth and death, if these are known. When a book has two or more authors, the name of the principal author only is given on this line.

Part II provides the description of the book: title, author's name (first name first), place of publication, publisher, and date of publication. Other data that may appear here include names of joint authors, editor's name, translator's name, and edition. Part III gives the size of the book, and the card shown in Figure 1 is to be read in this way: "Seven pages of introduction, one blank leaf, 114 pages of text. Height 20 centimeters."

Part IV lists the other headings or entries under which the book may be found in the catalogue. For example, the book we have been considering is also catalogued under these headings:

1. Education of adults
2. Church and education
3. Religious education of adults

Roman numeral I indicates that the book is catalogued under its title.

Part V supplies the several numbers assigned to the book by the Library of Congress, and sometimes the Copyright Office number along with the classification number in the Dewey Decimal System. (See p. 302.)

The title card consists of the author card with the title typewritten above the author's name, as in Figure 2.

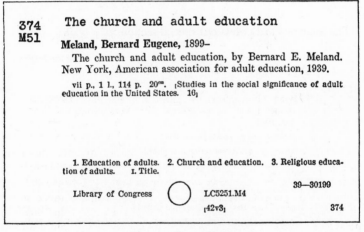

Fig. 2—Title Card

This card will be found in the catalogue under C instead of under M.

The subject card consists of the author card with a subject heading typed or written in red ink above the author's name. (See Fig. 3.) The book we have been using as an illustration has a total of three subject cards, as indicated in Part IV of the author card. Figure 3 shows the card as filed under "Education of adults."

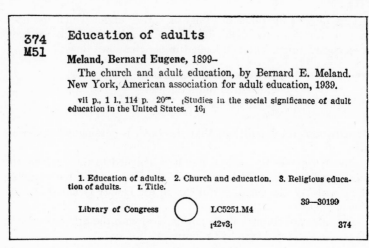

Education of adults

Meland, Bernard Eugene, 1899–
   The church and adult education, by Bernard E. Meland.
New York, American association for adult education, 1939.

   vii p., 1 l., 114 p. 20ᶜᵐ. ₍Studies in the social significance of adult
education in the United States. 16₎

1. Education of adults. 2. Church and education. 3. Religious education of adults. ᴵ. Title.

Library of Congress ◯ LC5251.M4

39—30199

₍42v3₎

374

Fig. 3—Subject Card

The analytic card points out special sections of a book:

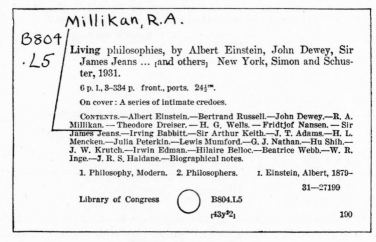

Millikan, R.A.

B804
.L5

Living philosophies, by Albert Einstein, John Dewey, Sir
   James Jeans ... ₍and others₎ New York, Simon and Schus-
   ter, 1931.

   6 p. l., 3–334 p. front., ports. 24½ᶜᵐ.

   On cover : A series of intimate credoes.

   Contents.—Albert Einstein.—Bertrand Russell.—John Dewey.—R. A.
Millikan. — Theodore Dreiser. — H. G. Wells. — Fridtjof Nansen. — Sir
James Jeans.—Irving Babbitt.—Sir Arthur Keith.—J. T. Adams.—H. L.
Mencken.—Julia Peterkin.—Lewis Mumford.—G. J. Nathan.—Hu Shih.—
J. W. Krutch.—Irwin Edman.—Hilaire Belloc.—Beatrice Webb.—W. R.
Inge.—J. R. S. Haldane.—Biographical notes.

1. Philosophy, Modern. 2. Philosophers. ᴵ. Einstein, Albert, 1879–

31—27199

Library of Congress ◯ B804.L5

₍43y²2₎

190

Fig. 4—Analytic Card

   The reference (or author cross-reference) card may be used for
an author writing under a pseudonym. (See Figure 5.)

```
Ward, Artemus, pseud.

see

Browne, Charles Farrar, 1834-1867
```

Fig. 5—REFERENCE CARD

Reference cards are also used if a subject is treated under another heading.

The editor card is like the author card, except that it is catalogued under the editor's last name, which is typewritten above the author's name, as in Figure 6.

```
821.48     Ward, Charles Eugene, ed.
D79 L
           Dryden, John, 1631-1700.
               The letters of John Dryden, with letters addressed to him,
           collected and edited by Charles E. Ward. ₍Durham, N. C.₎
           Duke university press, 1942.

               xvii, 196 p.  front. (port.) facsim.  22ᶜᵐ.  (Half-title: Duke university
           publications)




              1. Ward, Charles Eugene, ed.
              Library of Congress          PR3413.W3        42-5955

                                        ₍20₎                 928.2
```

Fig. 6—EDITOR CARD

SYSTEMS OF CLASSIFICATION

Two chief systems of classification are in use in American libraries: the Dewey Decimal System and the Library of Congress System. The Dewey Decimal System divides all knowledge into the following classes:

000	General Works	500	Natural Science
100	Philosophy	600	Useful Arts
200	Religion	700	Fine Arts
300	Sociology	800	Literature
400	Philology	900	History

These major divisions are each divided into ten parts and further subdivided wherever necessary. The Natural Science division, for example, is subdivided into:

500	Science in general
510	Mathematics
520	Astronomy
530	Physics
540	Chemistry
550	Geology
560	Paleontology
570	Biology
580	Botany
590	Zoology

These numbers may be extended by the use of decimals. A call number consists of a number such as 942.06 followed by a number indicating the author, e.g., M11a.

The Library of Congress System is based upon the alphabet and has these main divisions:

A	General works
B	Philosophy
BF	Psychology
BL-BX	Religion
C	Auxiliary history
D	History and topography except American
E-F	American history
G	Geography—Anthropology
H	Social sciences

J   Political science
K   Law
L   Education
M   Music
N   Fine arts
P   Language and literature
Q   Sciences
R   Medicine
S   Agriculture—plant and animal husbandry
T   Technology
U   Military science
V   Naval science
Z   Bibliography and library science

The Science Division is subdivided thus:

Q   Science (general)
QA Mathematics
QB Astronomy
QC Physics
QD Chemistry
QE Geology
QH Natural History
QK Botany
QL Zoology
QM Human anatomy
QP Physiology
QR Bacteriology

The complete call number includes the author's number. A typical Library of Congress call number is N6766.A4, in which A4 is the number assigned to the author.

ARRANGEMENT OF CARDS

In general it may be said that cards in the card catalogue are arranged alphabetically. But, as in indexes, dictionaries, encyclopedias, and the like, problems of arrangement sometimes arise. There may be a hundred or so cards under one heading—"Shakespeare," for example—and some familiarity with the principles of arrangement is necessary to avoid loss of time. Most cataloguers arrange cards according to these principles:

Books about a person precede books by a person; complete works precede individual works:

Harris, Frank, *Bernard Shaw; an unauthorized biography based on first hand information,* 1931.

Henderson, Archibald, *Bernard Shaw, playboy and prophet,* 1932.

Shaw, George Bernard, *The Apple Cart: a political extravaganza,* 1931.

When the same word is used for a person, a place, and a title, the cards are arranged in that order:

Sheffield, John
Sheffield, England
Sheffield Farms Co., Inc., of New York

Saints, popes, kings, and all others are arranged in that order:

John Chrysostom, Saint
John XXI, Pope
John II, King of Portugal
John, Augustus Edwin
John Dewey Society
John Paul Jones in Russia

Subject cards are arranged alphabetically by author's last name and the various subdivisions of a subject are alphabetized or arranged chronologically:

San Francisco
Himmelwright, A. L. A., *San Francisco Earthquake and Fire*

Taylor, William, *Seven Years Street Preaching in San Francisco, Cal.*

San Francisco. Committee of Vigilance
Royce, Josiah, *California*
Williams, Mary F., *History of the San Francisco Committee of Vigilance*

San Francisco—Description

San Francisco—Earthquake and fire 1906

San Francisco—History

San Francisco—Politics and government

Abbreviations are treated as if spelled in full, and a short word precedes a longer word of which it is a part:

McAdam, David	*Mad Monk*
Macadam Trail	Madagascar

THE REFERENCE LIBRARY

The following list of reference works, presented here in abbreviated form, will serve to indicate the wide range covered by such books. The user of the library should familiarize himself with these at least and should add any others that are to be found in his library. Full information about these and other reference books may be obtained by consulting either of these guides:

1. Shores, Louis, *Basic Reference Sources.* Chicago: American Library Association, 1954.
2. Winchell, Constance, *Guide to Reference Works.* 7th ed. Chicago: American Library Association, 1951. Periodic supplements.

Unabridged Dictionaries

Funk and Wagnalls' New Standard Dictionary of the English Language, rev. ed., 1952.

New Century Dictionary of the English Language, 2 vols., rev. ed., 1956.

New English Dictionary on Historical Principles, 10 vols., 1888–1933. Reprinted as the *Oxford English Dictionary,* in 12 vols. and supplementary vol., 1933.

Webster's New International Dictionary of the English Language, 2nd ed., 1934; 3rd ed., emphasizing current usage, 1961.

General Encyclopedias

Encyclopedia Americana, 30 vols.; plate revisions annually.
Encyclopaedia Britannica, 24 vols.; plate revisions annually.
Columbia Encyclopedia, 3rd ed., 1963.

Special Dictionaries

Allen, F. S., *Allen's Synonyms and Antonyms,* rev. by T. H. Vail Motter, 1949.

Bartlett, John, *Familiar Quotations,* 13th ed., 1955.

Brewer, E. C., *Dictionary of Phrase and Fable,* 8th ed., rev. by John Freeman, 1964.

Fowler, H. W., *Dictionary of Modern English Usage*, 2nd ed., rev. by Ernest Gowers, 1965.

Henderson, I. F., and Henderson, W. D., *Dicitonary of Biological Terms*, 8th ed., rev. by J. H. Kenneth, 1963.

Mathews, M. M., *Dictionary of Americanisms on Historical Principles*, 1956.

Partridge, Eric, *Dictionary of Slang and Unconventional English*, 5th ed., 1961.

Roget, P. M., *Thesaurus of English Words and Phrases*, rev. by R. A. Dutch, 1964.

Skeat, W. W., *Etymological Dictionary of the English Language*, 4th ed., 1910.

Special Encyclopedias

Bailey, L. H., *Standard Cyclopedia of Horticulture*, 1914–1917, 6 vols. Reissued in 3 vols., 1947.

Benét, W. R., *Reader's Encyclopedia*, 3rd ed., 1965.

Catholic Encyclopedia, 1907–1922. 16 vols. and Supplement. Reprinted with Supplement II, 1965.

Encyclopedia of Banking and Finance, edited by G. G. Munn (rev. by F. L. Garcia), 6th ed., 1962.

Encyclopedia of Educational Research, edited by Chester Harris, 3rd ed., 1960.

Encyclopedia of the Social Sciences, 1930–1935. 15 vols. Reissued in 8 vols., 1948.

Encyclopedia of World Art, 1959–. 10 vols.

Grove's Dictionary of Music and Musicians, 5th ed., 1954, 9 vols. Supplement, 1961.

Interpreter's Dictionary of the Bible, edited by George Buttrick, 1962, 4 vols.

Jewish Encyclopedia, 1901–1906, 12 vols.

Thorpe, J. F., *Dictionary of Applied Chemistry*, 4th ed., 1937–1955, 12 vols.

Van Nostrand's Scientific Encyclopedia, 3rd ed., 1958.

Yearbooks

American Year Book. 1910–

Americana Annual. 1923–

Annual Register. 1758–

Britannica Book of the Year. 1938–

New International Year Book. 1907–

306

Stateman's Year Book. 1864–
Who's Who in America. 1899–
World Almanac. 1868–
Yearbook of the United Nations. 1946–

ATLASES AND GAZETTEERS

Britannica World Atlas. 1963.
McGraw-Hill International Atlas. 1964.
National Geographic Atlas of the World. 1963.
The Odyssey World Atlas. 1966.

INDEXES TO PERIODICALS

Current newspapers and magazines are available in most libraries on the open shelves; earlier issues are usually bound and stored in the stacks. Each periodical is, of course, listed in the card catalogue, but special indexes have been prepared for the New York *Times* and for the periodicals. These indexes are kept up to date and are extremely useful.

Typical of the general indexes are these:

Reader's Guide. 1900–
Poole's Index. 1802–1906.
International Index. 1907–
New York Times Index. 1913–
Book Review Digest. 1905–

The following entry from the *Reader's Guide* (Vol. 42, no. 16, p. 123, March 10, 1943) will serve to indicate the arrangement of periodical entries:

> LACY, Creighton
> Democracy of China. Asia.
> 43:162–6 Mr '43
>
> LADEJINSKY, Wolf Isaac
> Food situation in Asia.
> Ann Am Acad 225:91–3 Ja '43
>
> LADY Bountiful; novel. See Carson, R.
>
> LA FARGE, Christopher
> Christmas, 1942; poem.
> New Yorker 18:20 D 26 '42
> Victim; story. New Yorker
> 18:14–18 F 6 '43

LAGE, Wilbur
    Parachute officer's golden rule.
    il por Flying 32:53   Mr '43

LA GUARDIA, Ricardo Adolfo de.
    See Guardia, R. A. de la

The abbreviations used to save space are explained in each volume of the *Reader's Guide*. In the fifth entry, for example, we are told that an article illustrated and containing a portrait appears in the March 1943 issue of *Flying and Industrial Aviation,* Volume 32, page 53.

The following entry from the *New York Times Index* (Vol. 31, no. 1, p. 87, January 1943) will indicate the arrangement of entries in this index:

LAND, Harold
    On Ger. efforts to control Norwe-
    gian schools; to lecture in collabora-
    tion with US Educ office, Ja 19, 4:1

LANDAUER, (Capt) James D.
    Named San Antonio Aviation
    Cadet Center acting exec officer;
    portrait, Ja 3, x, 2:3

LANDIS, Carole
    To wed Capt T C Wallace, Ja 5,
    15:5; wedding, Ja 6, 19:1
    To entertain US troops, North
    Africa, Ja 16, 3:4

LANDIS, (Dir) James McCauley.
    See US—Civilian Defense.

LANDON, Alfred Mossman. See
    Presidential Campaign of '36.

The abbreviations used in this *Index* are explained in each of the bound volumes. The second entry, for example, will be found in Section X of the Sunday edition of January 3, 1943, on page 2, column 3.

SPECIAL INDEXES

Special Indexes include the following:

Agricultural Index. 1916–
Art Index. 1929–
Dramatic Index. 1909–
Education Index. 1929–
Engineering Index. 1884–
Index Medicus. 1879–
Industrial Arts Index. 1913–
Technical Book Review Index. 1917–1929; 1935–

HOW TO PREPARE A LIBRARY PAPER

The preparation of a paper may be divided into two steps:
1. gathering the material, and
2. writing the paper in acceptable form.

The first step must, of course, be completed before the second step can be undertaken successfully. The writer must select a subject, limit it, draw up a tentative outline and a tentative list of source material, find passages in source books that will be pertinent to his topic, and take notes. He is then ready to write the paper, and, finally, to draw up a bibliography and perhaps a final outline.

The following practical suggestions are designed to provide a workable method for the beginning writer:

1. Read a short account of the subject in an encyclopedia or other reference work. (See p. 305–6)
2. Draw up a preliminary outline. (See p. 309–12)
3. Collect on bibliography cards a number of likely looking titles of books or periodical articles. (See p. 312–13)
4. Begin reading and taking notes on note cards. (See p. 314–15)
5. Revise the outline whenever necessary.
6. Write the paper, using the material on the note cards.
7. Use footnotes to indicate sources.
8. Draw up the final bibliography, using the entries on the bibliography cards.

THE OUTLINE

Two principal kinds of outline are in general use today: the Topic Outline and the Sentence Outline. It is advisable to begin each form with a one-sentence statement of the "theme idea." A composition that cannot be thus reduced to a single sentence is probably lacking in unity.

The **Topic Outline** makes use of nouns or noun equivalents to indicate the chief ideas in the composition. Use Roman numerals for these topic-headings and, if subdivision is necessary, adopt a consistent procedure as illustrated in the sample Topic Outline given below. Be sure that only parallel ideas are put in parallel structure. Remember, too, that subdivision means division into at least two parts.

Suppose that you intend to write about bookbinding. After reading a brief article on the subject, in an encyclopedia or other reference work, you should draw up a preliminary outline. Perhaps it will consist of something like this:

BOOKBINDING

I. Tools
II. Materials
III. The Process of Binding

As you continue your investigation of the subject, you may well decide to limit your topic, to a discussion of, let us say, how to rebind an old book. As you discover more and more about this technical problem, you will want to enlarge your outline. If you decide to limit yourself to the binding process itself, your outline may take a form something like this:

HOW TO REBIND A BOOK

Theme idea: Rebinding consists of two principal steps.

I. Forwarding

    A. Preparing the old book
        1. Collating
        2. Pulling to pieces
        3. Knocking out joints
        4. "Guarding" or mending
        5. End papers
        6. Pressing

B. Sewing and glueing
  1. Trimming the book
  2. Using sewing frame
  3. Fraying out cords
  4. Glueing up
  5. Rounding and backing
  6. Attaching boards
  7. Headbands

C. Preparing the cover
  1. Paring the leather
  2. Trimming the boards

II. Finishing
  A. Covering the book
    1. The paste
    2. The cover
    3. Tying up
    4. Pressing
    5. Mitring
    6. End papers

  B. Tooling
    1. Designs
    2. Lettering

The **Sentence Outline,** like the Topic Outline, begins with a statement of the "theme idea." The chief divisions of the composition are represented, however, not by nouns, but by complete sentences:

HOW TO REBIND A BOOK

Theme idea: Rebinding an old book involves two principal steps.

I. "Forwarding" includes all steps up to the actual covering of the book.

  A. The old book is first prepared for rebinding.
    1. The pages are collated.
    2. The book is pulled apart.
    3. The joints are knocked out.
    4. The book is mended.
    5. The end papers are prepared.
    6. The book is put in the press.

B. The prepared book is sewed and glued.
   1. The edges are trimmed.
   2. The book is stitched.
   3. The cords are frayed out.
   4. The book is glued up.
   5. The back is rounded.
   6. The boards are attached.
   7. The headbands are put in.

C. The cover is prepared.
   1. The leather is pared.
   2. The boards are trimmed.

II. "Finishing" includes all steps after the actual covering.

A. Covering involves six steps.
   1. Paste is applied.
   2. The cover is put on.
   3. The book is "tied up."
   4. The book is put in the press.
   5. The corners are mitred.
   6. The end papers are pasted down.

B. Tooling involves the use of metal dies.
   1. Designs may be stamped on the cover.
   2. Title and author's name may be stamped on the back and sides of the book.

THE BIBLIOGRAPHY CARD

The bibliography card is usually three inches by five inches in size. Using one card for each book or article, enter in ink the following information: author, title, facts of publication, and, if needed, the call number of the book in the library you are using. Figure 1 on page 313 is a typical bibliography card for a book.

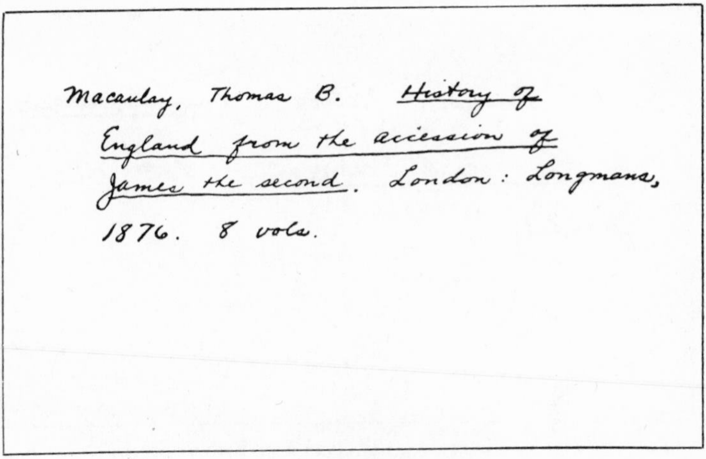

Macaulay, Thomas B. History of England from the accession of James the second. London: Longmans, 1876. 8 vols.

Fig. 1—Bibliography Card

This card you will use later in drawing up your final bibliography. Be sure to include all necessary information.

A bibliography card for a periodical article or for an article in an encyclopedia contains certain special information. Follow the forms shown in Figures 2 and 3.

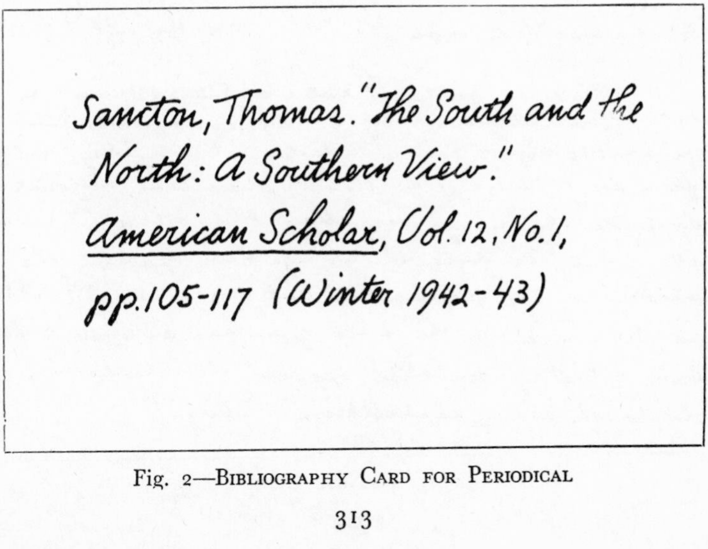

Sancton, Thomas. "The South and the North: A Southern View." American Scholar, Vol. 12, No. 1, pp. 105-117 (Winter 1942-43)

Fig. 2—Bibliography Card for Periodical

Smith, Bruce. "Police". *Encyclopaedia of the Social Sciences*. Vol. 12, p. 183.

Fig. 3—BIBLIOGRAPHY CARD FOR ENCYCLOPEDIA

THE NOTE CARD

The note card usually measures four by six inches and contains, in longhand, a paraphrase of the passage under consideration, some indication of the probable place the note will occupy in the completed paper, and a brief indication of the source. Figure 4 shows a typical note card:

Introduction of Street Lamps.   Mac: Hist. Engl. I : 337

Macaulay points out that when Edward Heming in 1685 offered to place a light "before every tenth door, on moonless nights, from Michaelmas to Lady Day, and from six to twelve of the clock" his scheme, although applauded by many was attacked by others "as strenuously as fools in our age have opposed the introduction of vaccination and railroads... [and] as strenuously as the fools of an age anterior to the dawn of history doubtless opposed the introduction of the plough and of alphabetical writing."

Fig. 4—NOTE CARD

The words "Introduction of Street Lamps" in the upper left show that the material given in the note is to be used in the early part of the paper. The words "Mac:Hist.Engl.,I:337" form an abbreviated indication of the source. The full details of this particular source will be transferred from the bibliography card (see p. 313) and given in the final bibliography. Observe that the words "before every tenth door, on moonless nights, from Michaelmas to Lady Day, and from six to twelve of the clock" and the words "as strenuously as fools in our age have opposed the introduction of vaccination and railroads" and "as strenuously as the fools of an age anterior to the dawn of history doubtless opposed the introduction of the plough and of alphabetical writing" are enclosed in quotation marks on the note card to show that they are the direct words of the author of the source book. Great care must be exercised in this matter of direct quotation, because most notes consist of a paraphrase of the original.

FOOTNOTES

Footnotes are used principally to give the exact source of borrowed material, whether used directly or indirectly. Footnotes are placed at the bottom of the page in order to prevent interruption in the flow of the text and are keyed to the text by means of numbers. If the paper is to contain a bibliography, footnotes are presented in abbreviated form; if no bibliography is to be included, footnotes must give all pertinent information: author, title, facts of publication, and date.

Footnotes may also be used to provide a definition or explanation of a word or term or to give further information about the passage in question—information which can be separated from the text itself. Footnotes of this sort offer no difficulty. Our concern will be with the footnote designed to indicate the source material.

The following are acceptable forms for footnotes:

Books:

Thomas Hardy, *The Return of the Native,* p. 12.

B. Sprague Allen, *Tides in English Taste,* II, 155.

Newspapers:

New York *Times,* November 19, 1913, p. 5, col. 6.

Encyclopedias:

Bruce Smith, "Police," *Encyclopedia of the Social Sciences,* Vol. 12, p. 183.

"Police," *Encyclopedia Americana,* 1932, Vol. 22, p. 301.

Pamphlets, Documents, or Bulletins:

Maxwell S. Stewart, "How We Spend our Money," *Public Affairs Pamphlet No. 18 (Revised),* p. 12.

Articles in Periodicals:

Thomas Sancton, "The South and the North: A Southern View," *American Scholar,* Vol. 12, no. 1, p. 106.

The following abbreviations may be used in footnotes:

Ibid. (Lat. *ibidem,* in the same place) is used when the footnote refers to the reference immediately preceding. If the second footnote is exactly the same, use *Ibid.;* if the second footnote refers to another page, use the form *Ibid.,* p. 3.

Op. cit. (Lat. *opere citato,* in the work cited) is used when the footnote refers to a work already mentioned in a previous footnote. It is used after the surname of the author and only when other references have intervened:

> [1]Allen, *op. cit.,* p. 100.
> [2]Macaulay, *op. cit.,* p. 49.

More modern practice is to replace *op. cit.* with a shortened form of the title.

Loc. cit. (Lat. *loco citato,* in the place cited) is used in subsequent references to articles in periodicals or encyclopedias. It is preceded by the author's name or, if the article is unsigned, by the title of the article or of the encyclopedia:

> [1]Stanley, *loc. cit.,* p. 6.
> [2]*Encyclopaedia Britannica, loc. cit.*
> [3]McAdam, *loc. cit.,* pp. 8 ff.
> [4]"Police," *loc. cit.,* p. 701.

Footnotes may be numbered consecutively throughout the paper or a new series may be used on each page.

The following sample page from a student paper shows how footnotes are used:

and in these factories "small children therefore worked their twelve or fifteen or even eighteen hours in the day."[1] But, although we associate child labor first of all with factories, we must not overlook the coal mines of eighteenth century England ". . . where conditions were peculiarly degraded."[2] It was not until 1802 that the first legislative measure designed to restrict child labor was adopted.[3]

Slum conditions prevailed in the manufacturing towns. The streets were squalid, unsanitary, and unsafe. It is true that street lighting had been introduced in London as early as 1685, when Edward Heming offered to place a light "before every tenth door, on moonless nights, from Michaelmas to Lady Day, and from six to twelve of the clock."[4] Despite the opposition of many who attacked the scheme ". . . as strenuously as fools in our age have opposed the introduction of vaccination and railroads"[5] the new lights helped make the streets somewhat safer. London has always had some police regulation, of course. The Act of 1585 providing for police protection in the city was re-enacted in 1737 and 1777.[6] But, says Paine,[7] "In spite of repressive measures until the end of the 18th century the conditions alike of London and the provinces were deplorable."

[1] Turberville, *English Men & Manners,* p. 159.
[2] *Ibid.*
[3] G. A. Johnston, "Child Welfare & Child Labour," *Encyclopaedia Britannica,* V:483.
[4] Macaulay, *History of England,* I:337.
[5] *Ibid.*
[6] W. Wyatt Paine, "Police," *Encyclopaedia Britannica,* XVIII:158.
[7] *Ibid.*

Final Bibliography

A **bibliography** is a classified list of the source material used in writing the library paper. It occupies the last page or pages of the completed paper and should be drawn up from the entries on the bibliography cards.

If the bibliography is short, the items may be arranged alphabetically according to authors' last names. If the bibliography contains a variety of reference material, items may be grouped in various ways and each group alphabetized. For example, a bibliography may consist of general reference works, such as encyclopedias, books, articles in periodicals, bulletins, and newspaper reports. Whichever plan is adopted, the bibliography should be made logical and clear. If the author's name is not known, the article should be entered alphabetically according to the first word of the title or should be labelled "Anonymous." The bibliography may include books and articles consulted but not actually referred to in the body of the paper. In any event, full information must be given: author, title. facts of publication, date, edition, and number of volumes.

The following forms may be used for reference:

BOOK:

Hardy, Thomas. *The Return of the Native*. New York: Harper & Brothers, 1922.

NEWSPAPER:

New York *Times*, November 10, 1964, p. 5, col. 6.

ENCYCLOPEDIA:

"Police." *Encyclopedia of the Social Sciences*, Vol. 12, pp. 183–190.

GENERAL REFERENCE WORKS:

World Almanac, 1966, pp. 80–84.

PAMPHLETS, DOCUMENTS, OR BULLETINS:

Stewart, Maxwell S. "How We Spend our Money," *Public Affairs Pamphlet No. 18 (Revised)*. New York: Public Affairs Committee, 1941.

ARTICLE IN PERIODICAL:

Sancton, Thomas. "The South and the North: A Southern View," *American Scholar*, Vol. 12, no. 1 (Winter 1942–43), pp. 105–117.

The following bibliography from a student paper will show how the items may be arranged:

BIBLIOGRAPHY

Encyclopedias

"Town and City Planning." *Encyclopaedia Britannica,* 14th edition, 1929, Vol. 22, pp. 332–335.

"Street." *Encyclopedia Americana,* 1932, Vol. 25, pp. 724–725.

Books

Allen, B. Sprague. *Tides in English Taste.* Cambridge, Mass.: Harvard University Press, 1937. 2 vols.

Botsford, Jay B. *English Society in the Eighteenth Century.* New York: Macmillan, 1924.

Bryant, Arthur. *Samuel Pepys.* New York: Macmillan, 1933–1938. 3 vols.

Lewis, Harold MacLean. *City Planning.* New York, Toronto: Longmans, Green, 1939.

Macaulay, Thomas B. *History of England from the Accession of James the Second.* New York: Harper & Bros., 1849–1862. 5 vols.

Traill, Henry D., (ed.) *Social England.* London, New York: Cassell, 1900–1901. 6 vols.

Turberville, A. S. *English Men and Manners in the Eighteenth Century.* Oxford: Clarendon Press, 1926.

Ware, Caroline F., (ed.) *The Cultural Approach to History.* New York: Columbia University Press, 1940.

ANSWERS TO THE EXERCISES

CHAPTER II (pages 54–58)

A.   (1) city
     (2) state
     (3) strait
     (4) island
     (5) sea
     (6) country
     (7) city
     (8) mountain range
     (9) river
   (10) country

B.   (1) turkeys
     (2) cargoes
     (3) knives
     (4) swine
     (5) sons-in-law
     (6) oxen
     (7) men
     (8) echoes
     (9) phenomena
   (10) indexes or indices

C-1. (1) road, man; (2) mountain, aspect; (3) hat, boat-cloak, anchor, face; (4) hand, walking-stick, leg, ground, point, interval; (5) day, officer, sort; (6) road; (7) heath, side, surface, parting-line, head, hair, horizon; (8) man, tract; (9) length, distance, front, spot, vehicle, way; (10) atom, life, scene, loneliness; (11) rate, advance, man; (12) van, shape, colour; (13) driver, van; (14) dye, tincture, cap, head, face; (15) colour; (16) man, meaning; (17) traveller, cart, reddleman, person, vocation, redding; (18) class, Wessex, present, world, place, century, dodo, world; (19) link, life.

C-2. (2) shoulders; (3) shoes, buttons; (4) inches; (8) eyes; (14) clothes, boots, hands; (17) farmers, sheep; (18) animals; (19) forms.

C-3. (6) long, laborious, dry, empty, white; (7) open, each, vast, dark, black, furthest.

C-4. (16) (17) (18) rapidly; (19) nearly, generally.

C-5. Sentence (6): intransitive; sentence (8): transitive.

C-6. (a) vehicle; (b) man; (c) van; (d) driver; (e) colour.

C-7. (18) becoming, filling.

C-8. (8) to gaze, to traverse; (9) to be; (10) to render.

D. (1) came IR, wished R; (2) turned R, replied R; (3) was IR, approached R, would have IR, contradicted R, was IR; (4) glared R, was IR; (5) had IR, allowed R.

E. (1) I went only as far as the corner.

(2) I had almost given up hope.

(3) I did not expect ever to have to do this again.

(4) Philip said to the policeman that he was merely waiting for a friend.

(5) She knows a girl who had almost the same kind of operation on her throat that she had.

(6) She had to stay in the hospital for nearly six weeks.

(7) She could see only her relatives.

F. (1) happy   (9) who
   (2) an   (10) its
   (3) an   (11) our
   (4) I   (12) us
   (5) is   (13) is
   (6) is; is   (14) would
   (7) me   (15) nor; has
   (8) whom

G. (1) shaken   (4) risen; fallen; torn
   (2) did   (5) broken; become
   (3) blown

H. (1) decided (finite verb); walking (gerund)

(2) strode (finite verb); scowling, looking, muttering (participles)

(3) may borrow (finite verb)

(4) were thrown (finite verb); glowing (participle)

(5) is (finite verb)

(6) tried (finite verb); to learn (infinitive)

(7) pored (finite verb); during (preposition)

(8) was forced, had been (finite verbs); to admit (infinitive); going (gerund)

(9) shall estimate (finite verb)

(10) believe, denies (finite verbs)

CHAPTER III (pages 92–96)

A.　(1) adverb   (6) noun
　　(2) adverb   (7) noun
　　(3) adjective   (8) adverb
　　(4) adjective   (9) adverb
　　(5) adjective   (10) noun

B.　(1) Martin, together with his friend David, has been seeing the sights of Pittsburgh.

　　(2) The part that interested them most was the two colleges they visited.

　　(3) The junction of the three rivers was an impressive sight, too.

　　(4) There are, in and around Pittsburgh, a great many steel mills.

　　(5) Each seems larger than the next.

　　(6) In order to reach David's home, it is usual to travel on one of the inclined railways that run to the top of the cliff.

　　(7) From the top, the visitor enjoys one of the most interesting sights that are to be found in the state.

　　(8) Neither David nor his parents were anxious for Martin to leave.

　　(9) At the bus station, there were an elderly couple and four soldiers waiting to start for Chicago.

　　(10) The bus for Chicago, like the other long-distance busses, was large and roomy.

C.　(1) DO   (6) DO
　　(2) PA   (7) DO
　　(3) PN   (8) DO
　　(4) DO   (9) DO
　　(5) PN   (10) PA

D.　(1) DEP   (4) IND
　　(2) IND   (5) IND
　　(3) DEP

E.　(1) S   (6) S
　　(2) CX   (7) CC
　　(3) CC   (8) CX
　　(4) S   (9) S
　　(5) S   (10) CX

F.   (1) subject
     (2) direct object
     (3) object of a preposition
     (4) object of a preposition
     (5) adjective

     (6) object of a preposition
     (7) verb
     (8) predicate noun
     (9) direct object
    (10) object of a preposition

ANSWERS TO DIAGRAMING EXERCISES

I.

(1)

Frank | chuckles

(2)

mother | looks

(3)

She | *and* — is knitting / (is) listening

(4)

you | are laughing

(5)

letter | is

(6)

letters | do amuse

(7)

Uncle Louis | writes

(8) <u>(you) | Open</u>

(9) <u>you | Do find</u>

(10) <u>Knitting | can be</u>

II. (1)

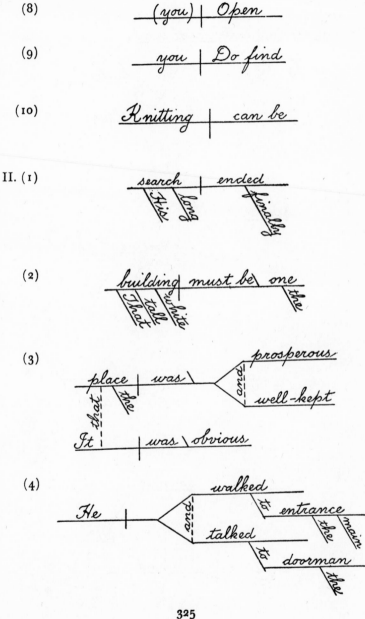

(2)

(3)

(4)

(5)

The uniform | was \ resplendent
with buttons (brass) and braid (gold)

(6)

Walter | asked
for the apartment Smiths'

(7)

The doorman and Walter | discussed number
of the Smiths in city the

(8)

the buzzer | sounded Finally
and
the door | opened

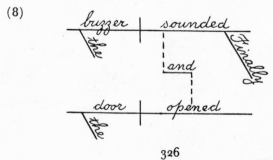

326

(9)

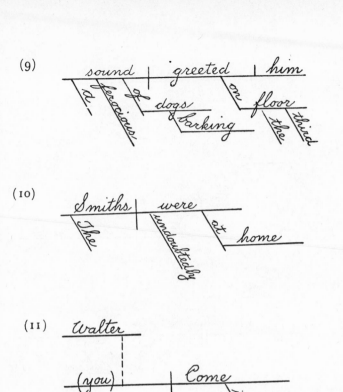

(10)

(11)

(12)

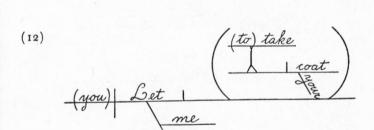

(13)

327

(14)

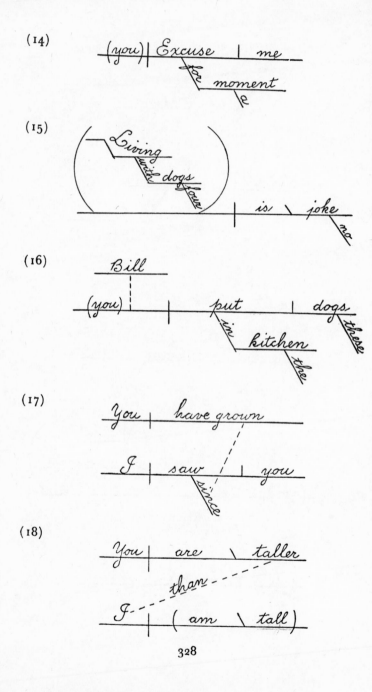

(15)

(16)

(17)

(18)

328

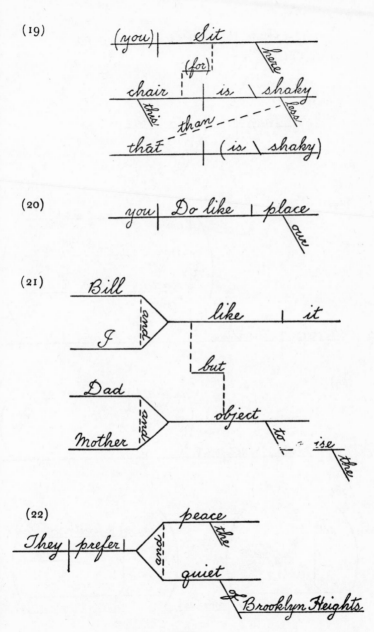

(19)

(20)

(21)

(22)

329

(23)

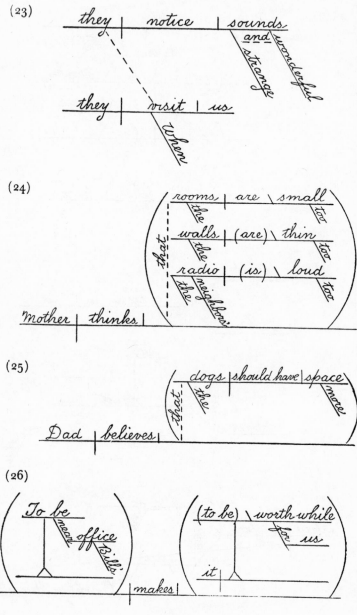

(24)

(25)

(26)

330

(27)

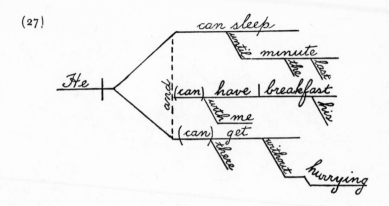

(28)

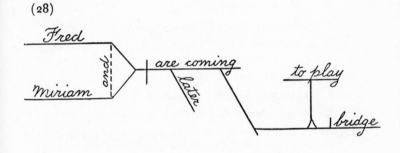

(29)

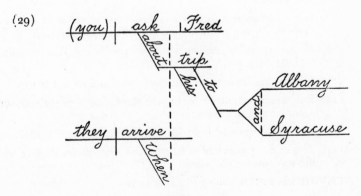

(30)

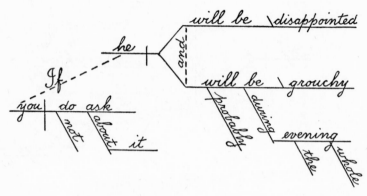

CHAPTER IV (pages 117–122)

A. (1) He taught grammar and spelling.

(2) Swimming and fishing are summer sports.

(3) If we have packed and if we get up early enough, we should get to the beach by ten.

(4) They were not only disappointed but also angry.

(5) I want both exercise and amusement.

(6) He offered to pay for it either now or tomorrow.

(7) As we were unfamiliar with the route and as darkness was approaching, we decided to ask for advice.

(8) He had not only attended many weddings but he had been best man twice.

(9) If we remember that when he first tried to enlist he was only thirteen, we ought not to be surprised at what happened.

(10) He had spent his previous summers travelling in Europe, sailing on Lake Erie, and visiting Mexico.

(11) Michael has brought his little girl a doll and an Easter egg.

(12) Sam wants to trade-in his bicycle and to buy a motorcycle with a sidecar and two horns.

(13) Billy's face was streaked with dirt and his feet were muddy.

(14) The critics praised McAdam for his short-stories dealing with the war and for his poems.

(15) He was neither willing nor able to pay.

B. (1) Dashing to the front window, we saw the parade come into view.

(2) Because his car was missing on two cylinders and backfiring badly, the driver stopped at the filling station.

(3) When he had diagnosed my case and had given me a prescription, I paid Dr. Robins and left.

(4) When I opened one eye a fraction, the room appeared empty.

(5) Taking our great Dane for his morning walk, I find the neighbor's cat a nuisance.

(6) When it was nicely browned on both sides, I removed the pancake from the griddle.

(7) When I reached the tender age of three, my parents moved to New Jersey.

(8) I went to a dance last night, and, as a result, I was late at the office this morning.

(9) Two months ago, after I graduated from high school, my grandfather gave me a gold watch.

(10) To open this door, give it a sudden push.

(11) Since he was unaccustomed to smoking, the pipe made him ill.

(12) If one is to learn French well, one must speak it regularly.

(13) When the essay is neatly typewritten and folded correctly, hand it to the teacher.

(14) When I was swimming half a mile out into the bay, the shore seemed distant indeed.

(15) We had just started the third rubber of bridge when, looking up, we saw Mrs. Green.

(16) Whenever he spoke of his experiences in New Orleans, Stephen's excitement made him stutter.

(17) After much frantic searching in my desk, I discovered the missing fountain pen.

(18) The fact that I had forgotten to change my shirt caused me much embarrassment.

(19) When they have been properly sprinkled, roll the tablecloths up and put them aside.

(20) Since she was not used to the water, she thought the small boat looked dangerous.

C. (1) Because he had made that speech a number of times, he was so accustomed to it that he couldn't understand the lack of applause.

(2) Just as I was reaching down to pick up my hat, I saw the two rattlesnakes.

(3) When we came within sight of the village, our car suddenly caught fire.

(4) The fact that he has been to college is no sign he is cultured.

(5) She felt as if she were walking on air.

(6) I am not sure that we ought to let him have that gun.

(7) The main reason I left early was that I was bored.

(8) Mr. Samuelson is the vice-president and Mr. Daniels is the secretary.

(9) Because of illness, he was obliged to postpone his vacation.

(10) Just as my cousin was recovering normally she had a relapse.

D. (1) Whenever we can, of course, we go to camp during the summer.

(2) Everyone appeared pleased about the outcome, especially the out-of-town visitors.

(3) Running, jumping, climbing on chairs, dashing in and out of rooms—the small boy was always active.

(4) Our literary club has only two officers, Mr. Dawson being president and Miss Gaines being secretary-treasurer.

(5) Living in the city is not always pleasant, particularly during the summer months.

(6) "We'll have to wait here," said Bill, disgustedly, "since they haven't left the door unlocked."

(7) His new clothes gave him a feeling of confidence such as he had never had before.

(8) There was one thing he couldn't tolerate, namely, neighbors who give noisy parties late at night.

(9) To live in New York, to feel that she was in the very center of things, to get away once and for all from small-town pettiness— this was her ambition.

(10) He hated foreign languages, especially Latin, French, and German.

E. (1) Talking to the mayor gave Elizabeth a new feeling of confidence. She felt it had done wonders for her.

(2) Since I was sure I'd get there on time, I walked confidently down the street.

(3) "I've never done any skiing before," Melvin whispered to me. "I'm rather disturbed at the idea."

(4) The sand was beginning to blow, and so we headed for shelter.

(5) She saved money by making her own clothes; moreover, she enjoyed designing them.

(6) My brother was obviously disconcerted by Mr. Simpson's flat refusal; so he turned away abruptly.

(7) Spending forty minutes on the subway every morning is no joke; to tell the truth, it's a fearful nuisance.

(8) They are still quite young; therefore they can afford to wait a year or two.

(9) "I was back in my hotel room by ten o'clock," stated the witness. "I did not go out again until the following morning."

(10) We saw her fall. We never want to see a sight like that again.

F. (1) It wasn't his idea. He should have known better than to do it.

(2) I can't quite picture him as a teacher. He isn't the type, somehow.

(3) We were tired and hungry; in fact, we were almost exhausted.

(4) We hesitated a moment or two but then decided to go in anyway. If worst came to worst, we could always mention Jack's name.

(5) Joan had never read any novels by Sinclair Lewis; so she bought a copy of *Arrowsmith*.

(6) The room looked wonderful. The rugs had just been vacuumed.

(7) I don't think it's his fault. He hasn't played tennis for three years and he's out of practice.

(8) He is taking a pre-medical course. To enter medical school is his greatest ambition.

(9) Kenneth may be able to tell you; on the other hand, you may have to ask Mr. Edwardson.

(10) Come inside at once. I'm tired of having to reprimand you.

G. (1) The librarian was extremely discouraged about the lack of funds.

(2) Our situation is wonderful.

(3) Trying to work when my roommate is playing his accordion is a great problem.

(4) The young girls wore ankle-socks. In spite of their odd manners and strange slang, they were, we found, essentially kind-hearted.

(5) She is very talented.

(6) Courses in science have more appeal for the college student today than have liberal arts courses.

(7) "From my boyish days I had always felt a great perplexity on one point in *Macbeth.* It was this:— the knocking at the gate which succeeds to the murder of Duncan produced to my feelings an effect for which I never could account. The effect was that it reflected back upon the murderer a peculiar awfulness and a depth of solemnity; yet, however obstinately I endeavoured with my understanding to comprehend this, for many years I never could see *why* it should produce such an effect."
—De Quincey: "On the Knocking at the Gate in *Macbeth*"

H. (1) Apparently, he was content to wait patiently outside the door.

(2) I wrote to my nephew and asked him to let me know about the horses as soon as he could.

(3) The membership committee are trying to make up their minds about Sidney's application.

(4) Both Sally and her sister saw the play, but Sally was disappointed in it.

(5) He took an oath never to reveal the secrets of the organization, no matter what happened.

(6) She lifted her eyes from the floor and stared out the window.

(7) I informed the policeman that I was always anxious to be of service.

(8) We went on a trip to Mexico. The Mexicans, we found, are a hospitable people.

(9) I have been reading *Henry Esmond,* a novel by Thackeray, who is one of the best authors of the nineteenth century.

(10) Having worked steadily at the sewing-machine for three hours and having finished stitching five dresses, she sat down wearily in the armchair.

(11) She is as old as Marion, if not older.

(12) We have talked to him and we will talk to him again about his plans.

(13) The broad fields were covered with white frost.

(14) She told us that she had difficulty in following the doctor's advice, although it seemed easy enough.

(15) I heard Wagner's *Die Meistersinger*. Wagner was, undoubtedly, a great composer.

I. (1) My sister, on the other hand, is happy in her new home.

(2) For some reason or other, the guests left early.

(3) His teacher is one person in whom he can confide.

(4) Just as we came out of the house, the rain began to fall.

(5) If you don't like it here, go away.

(6) That they will put much faith in his words is, to say the least, unlikely.

(7) He testified that he had attended grammar school, high school, and college.

(8) Lincoln's speech at Gettysburg was not appreciated at the time, but Lincoln's speech will live forever.

(9) The policeman informed us that he had told Edith of her mother's death.

(10) We think it is a worthy cause.

CHAPTER VII (pages 205–208)

A. (1) The Nobel Fund, through which prizes are awarded each year, was established by Alfred B. Nobel.

(2) Nobel, who was the inventor of dynamite, died on December 10, 1896.

(3) The fund which he established is now managed by a Board of Directors.

(4) It was designed to reward those persons who, in the opinion of the board, had contributed most, during the previous year, to the service of mankind.

(5) Prominent persons, including a number of Americans, are among those who have received the Nobel Prize.

(6) Although the Nobel Prize for Peace was not awarded in 1924, it was awarded the next year to Charles G. Dawes, an American, and to Sir Austen Chamberlain, an Englishman.

(7) Previously, in 1919, it had been awarded to Woodrow Wilson.

(8) Mme. Curie, who twice received the prize, is among the best-known winners.

(9) The discoverer of insulin, Dr. Banting, shared the prize in 1923 with Dr. McLeod.

(10) Sinclair Lewis, who has written many novels of distinction, was the first American to receive the Nobel Prize for Literature.

B. (1) Another famous trust fund was established by Cecil John Rhodes, a South African, who died in 1902.

(2) Originally, according to the provisions of the will, two scholarships at Oxford were established for eligible young men in each of the states in this country.

(3) In addition, scholarships were made available to the several states and provinces in Canada, South Africa, and Australia and to students in Newfoundland, New Zealand, Jamaica, Bermuda, and Malta.

(4) The fund, as subsequently modified, provides thirty-two scholarships each year to the United States, and the country, for the purposes of election, is divided into districts, each consisting of several states.

(5) Four scholars are chosen from each district yearly, but each scholar represents his own state.

(6) A candidate must meet certain requirements: he must be over seventeen and not over twenty-four years of age, he must be of at least junior standing in college, and he must show evidence of ability and interest in scholarship and athletics.

(7) Normally, a Rhodes Scholar remains at Oxford for two years, but he may apply for an additional third year.

(8) The Rhodes Scholars, numbering usually about two hundred, are, as a rule, fairly equally divided between the British Empire and the United States.

(9) The five scholarships which were awarded to Germany were annulled in 1916, later restored, and still later withdrawn once again.

(10) After the outbreak of the Second World War, the Rhodes Scholarships were suspended for the duration.

C. (1) Great trust funds for philanthropic purposes have been established in this country; there are some twenty-five such public trusts now in operation.

338

(2) Those established with an original endowment of more than $10,000,000 include the following: the Ford Foundation, the Rockefeller Foundation, the Carnegie Corporation of New York, the Juilliard Foundation, and the Duke Endowment.

(3) American foundations make possible research in a variety of fields: education, social welfare, medicine, public health, housing, economics, and many others.

(4) The Guggenheim Memorial fellowships are granted for research in many fields of knowledge; they are awarded to capable and talented persons, regardless of race, color, or creed.

(5) One of the many funds set up by Andrew Carnegie is the Carnegie Hero Fund Commission; it awards medals and sums of money to heroes and heroines or to their dependents.

D. (1) The Seven Wonders of the World are the Pyramids, the Hanging Gardens of Babylon, the Temple of Diana, the Statue of Jupiter Olympus, the Mausoleum, the Pharos of Alexandria, and the Colossus of Rhodes.

(2) The best-known of these is the Pyramids of Egypt.

(3) The great stone lion called the Sphinx was hewn, we believe, from a single stone.

(4) The Colossus of Rhodes must not be confused with the Coliseum: the former was a statue of Apollo; the latter is that great amphitheater which still stands in Rome.

(5) Another famous monument of antiquity is Stonehenge, a group of huge stones on Salisbury Plain, in England.

E. (1) The Monroe Doctrine, one of the important documents of history, was incorporated in President Monroe's message to Congress on December 2, 1823.

(2) The result of much consultation with the members of the Cabinet, the Doctrine asserted that "the American continents . . . are henceforth not to be considered as subjects for future colonization by any European powers."

(3) Jefferson, echoing the Farewell Address of Washington, declared: "Our first and fundamental maxim should be never to entangle ourselves in the broils of Europe."

(4) The Monroe Doctrine has been discussed, re-examined, and debated, both at home and abroad, during the last century.

(5) This discussion, we have every reason to believe, will continue.

F. It was near sunset, I repeat, and we were crossing the bay of Gibraltar. I stood on the prow of the vessel, with my eyes intently fixed on the mountain fortress, which, though I had seen it several times before, filled my mind with admiration and interest. Viewed from this situation, it certainly, if it resembles any animate object in nature, has something of the appearance of a terrible couchant lion, whose stupendous head menaces Spain. Had I been dreaming, I should have concluded it to be the genius of Africa, in the shape of its most puissant monster, who had bounded over the sea from the clime of sand and sun, bent on the destruction of the rival continent, more especially as the hue of its stony sides, its crest and chine, is tawny even as that of the hide of the desert king. A hostile lion has it almost invariably proved to Spain, at least since it first began to play a part in history, which was at the time when Tarik seized and fortified it. It has for the most part been in the hands of foreigners: first the swarthy and turbaned Moor possessed it, and it is now tenanted by a fair-haired race from a distant isle. Though a part of Spain, it seems to disavow the connection, and at the end of a long narrow sandy isthmus, almost level with the sea, raising its blasted and perpendicular brow to denounce the crimes which deform the history of that fair and majestic land.

—GEORGE BORROW.

G. (1) Halt! Who goes there?

(2) The new boarder (he's from Louisiana) speaks with a delightful accent.

(3) Everything important—life, liberty, the pursuit of happiness—seemed about to be lost forever.

(4) Freedom of speech, freedom from want, freedom from fear, freedom of religion—these, they felt, were great ideals.

(5) The applicant identified himself as follows: George Albert Wilson, 2205 Mill St., Smithtown, California.

(6) "It's—it's impossible!" stammered the young man. "Do you really think he'd . . . ?"

(7) Because of his abilities as a leader, Sam was more than just a likely candidate: he was the one man for the job.

(8) I have collected many things in my time: stamps, coins, arrowheads, books, and cigar bands.

(9) "I'll say he's upset," said my roommate. "He was shouting, 'Down with examinations!'"

(10) Our club's last meeting was devoted to a debate on the question, Shall the constitution be revised?

A. (1) On Saturday night, Joe Masters and his Rhythm Boys entertained the Yorkville Social Club.

(2) My cousin Robert has a decided French accent.

(3) He referred to his section of the Southwest as "God's Country."

(4) The street was named Sherman Street in honor of General Sherman.

(5) I remember that there was a Chinese boy in my class in Burton High School.

(6) Father and Mother both approve of the United Nations.

(7) Bill said, "Oh, there goes Dr. Jones now!"

(8) We wrote to Captain Anderson of the Ninety-fifth Coast Artillery.

(9) He has a book about the Stone Age.

(10) They stayed with their uncle from Thanksgiving until Christmas.

B. (1) In high school we studied physics, English, Latin, history, and civics.

(2) I suffer during the winter and go South if I can.

(3) Please go to the drugstore, Sally, and get Mother some ice-cream.

(4) The crew included Mexicans, Indians, Negroes, and Portuguese.

(5) He reads the Bible regularly and especially likes the letters of the Apostle Paul.

(6) Sometimes gypsies are called Bohemians.

(7) The area around Times Square is known as the Great White Way.

(8) Theirs is a platonic friendship.

(9) The Missouri River flows into the Mississippi.

(10) Mrs. McDermott, a high-school teacher, threatened to call in the Board of Health.

C. (1) Eighty-five pedestrians were killed on Linden Boulevard last month.

(2) The mountains form a splendid background for the University of Colorado.

(3) Charles Miller, Professor of Chemistry, will be fifty next January eighth.

(4) Enclosed please find one dollar.

(5) My address is 16 Fremont Street, Middletown, Ohio.

(6) His library contains 1,342 volumes.

(7) When he is in Chicago he goes sailing on Lake Michigan.

(8) The Fifth of November is called Guy Fawkes Day in England.

(9) Over ten thousand people saw the game between North Dakota and Nebraska.

(10) This box is two inches longer and three inches wider than the other one.

(11) Telephone me at Central 6-3000 at 5 P.M.

(12) They called on the Reverend Dr. Willis to arrange the wedding details.

(13) The word in question occurs in Chapter V., page 110, line 3.

(14) Christmas parties mean work for the doctors.

(15) Early last month he left for New Zealand.

D. (1) In the anteroom of the life insurance company's main office the workingman sat patiently for thirty-five minutes.

(2) He wore a light-gray suit and a four-in-hand tie.

(3) The filling-out of the application for an interview with the vice-president took up one third of his time.

(4) He had never been much of a letter writer, and it was with a feeling of self-satisfaction that he answered the last of the twenty-one questions.

(5) He handed the all-important document to the good-looking secretary and watched her as she went into the inner office.

E. (1) He preferred the *France* to the *Queen Elizabeth* for trans-Atlantic crossings.

(2) Did you enjoy *Together,* by Norman Douglas?

(3) The *w* in the word *Harwich* is not pronounced.

(4) They attended a performance of *Rigoletto* at the Metropolitan Opera House.

(5) The *Spirit of St. Louis* was one of the world's most famous airplanes.

(6) Like most epics, Milton's *Paradise Lost* begins *in medias res.*

(7) The story deals with his experiences en route to his Alma Mater.

(8) Johnson's *Rasselas* is a tale of Abyssinia.

(9) *Child Care,* a sixty-page pamphlet, has a chapter called "Clothing."

(10) The words *damask* and *calico* are derived from city-names: Damascus and Calicut.

Chapter IX (pages 276–281)

A. (1) The music critics were extremely interested in the concert and in one new species of composition especially.

(2) The football game began at four o'clock.

(3) I saw the old man when he was away down the road, and he seemed to be in bad shape.

(4) The workers agreed to the company's terms.

(5) Our grocer charges altogether too much for eggs, butter, and other things.

(6) Because he was not well, he stayed at home.

(7) The cashier has fewer dollar bills today than usual.

(8) When they are thrown into the water they cannot help swimming.

(9) An odd-looking person stood behind the desk talking to another odd-looking person.

(10) The child led the girl a kind of merry chase in the park yesterday.

(11) Except for Herbert, they are almost always eager to play bridge.

(12) His principal hobby these days is raising rabbits.

(13) She suggested that we sit down and estimate our chances of raising the money.

(14) "It is an illusion," said the instructor, "to think that this is as far as you can go."

(15) Her mother wasn't sure that Mildred should go about with older girls.

(16) They seem indeed to be a group of people whom you can't help liking.

(17) The data for the construction of the bridge have been put in the safe.

(18) Because of some misunderstanding or other, the dark-complexioned man was very late indeed.

(19) A "comma splice" is the name given to the error of joining two sentences with a comma.

(20) Hold the tennis racquet as Joe does.

(21) We seldom if ever go anywhere in the evenings.

(22) The reason he oversleeps is that he spends hours each night indulging in reminiscences.

(23) Try to return the book by Friday, will you?

(24) His parents wanted him to go to college and so did he until last year.

(25) The ticket collector suspected that we intended to try to slip by him.

(26) If my brother had sent me a telegram, I would have met his train.

(27) The poem sounds pleasant when it is read aloud.

(28) I know many people who will lend me an umbrella even if you won't.

(29) Mr. Watson lay on the couch all week.

(30) I like this game you've invented; I think it's most ingenious.

(31) The clerk said he would have some of this kind within a week.

(32) As soon as I finish work, we'll go to the zoo and spend the rest of the day there.

(33) Human beings, he is convinced, must learn tolerance.

(34) Reading about the plagues in the Middle Ages always has a depressing effect on me.

(35) Harvey and Paul get along with each other all right now.

(36) This chocolate cake surely tastes good.

(37) The two schemes are equally good.

(38) He was at a loss to explain the cause of these phenomena.

(39) The Norrises go to a great deal of expense each year entertaining friends in their home.

(40) He told her that she had no right to interrupt him.

(41) If things go wrong, they are likely to blame him.

(42) His uncle is angry about the new traffic regulations.

(43) The rain will have a good effect on our garden.

(44) They fully expected he would die of heart disease.

(45) I know several New Yorkers who hope to emigrate to Brazil.

(46) Johnny is in trouble, but I think I can arrange matters for him.

(47) Golf is a healthful pastime, but my father thinks it's inferior to tennis.

(48) She looked as if she were somewhat unhappy.

(49) I wrote to Mr. Mitchell with regard to the advertisement in yesterday's paper.

(50) Until last week, I was uninterested in his offers of employment; but, now that I am anxious to get employed, I suppose I'll have trouble finding a job, because of general conditions.

B. (1) While waiting for the other guests to arrive, my host and I talked about the new project.

(2) He dare not go anywhere nowadays.

(3) Regardless of what those people say, I'm going to go home now.

(4) He can't play the piano as well as he used to.

(5) This hat doesn't fit at all.

(6) He lent me the car himself.

(7) It was really kind of them to send me an invitation; I think I'll accept.

(8) Formerly, there was a stationery store on this corner.

(9) As we drove past the town hall, we noticed that it was later than we had thought.

(10) Decent people do not use coarse language.

(11) He is not the kind to show much enthusiasm about music.

(12) Let's leave this unpleasant town at once.

(13) She writes in her diary very faithfully every night.

(14) I wasn't sure whether I should take it as a compliment or an insult.

(15) It takes a great deal of skill and courage to drive cars like these.

(16) Do you plan to stay at home every night?

(17) If he had graduated from high school, he would have been able to get a better kind of job than the one he has now.

(18) He was convinced that there was no use continuing.

(19) The fortune-teller said he would either be drowned or hanged.

(20) "There ought to be a law," he said.

C. (1) harsh-sounding
(2) lukewarm
(3) glutted
(4) bountiful
(5) not destroyed
(6) impractical
(7) scurrilous
(8) selective
(9) simultaneous
(10) stamp-collecting
(11) nickname
(12) retentive
(13) surreptitious
(14) sweltering
(15) rashness
(16) courteous
(17) stealthy
(18) bold
(19) procession
(20) partiality
(21) close watch
(22) sonorous
(23) scattered
(24) changeable
(25) parasite
(26) laborious study
(27) witty retorts
(28) tomb
(29) stingy
(30) necessary
(31) compensate
(32) pithy
(33) earthly
(34) jesting
(35) freedom from punishment
(36) wise
(37) settled
(38) meddlesome
(39) unsophisticated
(40) silent
(41) odd
(42) menacing
(43) fat
(44) petitioner
(45) peevish
(46) flirts
(47) not genuine
(48) inexorable
(49) fellow-worker
(50) merry
(51) question
(52) peevish
(53) complaining
(54) revoked
(55) lying
(56) alert

INDEX

(In this index, italics are used for individual words discussed in the text)

347

348

351

354